PHILOSOPHY AND THE PUBLIC REALM

PROCEEDINGS OF THE FIFTH ONEONTA UNDERGRADUATE PHILOSOPHY CONFERENCE

EDITED

BY

DOUGLAS W. SHRADER

ONEONTA PHILOSOPHY STUDIES

HISTORICAL AND CULTURAL PERSPECTIVES

10 9 8 7 6 5 4 3 2 1

ISBN 1-586841-16-5

Library of Congress Cataloging-in-Publication Data

Title:	**Philosophy and The Public Realm**
Editor:	Douglas W. Shrader
Subject:	Philosophy, Confucianism, Liberalism, Pragmatism, Existentialism, Zen Buddhism, Ethics, Aesthetics, Abortion, China, Rights, Heidegger, Nietzsche, Whitehead, Wittgenstein

Cover design by Douglas W. Shrader – based on a bust of Marcus Aurelius in Ephesus Museum, Turkey.

Distributed by:

Global Publications, IGCS
Binghamton University
Binghamton, NY USA 13902-6000
Phone: (607) 777-4495 or 6104; Fax: (607) 777-6132
email: pmorewed@binghamton.edu
http://ssips.binghamton.edu

Dedicated to

STERLING BERNARD DONAHOE
(1918 – 1978)

Your dedication to the public realm and the power
of your smile lightened the loads of many.
In quiet moments, I still hear your voice –
I still see your face.

ONEONTA PHILOSOPHY STUDIES
HISTORICAL AND CULTURAL PERSPECTIVES

EDITOR IN CHIEF
Douglas W. Shrader

MANAGING EDITOR
Parviz Morewedge

EDITORS

Michael Green	*Achim Köddermann*
Ashok Malhotra	*Anthony Roda*

Department of Philosophy
SUNY ONEONTA
Oneonta, NY 13820-4015

http://www.oneonta.edu/~shradedw/ops.html

CONTENTS

Contents

Contents

PREFACE

I am always amazed by the energy and enthusiasm that students bring to our annual Undergraduate Philosophy Conference. If the fifth incarnation of this youthful exuberance (March 31-April 1, 2000) was an exception to the rule, it was only in the sense of "more so." We began Friday afternoon with an inaugural presentation by Ashok Malhotra (SUNY Oneonta) titled *Yoga: A Philosophical Demonstration and Guided Meditation.* In addition to providing an overview of the multidimensional nature of Yoga, including some of its most popular versions in the west, Professor Malhotra demonstrated a variety of physical and meditative exercises associated with Yoga. Sitting in a half-lotus position in a green Kurta Pajama, he encouraged the audience to join him on the carpeted floor of the Craven Lounge. Many did. Even those who opted to sit in chairs were amazed by the extent to which the Yoga helped them relax and get rid of some of those nervous jitters that haunt even seasoned professors on the eve of a presentation.

With some quick rearranging of the furniture, the room was readied for the first student presentations. In a session that prophetically carried the same title as this volume, Malinda Foster of the University of Michigan set the pace with a dynamic presentation about the silence of Philosophy in Plato's *Crito.* We had encouraged students to present their ideas to the audience in as engaging a manner as possible (vs. standing at the podium and reading from their paper), and Malinda had clearly taken the advice to heart. She walked back and forth in front of the room, conveying not only her ideas, but her enthusiasm as well. Katherine Collins (University of Massachusetts) and Tamara Johnson (Binghamton University) followed with presentations entitled "Arendt, Heidegger, and the Decline of the Public Realm" and "Political Noise and Vociferous Silence: Heidegger and Nazism."

Following a short break the audience reassembled, eager to see what goodies the second round of student papers might bring. The audience was primed, but nothing could have prepared them for the raw energy that John Kaag of Penn State was about to unleash. Leading the session on *Language Games* with a paper titled "The Mask Unmasked: The Role of Hypocrisy in the Dialectic of *Thus Spoke Zarathustra*," John was ready to burst at the seams. Rather than presenting his paper as such, he provided an angst-ridden account of the dialectical process that had brought him face to face with Zarathustra. Chiding his audience, he asked "Have we moved that far away from Hegel? ... Are we that worried about talking in the first person? Does philosophy mean nothing but a system we can evaluate?" Without waiting for answers to these rhetorical questions, he explained:

> I have this nice little highlighted paper. It's not going to work—because that's not what it's about. I'm going to talk about how I came to this paper, how I wrote this paper, how it affected me right away, what insecurities I went through. I'm not scared to say "This is how I felt." I'm willing to share it with all of you. And even in that there is hypocrisy.

Each paper is assigned a student discussant to raise questions, provide commentary, and offer alternative perspectives. Since John had strayed so far from his prepared text, his discussant had to assimilate the changes and provide a cogent on-the-spot assessment. Fortunately, John's discussant was a conference veteran, accustomed to some of the unanticipated twists and turns that come with authentic intellectual exchange. Dan Bristol (SUNY Oneonta) began with a single sustained word: "Wow!" Then, holding aloft a copy of John's essay, he instructed the audience:

> If any of you at any point get a chance to read this, do so. This is a perfectly marvelous piece of work. ... This is beyond all doubt the most beautifully written, clear, and masterful work on Nietzsche I have ever seen. You have done a perfectly wonderful job and I salute you.
>
> I also want to salute you for what you just did. ... Zarathustra says "I do not want to be read; I want to be learned by heart." ...
>
> "By heart" is what John just did. He took Nietzsche home.

Dan put it well: John "took Nietzsche home." He gave a presentation full of heart, not empty intellectual abstractions. For those who did not, like Dan, have the opportunity to ready John's manuscript, this volume represents a second chance. "The Mask Unmasked" is presented in its entirety on pages 127-142.

What was clear, long before John had finished his presentation, was that he had thrown down the gauntlet, issuing a challenge to all of the other participants to set aside personal insecurities or concern with appearances in favor of honest philosophical engagement. The next two speakers, Andrew Wilson and Zachary Haines, both of Macalester College, met the challenge with poise and resolve. By the time they had concluded their papers, "The Nature of Lan-

Preface

guage: Public and Private" and "Wittgenstein and Natural-ism," the entire assembly was ready for dinner. Around the tables in the Otsego Grille, conversations raged about all six of the presentations that had launched the conference. Those who would present the following day had seen any preconceptions they might have had about the conference blown out of the water. It was clear that this would be a weekend during which they would have to think outside the boxes.

That evening, we were all treated to a keynote presentation by Joanna Crosby of Morgan State University. In *Pragmatism and the Future of Confucianism in China*, Professor Crosby explained that life on the streets of China is more complex than many scholars care to acknowledge. Then, in an intriguing twist in cross-cultural studies, she proposed the possibility that American Pragmatism as well as Confucianism, both philosophies that emphasize practice over theory and actuality over metaphysics, can help heal the damage inflicted on Chinese culture by the Cultural Revolution.

Saturday morning began with a session on *Ethics: Theory and Practice*. While we could scarcely know it in advance, it was here that two of the presentations destined to receive President's Awards were delivered. Rachel Houchins of East Tennessee State opened the session with "Feminine Ethical Theories: Their Validity Tested." As a sensitive and perceptive student who planned to continue her studies in medicine rather than philosophy, Rachel was concerned not only with the manner in which traditional ethical theories have excluded women, but also with the practical application of alternative theories. Surprising many members of the audience, she took the theories of thinkers like Carol

Gilligan and Nel Noddings to task. Despite the surface appeal of an "ethics of care," Rachel argued that the approach simply fails to provide sufficiently clear, unequivocal guidance to resolve the complex issues with which health care professionals are forced to deal.

Rachel's paper was followed by "The Practice of Physician Assisted Suicide Supported by Kantian Ethics" by Seyra Ahmed of Virginia Commonwealth University. Because Kant's theories place strong emphasis on personal autonomy, and because the prohibition of Physician Assisted Suicide undermines the ability of individuals to exercise their autonomy, Seyra argued that a charitable reading of Kant's theories would support legalization of the practice. Because Kant also explicitly rejects suicide as morally unacceptable, discussion was spirited and robust.

The final paper of the session, by Michael Alan Payne of Virginia Commonwealth University, carried a title that made some of the participants a bit nervous: "A Father's Rights in Abortion: Proof That He Has A Say." Would this, they wondered, be a genuine philosophical investigation or a narrow-minded rejection of a woman's right to choose? To Michael's credit, he quickly won the confidence of even the most cynical skeptics. They may not have left the room agreeing with his final conclusions, but they did come to appreciate the honesty, integrity, and intellectual as well as moral commitment of this charming young man.

After lunch, students had to choose between two concurrent sessions: *Freedom, Happiness and the Human Condition* and *Truth and Beauty*. What a choice! In the first, Christine Cinquino of St. Vincent's College discussed "The Exhilarating Freedom! Hope in Existentialism," Malinda Foster returned to the podium to analyze "The Problem of Happiness in Nietzsche's 'Use and Abuse of History'," and Eric Bergmann of Binghamton University presented "The Extraordinary: Movements in Dostoevsky and Nietzsche." In the second, Scott Gleason of SUNY Potsdam discussed "Towards a Processean Aesthetics Within a Whiteheadian Metaphysics," Iain Tucker Brown of St. Mary's College followed with "On the Event of Truth: A Discussion of Art, Truth and the Primal Conflict in *Heidegger's The Origin of the Work of Art*," and Jason Baumgarth of the University of Minnesota concluded with "Tradition and Modern Meaning: Society and Relative Truth."

Each of the presentations was a unique, exceptional experience—for the audience as well as the presenter. During the break, students who attended Session A compared notes with those who attended Session B, then made their choices for the next, final session of student presentations. Would it be *Multiple Perspectives: The Search for Common Ground* or *Knowing Whereof We Speak: Language, Experience, and Truth*?

In the Craven Lounge, the same room in which the conference had begun the preceding day, Erin Cline of Belmont University presented "Incommensurability, Normative Vices, and the Comparative Language Game: A Wittgensteinian Model for Comparative Philosophy." Exhibiting an exceptional level of cognitive maturity as well as presentational poise, Erin analyzed various obstacles that plague comparative studies and placed Wittgenstein "in conversation with other key thinkers on the subject of different worldviews," including Alasdair MacIntyre, Donald Davidson, and Martha Nussbaum. She was followed by Katherine Collins of the University of Massachusetts with an enlightening assessment of "The Environmental Crisis Through a Buddhist Perspective."

In the adjacent room, Jayson White of Iowa State University talked about "Religious and Non-Religious Language, and Propositions About Human Rights." Justin Maaia of Suffolk University secured his place in the annals of conference history by becoming the first student to begin a presentation with a sax solo. Justin's paper, which is included in this volume on pages 145-171, is titled "The Experience and Expression of Truth."

With student presentations at a close all that remained was to grab one last cup of coffee and settle in for a rare treat: the concluding keynote presentation by Henry Rosemont, Jr. of St. Mary's College of Maryland. In "Whose Democracy? Which Rights?" Professor Rosemont systematically dissected a broad range of western values, modern philosophy, and social and political theory. At best, he suggested, Modern Western Liberalism vouchsafes first generation rights but falters in its attempt to take the next step, to second generation rights. Arguing that concepts like human rights, liberty, and individualism fail to capture what it is to be a human being, he then urged a careful reconsideration of Classical Confucianism. According to a Confucian perspective, our most basic rights are not civil or political, grounded in the view that we are autonomous individuals, but rather natural consequences of our membership in a community, with each member assuming a measure of responsibility for the welfare of all other members. It was a thought-provoking and fitting conclusion to an exceptional conference where students had pondered concepts of ethics, rights, social and political structures, and the value of comparative philosophy.

Preface

A Brief History

The conference itself took slightly less than two days. In truth, those two days are but a tightly compressed node of emotional and intellectual exchange in a remarkable fabric, the threads of which extend in untold directions in both space and time. In an important if somewhat simplistic sense, our conference began during the fall of 1995 when I invited a few students to tag along with me to a conference on Greek and Islamic Philosophy. They came back with a dream about holding a conference of their own, not for professors such as they had seen, but for undergraduates such as themselves. When I found that I could not discourage them, I agreed to work with them. We hosted our first conference the following spring, in March 1996. Even now I look back in astonishment at the unflagging commitment of our students, the enthusiastic response we received, and the remarkable quality of the papers.

By encouraging excellence, and by treating students with respect and professionalism, we have been rewarded in kind. Over each of the past five years I have found a small cadre of students willing to work long hard hours to bring this dream of an undergraduate conference to fruition. We have played host to students from a wide range of institutions throughout the United States and Canada. Many of our conference alumni have now gone on to graduate school. They are, in a very real sense, the future of our profession. As several of our keynote speakers have confided to me over the years, we have spoiled them. Having experienced a conference such as this, they will never accept the posturing or the stiff and boring presentations that occupy centerstage at many professional meetings. My response is simple and to the point: "I hope they don't."

Douglas W. Shrader

Seven of the twelve students whose papers are published in this volume received special awards, described below. The others, as will be obvious to anyone who reads the essays, made decisions concerning those awards especially difficult. Each paper represented an exceptional student's best work. In most cases, it was the first time the student had presented a paper beyond the confines of a classroom. The inherent intimidation of presenting one's work in public, combined with the knowledge that it would be subject to critical blind review, resulted in a significant measure of self-selection. I know many capable students who elected not to submit. But for those who summoned the courage, the experience was remarkable.

President's Awards

President's Awards honor student presentations that most clearly exemplify the standards and ideals of the conference. For 2000, these awards were presented to (alphabetic order):

> Erin Cline (*Belmont University*)
> Malinda Foster *(University of Michigan)*
> Rachel Houchins (*East Tennessee State University*)
> Michael Alan Payne *(Virginia Commonwealth University)*

Ninash Foundation East-West Awards

East-West Awards honor student presentations that exhibit special expertise and insight in Asian and Comparative Philosophy. For 2000, the award was presented to:

> Justin Maaia (*Suffolk University*)

Preface

To honor her role as student committee chair, especially her success in facilitating scholarly exchange concerning Asian and Comparative Philosophy, a second East-West Award was presented to:

Cynthia Budka *(SUNY Oneonta)*

Spirit of Conference Awards

Spirit of Conference Awards honor students who contribute to the conference in diverse, sometimes unexpected ways. Special consideration is given to contributions that enhance the academic, intellectual, and positive social atmosphere of the conference. For 2000, these awards were presented to (alphabetic order):

Iain Tucker Brown (*St. Mary's College*)

Gottlieb Jicha III (*SUNY Oneonta*)

John Kaag *(Pennsylvania State University)*

In my preface to *Children of Athena* (proceedings of the 1998 conference), I wrote about a student who was busy in another office, creating the program for our fourth annual conference. That he was doing so on his spring break, I noted, only serves to reinforce my conviction that somewhere, somehow, we must have done something right. That student, Gotti Jicha, was a member of a fraternity as well as the Rugby Club. To put it bluntly, he had a reputation for having a good time. When Gotti again devoted his spring break to work on the conference program the following (his senior) year, it only further served to increase my respect, admiration, and sense of wonder. By the time the conference arrived he had read and reread each and every paper. During the conference, he seemed to be everywhere at once: picking up students from the airport, making sure arrangements were just right, chatting with people about their presentations, and participating vigorously in the open discussions. Along with John Kaag who infused the conference with a dose of refreshing honesty and realism, and Tucker Brown who also earned the right to author the Student Preface for this volume, Gotti is sure to become a classic example of the enthusiasm and "beyond the call of duty" activity that merits a Spirit of Conference Award.

Proceedings and Acknowledgments

The proceedings are a natural extension of the conference. Accordingly, I try to approach the task of editing through the same lenses that I use for planning the conference. I ask myself repeatedly, "How can I help my students see beyond the inherent agonies and frustrations of the process by which a private opinion becomes a public position, to revel in the excitement and satisfaction of that process as well?" The result is a true labor of love. On the one hand, it always demands far more time and attention to detail than I have allotted. On the other hand, the students with whom I have worked—from other institutions as well as from SUNY Oneonta—have been sources of joy, inspiration, and delight.

For the proceedings of the fourth conference (*The Fractal Self*), I tried to teach students how to format papers using WORD. The idea seemed simple enough: we would combine content review with formatting. In practice, the students had so much trouble with WORD that there was barely any time left for serious discussion of the content. Thus, for the present volume, I modified the approach. Three of the four students who volunteered to help with the

Preface

editorial process had not been able to attend the conference. For them, this would be the first and primary encounter with these essays. Cindy Budka, who generously agreed to serve as conference committee chair for the second straight year, also agreed to provide preliminary formatting for many of the papers. That left other students free to focus on content. We met weekly, often in a comfortable coffee shop, to talk about the papers. I found myself giving impromptu lectures on everything from Heidegger to Feminism. By the end of the fall semester, we had page proofs ready to send to our authors.

A formal list of acknowledgments follows the student preface. Still, I would be remiss if I did not take this opportunity to thank my family (Barbara, Callie, and Sterling) for their patience, encouragement, and support. I also owe a special note of appreciation to Ashok Malhotra, Joanna Crosby, and Henry Rosemont, Jr. for gracing our conference with their presence, their insights, and their infectious enthusiasm. I am especially grateful to Joanna and Henry for allowing us the honor of including their presentations in the proceedings.

Without the assistance of faculty, staff, and administrators here at Oneonta, neither the conference nor this volume would be possible: thank you. Finally, I owe a note of gratitude to the students who provided editorial assistance for this volume: Cynthia Budka, Jason Ohliger, Elizabeth Verry, and Ann Williamson.

Douglas W. Shrader
Oneonta, New York

STUDENT PREFACE

In both the positive and pejorative sense, philosophy has been, perhaps, the most powerful impetus in my life thus far. My exploration began some three years ago when, as an eager—although unsuspicious—student, I read works whose titles carried the stamp of authors from whom I sought tutelage toward an avenue of personal growth (and with time and effort permitting, acceptance into their respective dialogic communities). Consequently, my induction into philosophical discourse, an attempt at Heidegger's *Being and Time*, lured me, unwittingly and without active discretion, toward the total admission of his thought. Questioning the personal relevance of Heidegger's ontological claims held a secondary stance with respect to the allure of his probing assessment of the self: a self which, although at first uncanny, I subsequently inwardly absorbed with full assurance. Heidegger thereupon became the solution, as I felt the need to establish a *Weltanschauung*, a world orientation.

Since the temptation of Heidegger's disciplined thinking disclosed for me the proper path of my own personal expression, I submitted to the Oneonta Undergraduate Philosophy Conference of 2000 a paper on his treatment of aesthetics. It is a paper that represents earnest effort, but beyond that reveals, compared with my present person, a self-struggle of doubt and a fear of my own absurdity. When I read, in preparation of presenting, the finished work (reflecting, too, on an idea/disposition I had been assuming), I began to wonder whether I could actively accept, or decisively agree with, Heidegger's philosophy, and what is perhaps even more, with the whole of *my* philosophical pursuit. It seemed, then, as if my work was all for naught: I, the unsuspecting student, embraced beliefs because of their veneration, not on account of my own volition. The conference, as I experienced it, bound three years of study within three days. Nonetheless, when I should have readied my speech, I sat, anxiously consumed by a newly felt sense of self-doubt. When I should have delivered my paper, I offered to the audience my reasons for not being able to do so. Though the emotional expression of my inability to furnish the assumed piece proved cathartic, I have learned, and wish to say decidedly, that I made a mistake, that I dishonored an obligation (that being the formal delivery of my written work).

Given now the means to suggest a few words of importance, I wish to submit that the significance of my internal questioning is not that of an admission of my dishonorable conduct, but rather stands behind my acceptance of self-doubt. In the acceptance of that doubt I saw, and remain to see now, the worth and weakness of philosophy and of myself. I've come to realize the accent of real possibility and expression: a sense of place both limited and boundless, but always steered by the will of one's own decision. As such, I chose, and continue to choose mindfully, of myself and of the other, from what is both necessary and possible. Self-doubt delivered me unto an understanding of what is, fundamentally, most intrinsically mine: personal will.

I should say, accordingly, that it was the conference, under the influential vibrancy of all those involved, that exfoliated what could be called a sort of self-reckoning. No other occurrence, as I surmise the sum of my life's experience, has ever forced an affect of such profundity. With that said, the struggle to make clear my inward-inquiry gives a definitive picture of those who have graciously given me their assistance and concern. So with this opportunity, I simply wish to offer my gratitude to the people of Oneonta and St. Mary's, as they have extended petition and care toward myself and other students of our philosophical communities. For their compassion and reassurance, I wish to thank Dr. Douglas Shrader and Dr. Henry Rosemont, both professors whose brilliance and sincerity I honor. To Daniel Bristol, I express laughter in his humor and extend an embrace for his fellowship. With similar gratitude I volunteer my indebtedness to Morgan Brenner, Rachel Houchins and Kevin McGarry, all individuals of love and limitless possibility. To Alan Paskow, John Schroeder, Jackie Paskow and Anne Leblans, I owe a tremendous amount of responsibility and respect, by virtue of their friendship and instruction. Lastly I would like to thank everyone who, subtlety and uniquely, helped to make this year's conference one of the most memorable and impacting moments of my life, and I am certain, that of others as well.

Iain Tucker Brown
St. Mary's City, Maryland

ACKNOWLEDGEMENTS

The conference and this volume depend on the contributions and good will of many. The following organizations and local merchants provided generous financial and/or professional assistance:

SUNY Oneonta Student Association
The Ninash Foundation
The Philosophy Club
Morris Conference Center
The Philosophy Department
Oneonta Philosophy Studies
Organization of Ancillary Services
The Marketing Club
The Video Production Club
Alpine Ski Hut
Elena's Sweet Indulgence
Gary's Flower's and Gifts
Hannaford Foods
Hummel's Office Supply
Office Max
Oneonta Bagel Company
P & C
Price Chopper
Stewart's Ice Cream Company
Stoeger Florist
Subway
The Village Printer
Wal-Mart
Woody's Market
Wyckoff's Florist

Acknowledgements

Special appreciation is extended to:

Ashok Malhotra, Joanna Crosby, and Henry Rosemont, Jr. for their time and inspiration

Cynthia Budka for leadership and commitment as student chair of the conference planning committee

The other students who served on the1999/2000 conference planning committee: Mark Ayotte, Morgan Brenner, Meghan Callahan, Gottlieb Jicha III, Molly Maroldo, Kevin McGarry, and Amanda Rasnick

Marjorie Holling for secretarial support

Cynthia Budka, Jason Ohliger, Elizabeth Verry, and Ann Williamson for editorial assistance

SUNY Oneonta faculty for patiently reviewing and evaluating a multitude of manuscripts—especially Michael Green, Michael Koch, Achim Köddermann, Ashok Malhotra, Anthony Roda, and Bram van Heuveln

SUNY Oneonta administration for support and encouragement—especially Dean Michael Merilan, Provost F. Daniel Larkin, and President Alan B. Donovan

Parviz Morewedge, IGCS, SAGP, SSIPS, and Global Publications for financial and in-house support of this series

Finally, a heartfelt **Thank You** is extended to all the Presenters, Chairs, and Discussants—for without them there would have been no Conference.

FREEDOM, HAPPINESS, AND THE HUMAN CONDITION

THE EXHILARATING FREEDOM!
HOPE IN EXISTENTIALISM

Christine M. Cinquino
Saint Vincent College

As demonstrated by the work of Sartre, Kierkegaard, de Beauvoir, and others, Existentialism offers a message of hope as well as a mechanism for constructing an authentic, meaningful life. In a society filled with despair and moral nihilism, the message takes on special significance and importance.

In our age, following what Nietzsche metaphorically referred to as the "death" of God, it is common for individuals to feel lost in a philosophical environment where all values are considered relative and where absurdity and anxiety seem to be the most powerful feelings life has to offer. In this moral climate, a temptation exists for some introspective young persons, who may be experiencing a phase of mental and emotional anguish from recent life experiences, to give in to a form of pessimistic nihilism. However, accepting an existentialist perspective does not necessitate the surrender of humanistic faith in the value of persons or of a meaningful life. The existentialist claim that "existence precedes essence" challenges each individual to create personal meaning and to reveal the value of all human beings.

After the black and white, good versus bad, "yummy or yucky" certainty of childhood, the world of gray and subjective values can be quite a shock to a young person. Suddenly, the young person realizes that parents are far from perfect, teachers do not have all the answers, and good does not always seem to win against evil, if such categories can be said to exist at all. Conversation with others quickly reveals that even the most cherished values seem relative, according to environmental background and personal views. The next decade of life is spent searching for ideas and values which fit the young person's emerging world-view.

In English classes, high school and college students may be introduced to existential themes through literature. Alienation, death, anxiety, and absurdity are several motifs of existentialism which have been expressed in literary form. These key terms and ideas are encountered in literature by students and young people, who may never read the philosophical works. Kafka's *Metamorphosis* and Camus' *The Stranger* are two commonly assigned texts which include "existential" themes representing the darker side of the human condition.

Through his grotesque characterization of the insect Gregor in *Metamorphosis*, Kafka deftly illustrates the sense of alienation from self, which human beings sometimes feel. Gregor is so paralyzed by others' expectations of him that he is incapable of making his own decisions. The anxious and pitiful man/insect does not know who he is. Trapped in a sluggish and revolting alien body, Gregor feels unable to communicate with his boss, with women, or with his family. His excruciatingly lonely life seems worthless, and even the reader feels more disgust than sympathy for the sniveling creature and his absurd situation.

Camus' novel, *The Stranger*, illustrates man's alienation from other men. Meursault is estranged from society, which he feels is false and pretentious. He refuses to fake emotions and go through the physical motions required of a son who is mourning the death of his mother. By refusing to put on the mask of insincere sentiment, Meursault becomes conspicuously alienated from society. Later, he is convicted of murder, not because of overwhelming evidence, but because he refused to conform to societal expectations. Meursault's display of what was perceived by society as "heartlessness" at his mother's death proved to that jury that he was cruel and inhuman. In prison facing the death sentence, Meursault seems cold and unfeeling toward his own impending death. The Stranger's individualist behavior, a threat to the citizens' peace of mind based on the illusion of community values, brought about his public execution.

This emphasis on alienation from self and others fits right in with the awkwardness and angst of adolescence and young adulthood. Life experiences, in the beginning of what Erickson refers to as the "identity versus identity confusion" stage of human development, are highly intense and often painful. Perhaps a first brush with death of a friend or loved one, the confusing loss of one's first love, or a frustrating struggle with physical or mental health has introduced the individual to personal tragedy. Or perhaps the young person feels marginalized and invisible around his or her peers, trapped and powerless in a stressful family situation, or stifled and bored in an unhealthy school environment. Emotional anguish from such experiences is easily generalized, in a rather melodramatic manner, to include the expectation that life will always seem and feel like it does at this moment. As high depression and suicide rates for young people suggest, a youthful lack of experience in keeping things in perspective can make life's struggles seem overwhelming.

Without the comfort of stable, unquestioned values, the world may seem cold and confusing. Every aspect of life, no matter how sacred it once seemed, can become questionable and susceptible to doubt. The restless individual, who has embarked on a journey in search of meaning, feels as though her ship is disappearing right beneath her feet, and experiences dread and gripping anxiety. In a subconscious state of panic, she instinctively reaches out for any system of thought which seems secure. In contemporary American culture, extreme emphasis on "scientific" certainty and rational understanding have eroded faith in intangibles to the point that, to a person in search, nihilism can seem quite sound. And the presence of emotional pain from recent life experiences, coupled with overwhelming evidence of the darker side of the human condition, often adds a discouraging light to the neutral meaning of nihilism.

Cynical messages of pessimistic nihilism offer potential disciples the paradoxical comfort of being relatively "right," compared with those who assert an ultimate, eternal, unchanging truth and value, in a universe which nihilists claim contains no true "right" or "wrong" nature. A sort of comfort can be found in resigning oneself to an empty world, because the restless search for meaning seems complete; it is just one more absurd quest in a valueless world of absurdity.

A pessimistic nihilist fancies herself excused from the exhausting search for truth. In a world lacking faith, love, trust, hope, and responsibility she is free to live her life on the amoral plane of hedonism or of complete indifference to pleasure and pain. When the pain or absurdity or boredom becomes tiresome, she may quietly end her valueless life in an indifferent manner, without a trace of tragedy. Why not squish the grotesque Gregor, who is miserable because of his human consciousness and acute sense of alienation from himself? Why mourn for Meursault, whose dying wish, "on the day of my execution there should be a huge crowd of spectators and that they should greet me with howls of execration," clearly revealed his complete apathy to his own meaningless life and death?

The young person's experience of existential vertigo, her feelings of confusion at the insufficiency of former beliefs, parallels the psychological climate of post-war Europe, from which existentialism gained a wider following. At first it seemed as though the period's main players could be easily characterized into good forces versus evil forces. However, horrible news of the carnage of technologically advanced warfare, the unspeakable cruelty of the Holocaust, and of the immense suffering of many individuals on both sides cast a decidedly gray light on any attempts at easy categorization. Throughout the twentieth century, this ambiguity was often expressed in literary form.

The message that often does not make it through these examples of one-sided "existential" literature is that absurdity and alienation are only half the picture. Perhaps our sentient existence in this world devoid of meaning seems absurd; at times, each of us feels alien in his own skin. But human existence, which possesses the unique abilities of rational thought and sentient emotion, can also be viewed with amazement and wonder. And a lack of pre-existing meaning does not prevent meaning from existing. The challenge of existentialism is to create meaning. It is up to the individual to take the raw material of existence and define his or her unique essence.

Existentialism cannot correctly be classified as a unified school of thought; rather it is a diverse mode of conceiving the world of Being. Developed partly as a reaction against absolute idealism, which was perceived by the new thinkers as irrelevant to human experience, existentialist thought focuses on Being and the human experience of this phenomenon. Three characteristics might be considered the "heart" of existentialism:

> the refusal to belong to any school of thought, the repudiation of the adequacy of any body of beliefs whatever, and especially of systems, and a marked dissatisfaction with traditional philosophy as superficial, academic, and remote from life. (Kaufmann 12)

If it were possible to name a central tenet of the existentialist perspective, one might look to the writings of Jean-Paul Sartre, a French philosopher who proudly accepted the generally unpopular title of *existentialist*. According to Heidegger, "Sartre formulates the basic principle of existentialism in these words: existence precedes essence" (Kaufmann 37). Those three words revolutionized the way a human being was perceived, transforming the conception from 'a member of the group called humans, with human nature' to 'an individual human who through free choices develops his or her own unique nature.' Thus, the only defining quality of a human being is that he or she possesses an individual free will.

In a similar manner, formal centralization of other concepts can be broken down. Instead of a natural law to be carried out through human laws and moral imperatives, passing mores and customs masquerade as universally necessary in an attempt to restrict the choices individuals can make. Aesthetically pleasing qualities in art or nature, formerly seen as a shared definition of true beauty, could now be considered to exist in the eye of the beholder alone. And the eternal presence of one universal truth is altogether denied; the meaninglessness of the universe is curtailed solely by our individually constituted perceptions of its nothingness.

It would seem that in the face of all this ideological decon-struction, each human being finds him or her self very alone in the universe. Without so much as a basic human nature to share with others, human beings seem alienated from everyone and everything. Even one's own skin some-times feels foreign. In *Being and Nothingness*, Sartre de-scribes the experience of seeing his hand as a "thing among other things" which "reveals to me the resistance of objects, their hardness or softness, but not itself. Thus I see my hand only in the way that I see this inkwell" (Sartre 402).

In addition to the disjointed feelings related to Cartesian dualism, the mind-body dichotomy reminds people of their mortality. Everything a person does and experiences is through the body, and when the body expires the individual no longer exists in the world. The mind knows, and perhaps has experienced, that the body can fail to work properly and is susceptible to a wide spectrum of physical ailments. Knowledge of this inevitable weakness leaves one feeling naked and vulnerable, powerless in the face of death.

Human beings possess the unique capability of rational thought, which brings each individual the joint curse and blessing of awareness that he or she will eventually die. The "awareness of the threat of *nonbeing*" is the main source of existential anxiety. In *The Meaning of Anxiety,* Rollo May quotes Paul Tillich's description of man as "the creature who is self-consciously aware of his being, but... also aware that at any moment he might cease to be" (May 15). May also quotes Kierkegaard's definition of anxiety as the "fear of nothingness." Anxiety lies not only in the physical threat of death, but also in the spiritual threat of meaninglessness in one's existence.

Pre-existing knowledge of one's ultimate death contributes to a gnawing feeling that the universe is absurd. Not only are humans doomed to die, but unlike any other animal, people are aware of the fact and feel anxiety because of it. Making decisions and achieving goals can seem pointless in the face of inevitable death. But inanely waiting for guidance or excitement to arrive, as Vladimir and Estragon did in Samuel Beckett's *Waiting for Godot*, seems more pointless and absurd.

Each individual possesses free will, a unique and powerful trait which causes a person to experience dread. According to Kierkegaard in *The Concept of Dread*, dread is the "dizziness of freedom" in which the shaken spirit "gazes down into its own possibility, grasping at finiteness to sustain itself." The possibility of freedom is the "alarming possibility of *being able*," a sometimes terrifying power which is accompanied by tremendous personal responsibility. Each individual is responsible for making the decisions which define that individual's present and future, and even the refusal to make a decision is a decision in itself. "In dread there is the egoistic infinity of possibility, which does not tempt like a definite choice, but alarms and fascinates with its sweet anxiety" (Kierkegaard 104-5). This overwhelming experience of anxiety can leave a person impotent in the moment of decision and action, and the spirit which "grasps at finiteness to sustain itself" is guilty of not rising to its potential.

While existentialism denies the traditional concept of a shared human nature, or model, according to Sartre, "there is nevertheless a human universality of *condition*, ... all the *limitations* which *a priori* define a man's fundamental situation in the universe" (Sartre 46). The human condition involves definitional limitations such as time, place, physicality, history, and situation. Every person finds himself in a body which needs food, water and sleep, in one historical

Christine M. Cinquino

time period and relative geographical locality. And human beings share similar feelings of anxiety, absurdity, loneliness, and dread. They find themselves facing universal spiritual and psychological problems related to alienation from self and others and from knowledge of death. These limitations define the myriad of possible choices each human being can make.

The human condition undeniably contains a dark element, but several of the philosophers whose work might be classified under "existentialism" offer joyful, life-affirming messages. Kierkegaard describes how the individual acts within a dynamic and ongoing process involving a gigantic leap of faith for those brave enough to make it. Nietzsche illustrates life as an exciting opportunity to dance, to fully experience both joy and pain, and to live deliberately. And de Beauvoir sees the "ambiguous" world as a canvas awaiting the creative artistry of each free individual.

Søren Kierkegaard examined the dark side of the human condition, concentrating on the problems of dread, anxiety, and despair. In *The Sickness Unto Death*, he wrote:

> there is not a single human being who does not despair at least a little, in whose innermost being there does not dwell an uneasiness, an unquiet, a discordance, an anxiety in the face of an unknown something, or a something he doesn't even dare strike up acquaintance with, an anxiety about a possibility in life or an [inexplicable] anxiety about himself. (Kierkegaard 52)

Having and being a self involves a constant and demanding process requiring courage and persistence in the face of anxiety and despair. But according to Kierkegaard, this struggle with despair reveals the human potential for hope, for "if there were nothing eternal in a man, he would simply be unable to despair" (51).

The Exhilarating Freedom! Hope in Existentialism

An individual is capable of overcoming despair by transcending the self and refusing to bow to the limits of reason; to achieve true freedom, one must make a leap of faith. Within specific material and spiritual situations, each individual negotiates his or her own existence. But true discovery of the self requires letting go of worldly, common sense and embracing a life of hope and faith. In *Fear and Trembling*, Kierkegaard described Abraham's transcendence with the words "he who expected the impossible became greater than all" (31). One who transcends the painful experiences of life and opens the self to the 'impossible' will be able to experience growth and joy beyond all expectation.

Friedrich Nietzsche was one of the first philosophers to celebrate the strong potential of the individual. In the narrative of the Madman, the consequences of the death of God are foretold. The death of God does not symbolize hopelessness or incurable emptiness. Instead, the refusal to submit to unquestioned, deceitful values is the first step in humankind's assumption of responsibility for the world. Each individual possesses power over his or her own life and has the opportunity to face the world, unfettered by traditional expectations of morality and social propriety.

In *The Gay Science*, Nietzsche challenges individuals to live each day *deliberately*. In aphorism 341, he praises the strength of individuals, who "*crave nothing more fervently*" than to fully experience "every pain and every joy and every thought and sigh and everything unutterably small or great in your life." This manner of living requires an active choice and some degree of optimism. The choice, actually a series of many choices, involves giving up the peace of mind which comes from a life of lethargic monotony and taking up an active life, one involving the spirit and the mind in all decisions and actions.

To live life *deliberately* requires much perseverance; one must constantly face the "question in each and every thing, 'Do you desire this once more and innumerable times more?'" This daring question brings "the greatest weight" and could "perhaps crush you," because it has the potential to paralyze all action. Nietzsche recognizes that there must be a limit to such analysis if life is to be lived. Thus, although "each and every thing" should theoretically be desired infinitely, "craving this ultimate eternal confirmation and seal" must involve a daily process. The individual should embrace every moment but recognize that there will be many more to come. Life is only meaningless and dark if the individual chooses to see it that way.

In *The Ethics of Ambiguity*, Simone de Beauvoir directly addresses the question of where existentialism leads, with regard to ethics and values. She asks,

> Is it true that this belief [in freedom] must lead us to despair? Must we grant this curious paradox: that from the moment a man recognizes himself as free, he is prohibited from wishing for anything? (Oaklander 390)

And her answer is an overwhelming *no*. Despair is not the inevitable result of the lack of preordained meaning. The passion of human beings, she asserts, "*has* no reason to will itself. But this does not mean that it can not justify itself, that it can not *give itself* reasons for being" (389). Clarifying two words commonly used in reference to existentialist thought, de Beauvoir emphasizes the difference between absurdity and ambiguity. "To declare that existence is absurd is to deny that it could ever be given a meaning; to say that it is ambiguous is to assert that its meaning is never fixed, that it must be constantly won" (393). Existentialism is better described by ambiguity, which she sees as a positive trait.

Ambiguity opens the door for creative vitality and embraces the endless details of daily life, which can never be adequately accounted for by an idealistic system such as Hegel's. Through a process of creation, each person justifies the world and fills it with value. De Beauvoir writes:

> Let men attach value to words, forms, colors, mathematical theorems, physical laws, and athletic prowess; let them accord value to one another in love and friendship, and the objects, the events, and the men immediately *have* this value; they have it absolutely. (403)

No value is static and unchanging; life involves ambiguity. The only universal value is freedom, which de Beauvoir calls "the source from which all significations and all values spring" (391).

Morality stems from embracing this freedom, struggling with ambiguity, and transcending the self. According to de Beauvoir, "To will oneself moral and to will oneself free are one and the same decision... But this living confirmation can not be merely contemplative and verbal. It is carried out as an act" (391). Individuals have the freedom to choose personal goals and values and the opportunity to live genuinely, according to those values. "It is up to man to make it important to be a man, and he alone can feel his success or failure" (390).

The knowledge that one is responsible for his or her life, through active decision making or the lack thereof, can place a lot of pressure on a person of any age. Young people face many difficult challenges as they navigate their way to adulthood. Important decisions must be made regarding educational and career goals, social and sexual identities, and personal beliefs and values. As a young person actively defines and develops the self through personal free choices, it might be helpful for that individual to keep in mind that everyone faces the 'existentials' inherent in the human condition.

Within the framework of the human condition, human beings possess a great degree of freedom, in that they are aware of their circumstances and have the power to act or react to the situations in which they find themselves. And while individuals are free to choose pessimistic nihilism, they are also free to embrace the terrible freedom of existential philosophy in a positive way, as some of the great 'existentialist' thinkers have done. The challenge of creating personal meaning can be especially liberating and invigorating to young people, who are in the process of discovering themselves and revealing their own values. People of all ages can be encouraged by the hope-filled, action-oriented process of grasping human freedom and choosing to create meaningful life on the blank canvas of existence.

REFERENCES

de Beauvoir, Simone. *The Ethics of Ambiguity*. Trans. Bernard Frechtman. Secaucus, NJ: Citadel Press, 1982. Rpt. in Oaklander, L. Nathan. *Existentialist Philosophy: An Introduction*. Englewood Cliffs, NJ: Prentice Hall, 1992. Pp. 387-403.

Camus, Albert. *The Stranger*. Trans. Stuart Gilbert. New York: Vintage Books, 1946.

Kafka, Franz. *The Metamorphosis and other stories*. Trans. Donna Freed. New York: Barnes & Noble, 1996.

Kaufmann, Walter. *Existentialism from Dostoevsky to Sartre*. New York: Penguin Books USA, 1989 (first printing expanded edition 1975). Pp. 11-51 and 83-120.

Kierkegaard, Søren. *The Concept of Dread*. Trans. Walter Lowrie. Princeton, NJ: Princeton University Press, 1957. Rpt. in Kaufmann, Walter. *Existentialism from Dostoevsky to Sartre*. New York: Penguin Books USA, 1989 (first printing expanded edition 1975). Pp. 101-105.

_____. *Fear and Trembling*. Trans. Walter Lowrie. Princeton, NJ: Princeton University Press, 1968. 26-37.

_____. *The Sickness Unto Death*. Trans. Alastair Hannay. London: Penguin Books Ltd., 1989.

May, Rollo. *The Meaning of Anxiety*. New York: W.W. Norton & Company, 1977.

Nietzsche, Friedrich. *The Gay Science*. Trans. Walter Kaufmann. New York: Random House, 1974.

Sartre, Jean Paul. *Being and Nothingness*: *A Phenomenology Essay on Ontology*. Trans. Hazel E. Barnes. Washington Square Press, 1993.

THE PROBLEM OF HAPPINESS IN NIETZSCHE'S "USE AND ABUSE OF HISTORY"

Malinda Foster

University of Michigan, Dearborn

This essay examines Nietzsche's "Use and Abuse of History," focusing on the problem of happiness. According to Nietzsche, in order for us to be happy in life we need history. Without history we will be unhappy. With too much history we will be unhappy. With just the right amount of history we may or may not be happy, but at least we will be tempted to think that happiness in life is possible—and the thought of that, Nietzsche says, will tend to make us rather happy.

In what follows I aim accurately to describe the main issue in Nietzsche's "Use and Abuse of History" as seemingly indicated by Nietzsche himself: the problem of happiness.[1] I suggest further that Nietzsche's essay and its hortatory content are directed at young students. Today, that would seem to translate into undergraduates in particular. These issues seem timely and appropriate because modern education, according to Nietzsche, leaves its pupils ignorant of the most important thing: the possibility of happiness in life.

Arguably, Nietzsche writes unconventional books. Consider his *Thus Spoke Zarathustra*. Is this a standard philosophical treatise? Not exactly. Might we not be tempted to characterize it as a work of literature? But to be considered as literature would it not need to contain a plot or narrative arc? Is there a plot to *Zarathustra*? Not exactly. Then if it is neither philosophy nor literature proper, what kind of a book is it? And the *Gay Science* with its prelude in rhymes and appendix of songs? Would this be Nietzsche's book on science? methodology? poetry? music? A little strange. One is prepared for this when turning to "The Use and Abuse of History."

Upon such a turn, the first reasonable question to ask is "Where is the Kaufmann translation?" The answer, of course, is that there is no Kaufmann translation. Why not? Why did he not regard it as important enough to command his attention as translator? Perhaps this could be resolved by saying simply that even Kaufmann has his limitations; translation, after all, is no easy task. Then again, it is difficult to overlook the fact that Kaufmann translated a substantial amount of Nietzsche's work and, for one reason or another, chose to attend to other texts instead of "The Use and Abuse of History."

Fortunately, there are alternatives; two of the more popular are those of Adrian Collins and R.J. Hollingdale. Strange, though, that this essay that is both commonly and comfortably referred to as "The Use and Abuse of History" is actually entitled *"Vom Nutzen und Nachteil der Historie fuer das Leben."* A fuller translation of the title, then, would be "The Use and Abuse of History *for Life.*" Is it not somewhat perilous to disregard Nietzsche's qualification— *fuer das leben*? The Collins translation does so freely.

Compounding the trouble, there is something a little strange about the silence surrounding numerous works of prominent Nietzsche scholarship—places where it seems legitimate to expect to see even a hint of a glimmer of an intimation of a reference to "The Use and Abuse of History." This includes, but is certainly not limited to, essays by Alphonso Lingis, Gilles Deleuze, Eric Blondel, Jacques Derrida, Sarah Kofman, Arthur Danto, and Richard Schact.[2] Wondering if the "Use and Abuse of History" suffers from neglect and confusion begins to seem increasingly justified.

Yet, the difficulties are in no way over, because there is an immediate complication when trying to engage Nietzsche by means of his text: the very first words are not Nietzsche's; they are Goethe's. Anyone with the slightest exposure to the *Gay Science* will recall aphorism 370 and wonder why Nietzsche, both in the foreword and throughout "The Use and Abuse of History," seems to ally himself with Goethe. In aphorism 370 of the *Gay Science* Nietzsche refers to Goethe as a demi-god of sorts (i.e., *not a full ally*) saying that he once made a mistake not only about Goethe, but also Wagner, music, art, romanticism, the motive force behind essential human needs, science, theories of being and becoming, destruction, and creativity; the list is long. "It may perhaps be recalled," he says, "at least among my friends, that initially I approached the modern world with a few crude errors and overestimations and, in any case, hopefully" (*Gay Science*, aphorism 370, pp. 327-31).

Keeping the Goethe problem in mind while setting the context, "The Use and Abuse of History" was published in 1873 when Nietzsche was approximately 29 years old and a full professor at Basel. Nine years later, after his taking leave from the university, the *Gay Science* was published in 1882. That would make Nietzsche 38 years old at the time. But aphorism 370 is in the fifth part of the *Gay Science*, which was not added by Nietzsche until 1887. That would make Nietzsche approximately 43 years old when writing about Goethe, art, science, romanticism, creativity, etc. in aphorism 370 of the *Gay Science*—as opposed to age 29 when he writes "The Use and Abuse of History."[3]

What all this means is that there is good reason to think that what Nietzsche says in "The Use and Abuse of History" reflects what he *once* thought, that is, when he was still young and, as he says, hopeful. It turns out that a critical portion of what he has to say in "The Use and Abuse of History" he will later refer to as a mistake. Accordingly, readers familiar with Nietzsche's more mature works of *Thus Spoke Zarathustra, Beyond Good and Evil*, and *Genealogy of Morals* must be prepared to face "The Use and Abuse of History" with a certain, profound naiveté.

Moving beyond Goethe's opening words, Nietzsche refers to his essay as a "meditation on the value of history" (59). It seems necessary to resist any temptation to be overly distracted with Nietzsche's use of the word "value" here, remembering that any revaluation-of-all-values education that might have been received from Nietzsche in the *Genealogy of Morals* would be the result of having read a book that will not exist for young Nietzsche for another thirteen or fourteen years.[4] To be understood, "The Use and Abuse of History" demands to be read on its own terms.

Returning to the essay, the problem, according to Nietzsche in "The Use and Abuse of History," is that modern education values the study of history to such a high degree that it no longer serves life (59). Modern men are suffering, he says, "from a consuming fever of history" (60). The result is sickness, because history studied as such serves death, and not life. The goal, Nietzsche indicates, is to put history in the service of life for the possible attainment of happiness.

The difficulty, according to Nietzsche, is that in order to be happy in life, history is absolutely indispensable. Without history, happiness in life is not possible. With too much history, happiness in life is not possible. With just the right amount of history, happiness in life may or may not be possible—but the thought that it just might be possible, Nietzsche says, tends to promote happiness.

Without history we are like cows, grazing in the pasture of life (61). Without knowledge of "yesterday and today," "neither melancholy nor bored," our happiness springs forth from an absence of suffering: we must be happy because we do not feel pain (60-1). Even if we were to suffer, we would quickly forget it because, like animals, we would have no memory beyond the last thirty seconds of life (61). Thus, he says, we would live, like animals, *unhistorically* (61).

To be brief, Nietzsche's problem with living a thoroughly unhistorical life is that, while a certain type of forgetfulness may be useful, there are also certain disadvantages (to life) because such an animal would not only forget that it suffers, but it would also forget that it lives (61). Only death would remind it that it once lived and Nietzsche wants happiness in life—not death (59, 61).

Alternatively, one can (as we modern men do, according to Nietzsche) have too much history (60). We are what he calls *historical* men (59, 65). We have been taught by Hegel and the subsequent Hegelian tradition that human beings suffer for a reason (104). Insofar as our suffering is not without purpose, we are to console ourselves, it is not without meaning. Therefore, we historical men glance behind, looking at the past, to understand and validate both ourselves and our suffering as meaningful in the present (65). For, as Hegel teaches, the justification of suffering (so that we will not think it devoid of meaning) necessitates a certain saturation and steeping of oneself in the study of history (65). Since history is the source of our redemption, we pursue it with the hope that—once understood—our suffering will have meaning (65). At best, it could be said that happiness is tantamount to a certain knowledge found at the end of our pursuit.

Nietzsche takes exception to living the life of the thoroughly historical man. Hoping to find happiness at the *end* of the process, the thoroughly historical man longs to relieve himself of the burdens and vicissitudes presented by life (i.e., human suffering and episodes of apparent injustice). The so-called end that the thoroughly historical man longs for is, ultimately, death. For only death would fully relieve him of the burden of life—a burden that Nietzsche indicates he would rather bear than shrug off (65).

A third possibility, according to Nietzsche, is to be "cured forever of taking history too seriously" by viewing the problem of meaning and suffering from what he calls the *suprahistorical* vantage point (65-6). In that case, we would learn from our study of history that there is "no salvation in the [Hegelian] process" of history (66). All suffering, we would learn, is in fact meaningless because, by virtue of having studied great historical events, we would be overcome by one, singular, nauseating thought: there is no justice (64).

History would teach us literally nothing. Life, for the thoroughly suprahistorical man, is nothing but death; there is no *meaningful* difference between the two. "Our being is pain and boredom," the suprahistorical man says "and the world is dirt—nothing more" (66).

What is most needed, according to Nietzsche, is history in the service of life, and not death (62). While this may be complicated, he says that it is possible that what he calls *monumental, antiquarian,* and *critical* history, properly employed, can be put in the service of life (62).

Firstly, *monumental* history promotes life. It is good, according to Nietzsche, because it gives us something to strive for (67). The man of monumental history "goes his way with a more cheerful step," because the thought that "X" great man or "X" great thing was once possible in the past, suggests to him that it might be possible again in the future (69). Happiness is found in a sense of continuity and connectedness.

Secondly, the man of *antiquarian* history also finds a certain joy in continuity (73). Upholding models of past greatness, history tells him that not only did the great things of the past once exist—but they also persist (73). Life, he learns to his satisfaction, is not fleeting and arbitrary chaos (74).

Lastly, *critical* history is needed as a source of questioning the things of the past (75-7). Blazing a trail for the novel, critical history breaks with tradition. Good, the man armed with critical history says; for now he can learn to see all that is still possible.

The Problem of Happiness

The difficulty, according to Nietzsche, is that along with the certain advantages that the three various histories can provide for life, there are also accompanying disadvantages. *Monumental* history can be bad for a number of reasons, he says, not the least of which is the realization that greatness always exists as part of the past. In doing so, it seems to dwarf the men of the present (68). *Antiquarian* history might also be bad because not all of our ancestors turn out to be good. Revering the bad simply because it is tradition can be disadvantageous (74). Additionally, the corruptive influence of the *critical* historian's questioning can also be extraordinarily impious. This is a problem because life, according to Nietzsche, requires a certain set of lies or myths (118-9). In other words, in order to live there are some questions that simply must not be asked.

Conceivably, Nietzsche could be considered to be disingenuous at this point. For, surely, someone might be tempted to submit, Nietzsche does not, himself, seem to be overly cautious about the types of questions that he tends to put forth for the reader to consider. In other words, someone might ask: How pious is Nietzsche? Does he, himself, submit to his own prescription?

Absolutely.

Again, the temptation is to think outside of the essay and in terms of *Beyond Good and Evil*; for example, where Nietzsche asks his fairly incendiary question: Why should we want what is good for us? Why not bad? Surely, there is no question that Herr Nietzsche—Mr. Rash and Curious, himself—refuses to ask.[5]

Let me put the answer in this way: Why is it again that, according to Nietzsche in "The Use and Abuse of History," we want life as opposed to death? Why is it that we want happiness? Why not unhappiness?

What more can be said? There are some questions that young Nietzsche does not ask.

Returning to the problem at hand, in addition to learning how much history is too much history, it seems necessary to learn the difficult task of balancing how much of one type of history is either too much or not enough in relation to the others (72). How shall we know? Nietzsche teaches that experience alone can act as educator (116-8). First, he says, we must learn to live. Next, we must learn to live well (i.e., learn what is good for life, learn to philosophize). Only then can we learn to put history in the service of life (116, 122).

Yet, on the whole, exactly what this extra-ordinarily balanced, life-serving type of history might turn out to look like is exceedingly mysterious. Instructing his readers by means of a parable, Nietzsche's answer seems ambiguous at best and seriously problematic at worst (122). For this reason it seems necessary to turn to those more experienced in such matters for assistance. Having hurdled the barrier of locating prominent, concentrated study and exegesis, the works of three conspicuous voices become audible: Hayden White, Walter Kaufmann, and Werner Dannhauser.[6]

Hayden White's answer to the problem of balance is quite straightforward. The answer is: there is no answer. In "The Use and Abuse of History," according to White, Nietzsche merely tells what such a life-serving type of history would *not* be; "he [does] not say what it would look like" (356). Ultimately, according to White, one must turn to the *Genealogy of Morals* for answers (356).

At the same time, White indicates that perhaps the most illuminating and fruitful comment that Nietzsche does make in "The Use and Abuse of History" is when he says that "...only if history can endure to be transformed into a work of art will it perhaps be able to preserve instincts or even evoke them" (Nietzsche 95-6 and White 352, 355). This makes sense because Nietzsche will say that to bridge the gap between life and history, or to find the correct life-serving balance of histories, it is necessary to turn away from science and scientific analysis (as they mask themselves beneath the guise of objectivity and therefore the supposed truth) and turn toward art or creativity (77-82). As White interprets, this bridging activity is to be done by the historian (50).[7]

Consequently, employing a sophisticated understanding of Nietzsche's *Birth of Tragedy* to support his arguments, when Nietzsche says in "The Use and Abuse of History" that "[t]he fine historian must have the power of coining the known into a thing never heard before and proclaiming the universal so simply and profoundly that the simple is lost in the profound and the profound in the simple," White interprets "[t]he historian thus conceived is the master of Metaphorical identifications of objects that occupy the historical field" (353). Meaning that the past is to be recreated at the hands of the historian in terms of metaphor, hiding the simple in the profound and the profound in the simple (353). "But this hiding is at the same time a revelation, a revelation of man's power to go into his present and do what he will with history" (353). Further, as White reads the text, the only prohibitions are

> from deifying the past at the expense of the present and the present at the expense of the future—that is

> to say, from writing uncritical Monumental or un-
> critical Antiquarian history, or, conversely, unheroic
> and irreverent Critical history. (White 356)

But, then again, White says, inevitably, one must turn to *The Genealogy of Morals* for more precise answers (356). Nonetheless, the long and the short of White's argument can be summed up in terms of history-as-metaphor.

Walter Kaufmann, who also acknowledges the limits of the text to provide precise answers, argues in a similar vein—save without White's sophisticated language and style (142, 152, 156). Also pulling his understanding of Nietzsche's "Use and Abuse of History" from his reading of the *Birth of Tragedy*, Kaufmann indicates that history looked upon as a work of art would take the shape of and serve as "timeless allegory" (152). Looking back on models of past greatness, contemplating "Aeschylus and Heraclitus, Socrates and Jesus, Leonardo and Michelangelo, Shakespeare and Goethe, Caesar and Napoleon, or Plato and Spinoza" history would reveal (to those of us who study it) the timeless questions, problems, and narrative debate relevant to humankind (152). So, Kaufmann's answer to the question of history as art can be summed up as history-as-allegory.

Werner Dannhauser, in many ways by contrast, is not so experimental. While he, too, acknowledges the limitations of the text to provide precise answers, saying that it is necessary to turn to *Beyond Good and Evil* for satisfaction, Dannhauser merely ventures an accurate description of Nietzsche's problem (829-35). Unlike Kaufmann and White, he posits no more certain answer in the face of Nietzsche's ambiguity. What he does instead, is frame his argument both in terms of his understanding of Hegel and his understanding of Hegel's subsequent influence upon

The Problem of Happiness

Nietzsche, and he does so by means of one word: *historicism*—a word I have yet to find in Nietzsche's vocabulary (832-4). That is to say, Dannhauser suggests that Nietzsche's need to turn away from science is essentially an attempt—*repeat, an attempt*—to escape the trappings of historicism. Further, Dannhauser wonders if it is at all possible for Nietzsche, based on his own arguments, to bridge this seemingly impossible gap between life and history, art and science, knowledge and truth. Eventually, he, too, will conclude that such conflicts are not resolved in "The Use and Abuse of History" (834).

So scholars agree that there is no firm answer to this question of what history as a work of art would look like. We must, they say, look elsewhere: White looks to *The Birth of Tragedy* and *Genealogy of Morals*, Kaufmann looks to *The Birth of Tragedy*, and Dannhauser to *Beyond Good and Evil*. But Nietzsche has already warned us to stick to the narrow confines of the text, lest he be misunderstood. Assuming that Nietzsche, too, is one of our betters, to whom shall we listen? Is possible that Kaufmann, White, and Dannhauser are not sufficiently naïve, sufficiently youthful, to hear young Nietzsche?

How is it possible that we could think Hayden White not sufficiently naive? He acknowledges Nietzsche's still intact innocence. Arguing for the thematic primacy of remembering and forgetting, White points out that there are some questions that young Nietzsche has yet to ask himself when writing "The Use and Abuse of History." As a result, the early Nietzsche is, he says, in some respects, surprisingly naive (348). Consider, for example, White's observation that Nietzsche has yet to begin to ask himself about the *source* of memory:

Malinda Foster

> Later on, in *The Genealogy of Morals*, Nietzsche undertook to explain, on historical and psychological grounds, how this ability to remember took root in man; but in 'The Use and Abuse of History' he took it for granted and asked what it implies for the living of a creative human life. (348)

Unique to White's presentation is a distinctly sensitive disposition to the hortatory nature of Nietzsche's essay. He maintains that Nietzsche is calling on the noble and the heroic to save modernity from its present crisis (i.e., the "consuming fever of history") (Nietzsche 60 and White 355-6). Moreover, according to White, it is the historians who are the nobles to save the day. They are the ones who are to step into the breach.

But is it not Nietzsche's point that before the historian can go to work, as it were, he must first learn how to live? Does Nietzsche not say that all study of history, heretofore, has ultimately served death, not life? Does he not say that because of this we no longer know how to live? Must we not learn this first? Moreover, does Nietzsche not think this—if at all possible—possible for the young only? Must one not be a child, of sorts, first? Does he not, at that point, indicate that one must then learn to live well; that is to say, one must learn to philosophize? At bottom, is not Nietzsche's argument not just a call out to the noble, but also a call out to the young and noble? This is puzzling because while White grants a certain naiveté to Nietzsche, he seems to function under a lack of it himself—presupposing more steps having already been taken on the way to the creation of history as art (i.e., history-as-metaphor).

Yet, Kaufmann may be able to help. His history-as-allegory reading may prove to be more instructive than White's history-as-metaphor. For unlike the device of metaphor, an essential, constituent element of allegory is a certain moral teaching or quality (Cuddon 22-4, 542-3, 676). Insofar as Nietzsche's concern is for living well and, therefore, philosophizing prior to any recreation of historical events at the hands of the historian, ethics and morality must play a significant role in any final version of any life-serving history, or history as art (Nietzsche 123). Additionally, note that Nietzsche instructs his readers by offering what he calls a parable in place of any concrete teaching (Nietzsche 122). While the line between parable and allegory is relatively fine, the line between parable and metaphor is significant (Cuddon). Therefore, Kaufmann's analysis seems more apt. But it is also strange. The original German is unambiguous: Nietzsche says "parable." Why, then, would Kaufmann suggest "allegory" as more appropriate? This is unusual. The merit, however, of Kaufmann's perspective is that he thinks back, as it were, one step further, with fuller recognition that before one can employ history in the service of life, one must know what is good for life—i.e., one must first learn to philosophize. Yet he does not seem to ask of the text *who* is to do this philosophizing.

Perhaps Dannhauser can help. How could one think him not sufficiently naive? For does Dannhauser make impositions on the text, as do Kaufmann and White? Saying that Nietzsche tries to transcend the problems that historicism presents by offering a creative (and therefore ennobling) interpretation of history, Dannhauser like White, hears a certain textual exhortation. Unlike White, and like Kaufmann, he acknowledges the need for the historian first to philosophize. But again, before we could philosophize, we would have to possess a certain youthfulness or appreciable naiveté.

In the end, precisely what shape might this youthful, artistic history take? Scholars say the answer is that there is no answer. Not in "The Use and Abuse of History." If at all. Then perhaps we need to change the question. For since when has Nietzsche ever been known to be a precise writer? Thorough, yes. Comprehensive, yes. Rich and full, yes. Poetic and often licentious, yes. Exacting and precise? Since when? Perhaps we also need to change our ways. Perhaps Nietzsche's answer is vague for a reason. What? We expect him to supply us with a formula? When Nietzsche says turn from science and toward art, we should abandon our slide-rulers and calculators and periodic charts, but we are to impose sophisticated terminology, specialized meanings, and alternate terms (historicism, allegory, metaphor)? How can we expect this to be the path? How is this possible?

Perhaps the limitations do not exist wholly within the text; perhaps we bring a few of them with us. Perhaps the precise answer, to be precise, is that there is no *precise* answer. Lacking such precision we might at least say that the youth to whom Nietzsche addresses his exhortation are, like him, untimely (60, 67). Moreover, any artistic life-serving history at their disposal would reflect their untimeliness (122).

But what does this mean to be untimely, falling like a day out of season? If we watch for the lightning in February, sleet in May, the smell of dead leaves in August, rain in January, and of course Indian Summer perhaps these will yield the best clues. What? Are we leaving the text? Well, that is the exhortation is it not? Shall we not enter the unique workshop of the unique master—nature—to learn (118)?

I suspect that the first time our ski trip is canceled on account of rain, or a hard frost is cast about the tender rosebuds of our garden, or a bolt of lightning strikes our furnace on a cold, cold, very cold winter night, then we might appreciate to whom Nietzsche is talking and what he is saying. Most of us will damn the rain, damn the frost, and damn the untimely bolt of lightning, fleeing to our local meteorologist demanding an account of such unseasonable phenomenon as justification for all the suffering and inconvenience we have experienced on its account. Only a few, a rare few, will stand on the front porch with skis hoisted upon their shoulders, watching the rain melt the snow and say with a smile, "best when it rains in January; thus it is, thus it shall be" (106). Yet it is to such a man that history—and, therefore, happiness—belongs (61).

No. To be precise, Nietzsche does not promise precision. He does not promise that our strange and unorthodox education will be easy, effortless, or without suffering (121). In fact he suggests that we are likely to find it intensely difficult (116, 121, 123). At the same time, knowing that the "path to redemption ... lies only through cheerfulness," our suffering will at least remind us that we are alive (61, 111). At best, the recognition and increasingly fuller appreciation for the fact that *we do live* encourages us to think that happiness is possible.

Happiness in life as possible ... the very thought, he says, makes a youthful heart laugh with joy (59-60, 111, 122-3).

Malinda Foster

NOTES

[1]   All page references to "The Use and Abuse of History" correspond to R.J. Hollingdale's translation which uses the title, "On the Uses and Disadvantages of History for Life." Parenthetic citations, unless otherwise specified, are to this text.

[2]   See for example: David B. Allison, ed. *The New Nietzsche.* (Cambridge: MIT Press, 1994); Robert C. Solomon and Kathleen M. Higgins, ed. *Reading Nietzsche.* (New York: Oxford University Press, 1988); Richard Schacht. *Nietzsche.* (New York: Routledge, 1996); Carl Pletsch. *Young Nietzsche: Becoming a Genius.* (New York: The Free Press, 1991); and Bernd Magnus and Kathleen M. Higgins, eds. *The Cambridge Companion to Nietzsche.* Cambridge: (Cambridge University Press, 1996).

[3]   For chronology, see *The Portable Nietzsche*, pp. 20-3.

[4]   Specifically, aphorism 6 of Nietzsche's preface to *Genealogy of Morals.*

[5]   See *Beyond Good and Evil* (aphorism 190, p. 103) and *Genealogy of Morals* (114).

[6]   Hayden White, *Metahistory*, pp. 346-56; Walter Kaufmann, *Nietzsche: Philosopher, Psychologist, Antichrist*, pp. 138-56; and Werner Dannhauser, "Friedrich Nietzsche," *History of Political Philosophy*, pp. 829-50. Unless otherwise noted, all citations for White, Kaufmann, and Dannhauser are to these texts.

[7]   Also see Hayden White, *Tropics of Discourse: Essays in Cultural Criticism*, pp. 28-9.

REFERENCES

Allison, David B, ed. *The New Nietzsche.* Cambridge: MIT Press, 1994.

Cuddon, J.A. *Dictionary of Literary Terms and Literary Theory.* Third Edition. Penguin Books, 1991.

Dannhauser, Werner. "Friedrich Nietzsche." *History of Political Philosophy.* Third Edition. Ed. Leo Strauss and Joseph Cropsey. Chicago: The University of Chicago Press, 1987.

Kaufmann, Walter. *Nietzsche: Philosopher, Psychologist, Antichrist.* New Jersey: Princeton University Press, 1974.

Magnus, Bernd and Kathleen M. Higgins, eds. *The Cambridge Companion to Nietzsche.* Cambridge: Cambridge University Press, 1996.

Nietzsche, Friedrich. *The Use and Abuse of History.* Trans. Adrian Collins. New York: Bobbs-Merrill. 1957.

_____. *Beyond Good and Evil.* Trans. Walter Kaufmann. New York: Vintage Books, 1966.

_____. *The Gay Science.* Trans. Walter Kaufmann. New York: Random House, 1974.

_____. *Thus Spoke Zarathustra.* Trans. Walter Kaufmann. Penguin Books, 1985.

_____. *On The Genealogy of Morals.* Trans. Walter Kaufmann and R.J. Hollingdale. New York: Vintage Books, 1989.

_____. *The Birth of Tragedy.* In *Basic Writings of Nietzsche.* Trans. and Ed. Walter Kaufmann. New York: Random House, 1992.

_____. "On the Uses and Disadvantages of History for Life." *Untimely Meditations.* Trans. R.J. Hollingdale. Ed. Daniel Breazeale. Cambridge: Cambridge University Press, 1997.

_____. *The Portable Nietzsche.* Ed. and Trans. Walter Kaufmann. New York: Penguin Books.

Pletsch, Carl. *Young Nietzsche: Becoming a Genius.* New York: The Free Press, 1991.

Schacht, Richard. *Nietzsche.* New York: Routledge, 1996.

Solomon, Robert C. and Kathleen M. Higgins, eds. *Reading Nietzsche.* New York: Oxford University Press, 1988.

White, Hayden. *Metahistory.* Baltimore: The Johns Hopkins University Press, 1973.

_____. *Tropics of Discourse: Essays in Cultural Criticism.* Baltimore: The Johns Hopkins University Press, 1978.

TRADITION AND MODERN MEANING: SOCIETY AND RELATIVE TRUTH

Jason Baumgarth

University of Minnesota, Duluth

Kobo Abe and Walker Percy develop the ideas found in traditional Continental Existentialism in *The Woman in the Dunes* and *The Moviegoer*. Though not traditional philosophers, Abe and Percy provide Japanese and American perspectives on the problems which threaten the individual in modern society. Abe's *The Woman in the Dunes* addresses the confines of a society bound by tradition and the risks such a society poses to the individual. Percy's *The Moviegoer* examines the effects of American society on individual freewill and authenticity. Both Abe and Percy provide permutations to Continental Existentialism which reflect their respective cultures and further the ideas of writers such as Sartre and Camus. In helping to identify the downfalls of the society we have created, Abe and Percy add to the groundwork of Existential literature and begin the search for solutions to the problem of finding authenticity in a systematized world.

Kobo Abe and Walker Percy enter into the history of existential literature in the 1960's providing two distinct permutations to the primarily Continental basis of Existential philosophy. Kobo Abe in *The Woman in the Dunes* addresses the concerns of living in a culture focused heavily on tradition. Walker Percy, providing an American perspective to traditional existentialist views, relies on the underlying concepts found in Continental existentialism to address the problems both tradition and popular culture pose to the American individual. Earlier existential literature, found in writings from Nietzsche, Kafka, Kierkegaard, Sartre, and Camus, approach the problem of individual freedom in the context of a society steeped in modern mass culture. Due to the cultural differences between Europe, America, and Japan, however, Abe and Percy must approach the situation of the individual differently from the Continental philosophers. Europe faced new problems with the advent of the Industrial Revolution, in particular, an internal upheaval of values on a continent formerly ruled by monarchy and theocracy. Japan, relying to this day on traditional approaches to culture and society, did not suffer as much from the advent of the Industrial Revolution; rather the individual was left with the oppressive nature of a tradition which demanded compliance and conformity.

America, as a young country compared with both the European nations and Japan, was formed near the beginning of the Industrial Revolution and, as a result, does not have the historical perspective of the European nations or the singular traditional basis of the Japanese culture. America, due to its heterogeneity and lack of history, was formed as a model of the scientific approach to social interaction as a common basis upon which we could understand each other on an equal basis. The heterogeneity of the United States also gave rise to unique traditional cultures, especially in the south where a rigid class hierarchy was developed as a result of the slave trade and agrarian lifestyle, which became oppressive in their categorization of individuals based on familial status alone. Despite the unique approaches to Existential philosophy found in *The Woman in the Dunes* and *The Moviegoer*, Abe and Percy adhere to the main precepts set forth by their Continental counterparts in developing their respective existential approaches to the individual in society.

Abe and Percy, in following with Continental Existentialism, react to the problems which have arisen as a result of
modern social structures. Following the Industrial Revolution, science and economics began to replace traditional
sources of value through their ability to systematically
analyze the nature of the world in which we live. The sys-
temized methods of the new objectivity of modern society
promoted the increasing power of mass culture. Categorization and quantification of nearly all aspects of our world,
through scientific study, popular art and media, mass production, and bureaucracy, aided the rise of mass culture by
removing the importance of individual differences.

Standardization and bureaucracy allowed governments,
businesses, and other groups to lower the criteria needed in
filling a position. For instance, a manufacturer, prior to the
industrial revolution, might have needed a worker who was
skilled enough to build an entire clock. Such a worker
would have to know not only how a clock works, but also
how to build a clock from start to finish. With the systemi-
zation of industry during the industrial revolution, the same
manufacturer could hire workers who needed to learn only
one part of clock-making, putting the hands on the face of
the clock or hanging the pendulum, for example. The sys-
temization of industrial, governmental, and social processes
increased the replicability of the individual. Individual replicability effectively levels the playing field by allowing
any individual to perform virtually any function, but it also
renders personal talents null and void. Any functional person could step into an assembly line job and help to create
something he would be unable to create outside the assembly line structure of modern industry. On the other hand, a
worker who once was secure in his clock-making position
because of his knowledge of the entire process could now
be viewed as dispensable since any worker could be taught

to create their little part of the bigger process. The replicability of the individual resulting from the structural shifts in the Industrial Revolution leaves the individual with a certain anxiety, a loss of personal identity in the face of an omnipresent mass culture.

The main characters of *The Woman in the Dunes*, Niki Jumpei, and *The Moviegoer*, Binx Bolling, demonstrate the difficulties which face the individual in modern society. Both Jumpei and Bolling face societal traditions which have lost their moorings in the sea of mass culture. The characters fall victim to residual practices of displaced traditions which have lost their original basis for justification. Jumpei finds himself caught in a tradition that maintains a lifestyle which has become not only impractical, but also illogical with the advent of modern technology. Despite the strangeness of Jumpei's situation, his predicament demonstrates the nature of traditions which are still pursued despite their loss of justification. Bolling's situation, perhaps, strikes a chord more in tune with our own experiences dealing with cultural hierarchies which have become obsolete as a result of the equality stemming from mass society. Bollings, continually pressured to fit into a class structure which no longer makes sense, becomes a spectator to a world devoid of personal meaning.

Kobo Abe illustrates the modern human condition through the character of Niki Jumpei, a teacher and amateur entomologist. Jumpei falls victim to the villagers of a small town built on the sand dunes of the Japanese coast. Looking for a place to stay while out on an expedition in search of a new species of insect, Jumpei approaches the head of the village in hopes of finding accommodations for the night. He is put up for what he thinks will be the night at the home of a single woman on the outskirts of town, which

lies at the bottom of a pit formed by the incessant movement of the sand upon which the village is built. Abe develops the pit, which is to become Jumpei's prison, into a
metaphorical representation of the modern human condition, a condition in which the individual is arbitrarily subjected to the oppressive nature of the society around him.
The combination of the pit and the sand that forms its rim
allows Abe to show the quagmire into which we have
fallen. Jumpei is subjected to unwilling imprisonment, simply for the fact that he is capable of digging sand, through a
seemingly harmless request which strikes him as common
decency. The sand pit, like modern society, is a seemingly
inescapable prison in which the only way in or out is not
within the realm of our control. The arbitrary nature of each
individual's situation seems to be determined by the influences of those around us rather than by the ability to freely
choose who, what, and where we want to be. As a prisoner
of the village, Niki Jumpei stands as a representative of the
modern individual in society.

The villagers by whom Jumpei is imprisoned show the
danger of adherence to meaningless tradition. Built on the
dunes of the Japanese coast, the village developed a tradition in which each person assisted in digging the drifting
sand away from the houses. If the drifting sand was not
cleared away from the houses each night, the sand would
surely bury the houses. By involving every villager in the
nightly ritual of digging out their own house, the town was
able to keep the sand at bay. It would seem that with modern technology, however, a better method of reclaiming the
areas around the houses could be devised. For instance, the
houses could be built on stilts, above the blowing sand, or
perhaps a wind block could be constructed which prevented
the sand from entering the pits in which the houses were
built. The village tradition, which may have started prior to

technologies that would make other options feasible, does not make sense in a world filled with alternative options. There does not seem to be any reason other than obsolete village tradition why the houses are not built elsewhere away from the dangers of the sand.

Abe's choice of sand as the medium of entrapment in *A Woman in the Dunes* effectively shows the nature of the oppressiveness of a society based on tradition. Tradition carries with it the assumption that all individuals who acknowledge that tradition or are present in the culture in which it is followed will continue to follow the rules, both explicit and implicit, which result. When a society is based on a particular cultural history, the society is active in the development and continuance of the practices which are in place, and emphasis is placed on promoting the ideas of the culture itself rather than the interests of the people who make up the culture. Thus the individual is expected, at times, to adhere to an ideal which is not in the individual's best interests. The difficulty lies in escaping the expectations of the society based upon tradition, however, as the society, promoting its own ideals, attempts to maintain traditional practices despite their individual effects.

Abstraction of societal ideals through tradition discounts the individual as unimportant in the grand scheme of things as long as the ideal itself is mostly intact. To escape the expectations of society, then, is much like trying to escape the sand pit. By trying to directly escape the confines of a social system of which you are a part, the system is changed to accommodate for the actions taken in your efforts. In effect, the harder you try to dig yourself out of the sand pit, the more sand you have to dig, as Niki Jumpei saw when he was buried in his attempt to escape. When the individual fights against the oppressive nature of society, society reacts by increasing the restrictions on the individual to maintain social order and keep the thread of tradition intact. Thus, the system upon which society is based, while seeming to be concrete, is, much like the sand in which Jumpei is imprisoned, very fluid, changing with each challenge to the integrity of the whole. Jumpei, a representative of the individual in modern society, is left with a choice between following a meaningless tradition or creating his own meaning, but where is he to look for meaning?

The Woman in the Dunes also touches on the status of women in modern society, depicting the woman in the dunes as simply an object for sexual satisfaction. Women, as a result of increasing commodification and the patriarchal structure of society, have become symbols of raw sexuality for consumption by the modern male. In the modern social structure, men are viewed as the primary source of income for a family, a situation which elevates the interests of men due to society's emphasis on economic measures as indications of stature and progress. As a result of the primary importance of the male in an economically based system, women have been relegated to a supporting position which involves satisfying the desires and needs of men. Abe illustrates the modern position of women in society through Jumpei's reactions to the woman in the dunes. Jumpei is shown throughout the novel doing very little in respect to the woman. The woman cooks, shovels the sand away, brings Jumpei whatever he desires, and eventually offers herself as fulfillment of his sexual desires. The woman's actions are not viewed as anything which goes above and beyond what is expected of her; instead, Jumpei is agitated when her actions are not effective in supporting his needs. Jumpei, as is seen throughout *The Woman in the Dunes*, views the woman as an object and thus treats the woman as he might treat any other object in his possession.

The objectification of women helps to illustrate the plight of every individual in society, while pointing out the additional categorization women face due to their sex. This view of women, like all other individuals, results in their use simply as tools used as means toward reaching an end goal. In such a position, individuals are not seen to have intrinsic value or, in following, any of the rights resulting from individuality. Their worth, instead, lies in their usefulness in attaining a desired goal. The view Jumpei holds of the woman in the dunes extends to all others in some form. Women are uniquely viewed as means toward fulfillment of sexual ends and thus become sexual commodities, but all individuals are viewed primarily as tools valued only so far as they are useful in a system.

The townspeople's treatment of Niki Jumpei shows the lack of intrinsic value of the individual in the context of society. The fact that Niki Jumpei was imprisoned by the townspeople to be the woman's mate and to assist with the daily chore of digging, without any prior knowledge of Jumpei's individual characteristics, indicates that unique individual traits are of no importance in choosing who should fill the open spot in the community. Any man could have filled the spot Jumpei finds himself in and met the only criteria deemed important by the townspeople. Further evidence of the replaceability of the individual as a piece of a system presents itself in the revelation that the woman had another man filling Jumpei's role before Jumpei arrived. Jumpei, in essence, is simply a replacement part for the man who once lived with the woman in the dunes and so long as he meets the basic criteria needed to fill the part, it is unimportant what characteristics or talents he may bring to the community. *The Moviegoer*, while viewing the predicament of the individual in modern society from a slightly different perspective, arrives at many of the same conclusions as *The*

Woman in the Dunes. Walker Percy illustrates the problem of expectations derived from modern abstraction when applied to the traditional values of Southern culture. Through the relation of Binx Bolling to his secretaries and his arbitrary decision to marry Kate Cutrer, his cousin-in-law, he also shows the sexual objectification of women resulting from a society seeking homogeneity. Percy, however, also points out the arbitrary nature of truth and meaning in *The Moviegoer* and shows the shallow approach to human relationships which evolves from alienation and a lack of interest in establishing truth based on other individuals.

Using New Orleans, with its convergence of rigid Southern aristocratic culture and bustling modern industry, Percy develops the life of stock broker Binx Bolling to illustrate the expectations and generalizations present when viewing individuals through the lenses of tradition and post-industrial social approaches. Traditional Southern culture developed as a result of the agrarian heritage of Southern families and heavy utilization of the slave trade in the production of goods. Use of Negro slaves in the Deep South allowed cotton farmers to produce large quantities of high quality cotton very inexpensively, resulting in the emergence of two distinct classes: the newly aristocratic slave owners and the slaves themselves. With the emergence of distinct classes within the society, expectations arose for each class. Certain jobs, education levels, and neighborhoods were deemed appropriate for individuals based upon the stature of their family in the Southern class structure. With such a rigid class structure in place, the abolition of the slave trade simply removed any logical grounds for an individual's stature within society, yet the class structure lingered on, determining, in part, what experiences an individual should and could have.

Tradition and Modern Meaning

Expectations of what an individual should be or do remaining from traditional class roles have come into conflict with individual freedom of choice afforded by modern society. Post-industrial social structures, through their de-emphasis on individual talents, have given the individual greater freedom in choosing what to do with their lives. Bureaucratic models of social organization neutralize individual talents which in pre-industrial society effectively limited the choices an individual had in regard to his or her position within society. Through the same process which leveled the playing field, however, the meaning behind cultural traditions was lost. Most cultural traditions depend upon individual differences, which are used to benefit society. For example, the Amish tradition of barn-raising brings the entire community together and allows each individual to utilize their unique talents so as to build a barn. One individual who, for instance, has a particular aptitude for building roofs, would not be able to build a sturdy barn alone. In order to build a sturdy barn, he will need the assistance of individuals who each know how to build other parts of the barn. The tradition of barn-raising, then, accomplished things which could not otherwise be done by making use of individual differences and working together. With the institution of division of labor, however, an individual could be trained to perform one very specific function and was expected to perform only that function within the entire process. The fragmentation of the process alienated individuals from one another by removing the common goal of the group. The goal of the individual instead became the fulfillment of a small function in a whole which he or she did not understand.

The difference between the barn-raising example and the modern approach can be understood if we look at the individual goals of a person in each system. An individual in the barn-raising example performs his function in the building of the barn while keeping a view toward the entirety of the barn. An individual in a modern system repeats the same function, i.e. nailing a board on a wall of the barn, without having to know what the final goal of the process may be. The difficulty such a shift poses to tradition lies in the underlying meaning which originally justified the tradition. By eliminating the need for individual talents, the barn-raising seems to have lost the logical justification for its continued practice, yet the expectations of the continued practice remain even without a justification of the tradition itself. The individual is thus left subject to the expectations of a meaningless tradition, yet offered no other sources of meaning from which to choose.

Binx Bolling, a member of his father's aristocratic family, illustrates the conflict of tradition with post-industrial structure in dealing with the expectations of his class stature pressed upon him by his aunt. He is faced with living up to expectations which he may not desire to or be able to meet. Throughout our glimpse at Bolling's life, various people, in particular his aunt, suggest he go into biological research despite his previous resistance to that very idea. It seems his family assumes that as a result of his family's stature, not only would Binx be a good researcher because of the intelligence he is assumed to possess, but he *should* be a researcher as it is a respectable job for a member of the upper class.

In addition to the traditional class-based assumptions, Percy shows the prevalence of post-industrial abstractions. As in *The Woman in the Dunes*, Percy points out the interchangeability of the individual as a result of bureaucratic division of labor. One example of this is seen at a stock brokers' convention in Chicago when Binx is asked to present a talk on "Selling Aids" in front of other brokers. Bolling is approached the night before the presentation by another participant at the conference who asks him to present the talk for no other reason than the fact that Bolling happened to be in the right place at the right time. The fact that Binx was asked to present by a man who had no knowledge of his background or expertise demonstrates the interchangeability of the individual even in dealing with matters of utmost importance in modern economic society. The importance of the conference had been expressed to Binx by his uncle prior to Bolling's attendance, yet the fact that presenters are not chosen based upon their knowledge and expertise would seem to indicate that the content of the conference is not.

The arbitrary nature of modern human experience extends its influence to the realm of truth and meaning. The industrial revolution, with its vast technological and scientific advances, initially provided an alternative method of determining truth based on evidence which could be rationally interpreted, as opposed to the traditional religious basis of truth. As the base of scientific knowledge rapidly grew, however, the only accurate basis for determining truth became individual rationality based upon facts provided. The difficulty with an individual basis for truth derives from the individual's limited ability to research facts. The individual simply does not have enough time or expertise to analyze all aspects of the things around them, so they are forced to make assumptions based upon the information to which they have been exposed. Since experience and, thus, exposure to various information is arbitrarily determined in modern society, individual truths lose their objective basis. Each individual is also faced with a different battery of experiences and uses what he or she knows in order to determine truth. The differences in experience between individuals lead to a highly relativistic truth upon which we base everyday actions, social relations, and long-term plans. Despite the relative and arbitrary natures of truth resulting from individual experience and the lack of unification of information either through church or state institutions, individuals approach their own truths as universal abstractions upon which all actions should be based.

The nature of truth is shown in the preconceptions of Binx and Kate seen in *The Moviegoer*. The basis of the preconceptions held by Aunt Emily, Jules, and other members of Binx and Kate's families are based upon what is thought to be true as opposed to what in fact is true. Aunt Emily bases her notions of what would be best for both Binx and Kate upon the truth of Binx's intelligence and ambition and the truth of Kate's confusion and suicidal intentions, truths which are created within Emily's mind, but are not deemed accurate by either Binx or Kate. Emily acts according to these very truths and illustrates the relative nature of truth and the modern reaction to such relativism. As products of the factual basis of modern rationality incapable of acquiring much of the information available, we are forced to act as if we had access to definitive ultimate truths while relying on our individual relative truths.

The conflicts of relative versus absolute truths and the lack of meaning in the traditions which riddle the world around us help to create a society in which we relate to one another on a purely superficial basis. By universalizing individually relative truth, we run the risk of disproving the foundations of all meaning by delving into the personality of another individual. As truths are a part of an individual's personality and the fundamental basis upon which meaning is built, to learn what another person holds to be true may put the truths and meanings of another person in conflict with our own. By associating with others on a shallow level, an individual is not required to learn the underlying truths and meanings which make up the other's personality and thus is able to protect the validity of his own construed truths. The shallowness of modern human relations can easily be understood in the instance of strangers, but love relationships, which traditionally involve each individual divulging all truths, secrets, and meanings they may hold true as a method of strengthening the bond of trust, would seem to be exempt from such shallowness if viewed in the traditional sense. The abstraction and generalization of the individual in modern society, however, has changed our perceptions of the uniqueness of the love relationship into an unromantic union of any male with any female for the quantifiable mutual benefits of money, status, and power. The commercialization of the institution of marriage, while being promoted as representative of love, has resulted in a more self-centered approach to marriage in which each individual protects him or herself first and then pursues what lies in the other's interest.

Percy illustrates the modern roles of love and marriage through Bolling's relationships throughout *The Moviegoer*. Binx seeks a relationship with his secretaries simply for sexual fulfillment and self-satisfaction. It appears that Sharon, Binx's secretary, views relationships in the same light, simply as methods of achieving some sort of self-fulfillment, a sort of temporary meaning to fill a psychological void left over from the de-emphasis of the individual. A more glaring difference between expectation and actuality is seen in Binx's proposal to Kate Cutrer. Marriage is thought to be pursued for some reason in both traditional and more modern conceptions; yet there seems to be no apparent reason for Binx's proposal to Kate. Reasons of love or economy are not found in the union of Kate and

Binx; it seems as if Binx proposed simply because he didn't have anything else to do, an arbitrarily chosen alleviation to his general boredom. It would seem, then, that love, like other relationships between individuals, has lost its basis as a union of trust between people.

Kobo Abe and Walker Percy, while following the general precepts of existential thought put forth by their Continental counterparts, offer unique permutations of the modern human condition resulting from the confluence of traditional values which have lost their underlying basis and the individual abstraction following from the rise of instrumental rationality. Modern social currents have become both liberating and oppressive to the individual, creating a web from which it is nearly impossible for the individual to escape. Meaning and individual uniqueness has been superceded by freedom and equality, but freedom without other available options. Relativistic truth has resulted in increasingly shallow relationships based solely upon the arbitrary truths we create to provide meaning to lives which seem to occur purely by chance. We are left with a society which judges based on universal truths and meanings which have no underlying basis or continuity. The arbitrary nature of truth leaves the individual with little hope for understanding the basis upon which he or she is to be judged as it can be changed as easily as it was created, with no explanation needed for justification. The only true meaning we are left with, then, is highly relativistic individual meaning created with individual truths. If we are to accept relativistic meanings and truths, however, we must recognize them for what they are and not lose ourselves to the arbitrary mundane character of the society which we have helped to create.

REFERENCES

Abe, Kobo. *The Woman in the Dunes*. Trans. E. Dale Saunders. New York: Vintage-Random, 1991.

Percy, Walker. *The Moviegoer*. New York: Vintage-Random, 1998.

ETHICS:
THEORY AND PRACTICE

ETHICAL THEORY RECONSIDERED: AN EVALUATION OF THE ETHICS OF CARE

Rachel Houchins

East Tennessee State University

Numerous commentators agree that many ethical theories have not only excluded women, but also degraded them, portraying women as morally deficient. This tendency has prompted Carol Gilligan, Nel Noddings, and others to provide new answers for the question: "How do women fit into ethical theory?" Although I applaud these efforts, I also fear they perpetuate many detrimental assumptions about women, and thus indirectly support the subordination of women. Specifically, Gilligan's ethic of care is not useful in many fields of applied ethics. This can be vividly demonstrated by studying the ramifications of the ethic of care on the field of bioethics.

I argue that ethical theory must be redefined and the manner in which it is grounded must also be reconsidered. In order for this refiguring of ethical theory to be successful, I believe that care and justice ethics must be integrated. While other philosophers (Held 1995 and Tronto 1995) have attempted to integrate justice and care ethics, the most beneficial type of integration has not been attempted. I suggest an integration of the two theories which rests on the autonomy of the individual. While many feminists have attempted to reject the idea of autonomy as a patriarchal construct, I will show that this rejection has been unsuccessful and unnecessary. We will begin by examining Gilligan's ethic of care.

* * *

Ethical Theory Reconsidered

> If one does not have a voice, one cannot speak on one's own behalf. – Barbara Houston

As Susan Hekman says, "It does not overstate the case to say that Gilligan's work has revolutionized discussions in moral theory, feminism, theories of the subject, and many other related fields" (Hekman 1). Gilligan's theory picks up where many women philosophers have stopped: with the realization that women fail to fit any of the existing models of moral development and ethical theory. Gilligan's book *In A Different Voice* was written largely as a response to her mentor, Kohlberg, publishing a new theory of human development. Under Kohlberg's scheme of human moral development, women consistently scored lower than men; this association was first noted in a 1971 study in which a group of high school students yielded an average score of level three for girls and level four for boys (Gilligan 1993: 348). This low score of level three for girls reflected what Kohlberg saw as a "deficient" level of moral development. This demonstrates that the problem is not merely that women are excluded from the creation of moral development theory, but there is also a tendency for any lack in success equal to that of men in such moral development tests to be interpreted as a "natural" shortcoming in women.

After noticing these problems in Kohlberg's theory, Gilligan set out to determine what could be done to make the system for evaluating ethics and morals more inclusive of women. Gilligan claims that we first have to realize that women develop theory differently and define themselves differently than men. Gilligan says "...in any given society, feminine personality comes to define itself in relation and connection to other people more than masculine personality does" (Gilligan 7). In the interviews that Gilligan conducted, women presented morality largely as a series of obligations rooted in these relationships. On the other hand, men presented the moral person as someone who valued rights, justice, and themselves. From this divergence in self-definition a different ethic emerges for women and men.

Gilligan claims that women are thus more apt to practice an ethic of care than an ethic of justice. Gilligan states

> This conception of morality as concerned with the activity of care centers moral development around the understanding of responsibility and relationships, just as the conception of morality as fairness ties moral development to the understanding of rights and rules. (Gilligan 19)

Although Gilligan's claims seemed quite persuasive, I found myself questioning them, asking: "Why are women more likely to appeal to an ethic of care?" and "If women are not happy with their position in society, why should they base a moral and ethical theory on how they have been socialized to handle ethical dilemmas?"

> When I reflect on the history of women, I realize how much our caring has nurtured and empowered others. I see how good it has been for others. However, I also see how terribly costly it has been for women.
>
> And so the first question that arises for me is one that arises for many of Gilligan's subjects. Can an ethics of care avoid self-sacrifice? – Barbara Houston

One of my central concerns with Gilligan's work is her seemingly complete acceptance of care as an ethical maxim. I believe women have adapted to accept caring as part of their nature largely because it is inherent in all the roles that they are encouraged to adopt. In viewing women as more apt to select an ethic of care without mentioning the possible detrimental effects, Gilligan perpetuates the repression of women by labeling the values that society has imposed on women as highly ethical. I am not arguing that caring should not be considered an ethical action, but rather that caring should not be encouraged to be the basis on which ethical judgments are made, especially because of its close ties to women's subordination. Throughout history, the social roles that women have been encouraged to adopt have included caring; teacher, nurse, and mother are all roles that connote care. This demonstrates that justice ethics have been denied to women not only because of their exclusion from the theories, but more importantly, because of the exclusion of women from the realm of politics and hence justice.

Another shortcoming of Gilligan's ethical theory stems from her claim that something is ethical insofar as it is a caring and responsible thing to do. In making such a general claim about ethics, Gilligan encompasses many acts that she would likely regard as unethical. People's ability to find any action caring and responsible is amazing. "Care" is such a loosely defined term that there is great danger in associating it with an ethical theory. Nel Noddings clearly acknowledges this lack of principles, but does not discuss the implications; she says,

> It is this ethical ideal, this realistic picture of ourselves as one-caring, that guides us as we strive to meet the other morally. Everything depends upon the nature and strength of this ideal, for we shall not have absolute principles to guide us. (Noddings 5)

Not only are there no parameters within which caring must be constrained, but if justice and all other principles are abandoned, there are no repercussions for blatantly uncaring actions committed in the name of care. Thus the ethic of care is inapplicable in many fields of applied ethics. Bioethics provides an excellent example for several reasons. Not only is bioethics an increasingly important field with the advent of new technologies and techniques, but bioethics is also a field that wants to be depicted as "caring."

✲ ✲ ✲

It is not a great pleasure to bring pain to a friend.
–Sophocles

Many health care professionals [HCPs] have embraced an ethic of care without realizing the ramifications while others take strong stances against the ethic of care; as an example, Howard Curzer argues that "Care is not a role virtue for HCPs. Indeed, it is a vice. In their professional capacity, doctors, nurses, and other HCPs should not care for their patients" (Curzer 55). Although I do not advocate such a radical stance, I do believe that an ethic of care is a less reliable and effective manner of evaluating bioethical dilemmas than an ethic of justice. In order to demonstrate this, let us look at a very popular modern ethical question: physician-assisted dying.

Marcus, a patient that Dr. McGall has known for over thirty years has developed terminal cancer. Dr. McGall has been treating Marcus for six months and Marcus is near the end of his life. On his most recent visit, Marcus complained to Dr. McGall that he was taking the maximum amount of pain reliever prescribed, but that the pain was still not wavering. He also complained of burdening his wife and children and requested that Dr. McGall either "make me feel better or help me die." When Dr. McGall discussed with him what he meant by this statement, he said "I am in constant pain and I am nothing but a burden to the people that I love. I think that it would be best if you would help me die." What should Dr. McGall do in this situation?

The ethic of care has a solution that may seem good on the surface, but that in fact raises a plethora of questions and problems. The solution is, of course, to do whatever is the most caring for all of the individuals involved, but what is that? One of the central problems with an ethic of care is that it ignores the issue of how one determines what is ethical in any given ethical dilemma. How does a physician determine what is caring? Basing an ethical theory on such a subjective and emotionally loaded term is not at all helpful in resolving a specific ethical dilemma. In fact, this demonstrates one of my major theoretical concerns: almost anything can be legitimated under an ethic of care. Take Marcus's case as an example: Dr. McGall could determine that the most caring thing for all people involved is to help Marcus commit suicide because: (1) it would alleviate Marcus's suffering, (2) it would release Marcus's family and the community from their obligations to care for him, and (3) it would relieve Marcus and his family from any further financial burdens. But Dr. McGall could as easily argue that the most caring action is to convince Marcus not to kill himself because: (1) Marcus's family and friends may not want Marcus to end his life, (2) it would put more of an emotional and psychological burden on Marcus's family, and (3) it is the most caring thing that Dr. McGall can do for himself, since he may not want to help Marcus commit suicide. Thus, no guidelines or absolutes for approaching the case are defined. The physician or HCPs must take on the responsibility of determining which actions are "caring" and which ones are not.

On the other hand, principlism evaluates cases under a much more consistent form. This form is better because it allows HCPs and ethics committees to have a set way of approaching each case. While everyone wants an ethic that allows for personal input, caring gives personal narrative too much weight. An approach closer to an ethic of justice has more concern for fairness and equality, both of which have been powerful tools for social change and development. As an example, principlism sets forth four principles that should be consulted in making ethical decisions: (1) Beneficence, (2) Nonmaleficence, (3) Autonomy, and (4) Justice. It is only when these principles conflict that one faces an ethical dilemma. Even in the case of a dilemma, there are more concrete ways of evaluating these principles than there are for evaluating "caring." There are socially accepted standards of what we mean when we say that something is beneficent, but what does one truly mean when they say an action is caring?

In addition to valuing the structure of principlism, I also find the epistemological grounding of principlism much more convincing than the empirical grounding of care ethics. Principlism is built around a system that values, ideally, autonomy (though this is debatable with the rise of distributive justice and healthcare economics). A person's ability to make decisions for him or herself is vital to his or her freedom and well being; principlism is a rights-based approach. The epistemological grounding for principlism can largely be traced back to the liberal tradition. Liberalism uses universal human rights to ground its ethics. From Locke, the forefather of liberalism, to modern liberal thinkers such as John Rawls, autonomy is the undeniable right. Every human has the right, and in fact the responsibility, to make his or her own decisions. Branching from this sense of autonomy and universal rights are certain political and social institutions, including ethical standards and principlism. On the other hand, Gilligan's empirical method involves evaluating the way in which people reason in moral situations, and then modeling a theory after it; it is an inductive approach. Once again, this approach seems questionable because of the constrained methods of moral reasoning available to women. Why should a new ethical theory be modeled after an empirical reality that is biased and unfair? Because of the philosophical and practical reasons that I have raised, Gilligan's ethic of care must be altered if it is to be of use to us philosophically.

Self-development is a higher duty than self-sacrifice.
–Elizabeth Cady Stanton

So, if an ethic of care is not the solution to the largely male-biased history of ethics, what is? I believe the answer lies in restructuring the application of both justice-based ethics and feminine ethics. In doing this, one of the first questions that must be answered is: Are these two theories mutually exclusive? Gilligan seems to think not, and I agree. While Gilligan sees that men may sometimes appeal to an ethic of care and women to an ethic of justice, she does not follow the implications of the ethics being able to coexist to the best outcome. It seems to me that the two ethics not only coexist vertically (that is to say in different people at the same time or in the same person at different times), but also horizontally (both care and justice can be active forces in making an ethical decision). To use a model from the physical sciences, we would say that both care and justice ethics give us models that are linear, like vectors. Individuals occupy certain positions on each of these vectors, and these positions may be influenced by sex, gender, class, race, and other variables. The important thing, though is that these vectors are additive. We can calculate the net force, length, and path of the resulting vector. In this manner, a personal ethic is formed by combining the vectors. Thus care and justice ethics can and should be integrated, for as Sara Hoagland says in *Lesbian Ethics*,

> ...emotions and reasoning aren't so easily separated...My point is that the two go together. Thus, efforts to rest either in the emotion without the judgement or in the reasoning without the emotion will fail. (Hoagland 187)

But it is also important to realize that the vector is still within a grid, an area that it cannot overstep. Therefore the ethic is not completely relativistic. I cannot form an ethic under this methodology that consents to genocide, rape, or other obviously unethical actions. But, what defines these boundaries?

These boundaries must be common to both an ethic of justice and an ethic of care, so where is the common ground? I propose that the common ground resides in the conception of the individual, namely in the autonomy of the individual. Though many feminists attempt to reject autonomy as a masculine construct, the autonomous individual (whether constructed or not) is an ethical maxim upon which both theories rest. Gilligan speaks often in her book of the personal narrative, and what is this if it is not a narrative from an autonomous individual about the decisions that he or she has made? Likewise, when Noddings speaks of the ethical self, she says

> The ethical self is an active relation between my actual self and a vision of my ideal self as one-caring and cared-for. It is born of the fundamental recognition of relatedness; that which connects me naturally to the other, reconnects me through the other to myself...My very individuality is defined in a set of relations. This is my basic reality. (Noddings 49-51)

Though this quotation may initially seem to deny the existence of an autonomous individual, in actuality it does not. Rather, we will observe that it is very similar to the liberal conception of the individual, which also requires interaction with a community of others. Locke describes the individual, saying

> God having made Man such a Creature, that, in his own judgement, it was not good for him to be alone, put him under strong Obligations of Necessity, Convenience, and Inclination to drive him into Society, as well as fitted him with Understanding and Language to continue to enjoy it. (Locke 318)

So, though feminists have attempted to divorce themselves from this conception of the individual, I do not believe that it has been successful or necessary.

The sense of autonomy that I am attempting to invoke does differ somewhat from traditional conceptions of autonomy, though. In many ways, this conception of autonomy is what is referred to as "relational autonomy." It relies on the assumption that the individual is affected by his or her social, political, and cultural climate. Thus, the autonomy of which I speak is much like that of Carolyn McLeod and Susan Sherwin, who

> understand relational autonomy to involve explicit recognition of the fact that autonomy is both defined and pursued in a social context...In relational autonomy, it is necessary to explore an agent's social location if we hope to evaluate properly and respond appropriately to her ability to exercise autonomy. (McLeod 259)

Hence, this model does not undermine a conception of community and the degree to which the community can alter the individual. Under this model, it would still be legitimate to claim that women have been socialized and have had a different conception of the political, the social, and the community than men. Thus, this new vision of autonomy accounts for my ability to reconcile the differences between liberal and feminist definitions of the autonomous individual.

Arising from a discussion of autonomy is usually the recognition that others are autonomous individuals, and thus a consideration of equality. Instead, I believe that this sense of autonomy should focus attention on justice rather than equality. As Jane Flax indicates, justice is more useful to us in such cases because it allows for a consideration of differences, which equality does not. Equality incorporates a measure of sameness, while justice does not require this measure, but rather demands that we treat people fairly. This encourages a respect not only for others, but also for their ethical decisions. Referring once again to the vector model, we see that an individual ethic is acceptable and expected as long as it does not deny another his or her right to make an autonomous ethical decision. This formulation of an individual ethic utilizes principles of both traditional ethics and Gilligan's ethic of care while simultaneously keeping individuals from slipping into relativism. This dynamic model thus fits the manner in which we actually think about and conceptualize ethics much better than either an ethic of care or an ethic of justice individually.

REFERENCES

Curzer, Howard. "Is Care A Virtue For Health Care Professionals?" *The Journal of Medicine and Philosophy.* 18:51-69. New York: Kluwer Academic Publishers, 1993.

Gilligan, Carol. "In a Different Voice: Women's Conception of Self and Morality." *Women and Values.* Pp.342-367. Belmont, CA: Wadsworth Publishing Co, 1993.

_____. *In A Different Voice: Psychological Theory and Women's Development.* Cambridge, MA: Harvard University Press, 1982.

Hekman, Susan. *Moral Voices Moral Selves: Carol Gilligan and Feminist Moral Theory.* University Park, PA: The Pennsylvania State University Press, 1995.

Locke, John. *Two Treatises of Government.* Ed. Peter Laslett. New York: Cambridge University Press, 1988.

McLeod, Carolyn and Susan Sherwin. "Relational Autonomy, Self-Trust, And Health Care for Patients Who Are Oppressed." *Relational Autonomy: Feminist Perspectives on Autonomy, Agency, and the Social Self.* New York: Oxford University Press, 2000.

Hoagland, Sara Lucia. *Lesbian Ethics: Toward New Values.* Institute of Lesbian Studies, 1989.

Noddings, Nel. "Ethics from the Standpoint of Women." *Women and Values.* Pp. 379-390. Belmont, CA: Wadsworth Publishing Co, 1993.

PROOF OF PATERNAL RIGHTS IN ABORTION

Michael Alan Payne

Virginia Commonwealth University

Taking its cue from a case study in *Well and Good*, this paper argues that a man as well as a woman may have the right to object to an abortion. The argument assigns special importance to the teleological function of sex, the concept of autonomy, and the equality of the genders. Several potential counterarguments are considered and rejected.

During the course of our lives, abortion has sparked controversy on the many stages of our society. The issue has taken precedent in our courts, in our pulpits and even at our lecterns. We as a society and as a new generation of philosophers must strive to find the moral center of this issue and the answer to many questions such as this. It is our obligation and our ethical responsibility to answer these problems on the broad ranging topic of abortion, above all others, before we delegate their weight to the shoulders of our offspring and our grandchildren. This paper distinguishes a view on abortion as observed in a specific light, however, there does appear to be a universal rule which can be drawn from my writing in order to settle at least one of the many facets of abortion. I encourage you as a reader to look beyond the pre-conceived notions of our society and to lay aside—as I have done many times myself—the personal opinions that have been formulated on your own. I ask you to do this for the time being in an effort to further understanding and, if desired, to take insight into my claims and views in an effort to solve this social enigma.

Paternal Rights in Abortion

Case study 2:1 on page 75 of *Well and Good* describes a unique situation in which the morality of abortion without the consent of both parents is uniquely highlighted. Though difficult to do, I will argue that a father does have rights concerning the pregnancy of his child, and that the choice to continue the pregnancy is a necessary decision anytime a couple disagrees over whether or not to have the abortion. This will be argued for using predominantly teleological means of argumentation for justification of my claims.

First I will list the most important facts drawn from the case study along with a slight overview of the study itself. The second section will cover my reasoning behind allowing the father to have a say in the pregnancy. In the third section I will lay siege to my own arguments using the most powerful arguments that popular methods of philosophy use to undermine my claims while attempting to show where these arguments are flawed. Finally, I shall espouse the rule that was created when all sections were taken into account and explain a simple extrapolated rule from this, which simply implies that the life of the child must be spared at any point at which parents are in disagreement over aborting the pregnancy.

It is important when reading this paper to include only the facts that the case study itself offers. As is the flaw to many views on abortion, the larger issues supported by facts of a particular incident are often lost under the thousands of personal opinions and lesser "what ifs" expressed by outside individuals and thereby progress is lost when dealing with this troublesome issue. For example, when we hear about a controversial case involving abortion, we are most often given the opinions of strong activists on both sides. Their statements are usually highly sentimental and based only on the grounds of, "I'm right and if you don't agree then you're wrong." As such it follows that, when arguing philosophy on the topic of abortion, eventually there comes a point when a person cannot think of any further way in which to promote their assertions or defend from the attack of another argument. Most often the answer is quite simply, "I don't know why this view is right.... it just is." The statements of such individuals are often conflicted or skewed to such a degree that any universality of their arguments is lost. Moreover, the ethical issues of abortion are lost in personal 'beliefs,' religious translation, and general controversy over how abortion is argued and not the issue of abortion itself. We force ourselves to be caught in webs of our own creation and arguments quickly slide into slippery slope faults in which there is no decisive point where we can draw a line. By failing to consider *only* the facts, we fail ourselves: progress, perhaps the only true prize of philosophy, is lost.

The following facts of the case were weighed heavily when deciding if my views were ethical, but no fact was considered more important than the description the case study gives of the couple which describes them as being the, "paradigm of [a] shared parenthood" (75). This fact is exceedingly important and cannot be underestimated in its explanation of the setting we are dealing with because it verifies with certainty that this marriage is a stable, caring relationship in which the parents have both demonstrated their commitment to their children and to each other. It establishes, most of all, the credibility of the father when considering whether or not he has a serious enough investment in both the relationship and the conception of the child to warrant having a strong say in whether or not to pursue an abortion.

Paternal Rights in Abortion

Among other facts taken into consideration were that the father is employed as an Associate Professor of History, indicating that he is secure in a middle class job and has above average intelligence. This indicates that under normal circumstances he is capable of rational, logical thought. Furthermore, we are given that the he has unfairly told the other two children of the mother's expectancy, which has caused undue stress on his wife to continue the pregnancy. In addition, the mother has clearly indicated that her sole reason for an abortion is that she wished to return to the career she previously left in order to raise her other two children. The case study also indicates that the couple was actively practicing "safe sex" in the form of an IUD (Intra-Uterine Device) and that both had agreed that for the moment two children were enough. The father, however, at discovering the pregnancy reveals that he had secretly wanted the third child at any time (the wife had been open to a later pregnancy) and that he was overjoyed by this unexpected turn of events. Ultimately, we are informed that the woman did proceed with the abortion against her husband's and children's wishes. Consequently, we are led to see that both major parties involved elicited highly selfish motivations.

My assertion, namely that a man has a right in the decision making process concerning his child and abortion, takes its strength from teleological ideology. Formally defined, teleology is "the science or doctrine that attempts to explain the universe in terms of ends or final causes" ("Teleology," *Microsoft Encarta Encyclopedia*). Teleological theories are also incorporated in consequentialist theories. "A teleological theory of obligation posits one and only one fundamental obligation and that is to maximize the good consequences and minimize the bad consequences of our actions" (*Well and Good* 13). It is important to understand that teleological theories can only be drawn from theories of value and are therefore dependent on them.

Teleological thinking gives merit to my assertions in the following way. It would have us believe that the reason for having sexual intercourse is to have children. Naturally, children are often the result of sexual intercourse, and until cloning techniques are effective enough to be utilized, sexual intercourse will be our species' only way of reproduction. Indeed, only society has evolved the concept that human sexuality is for self-expression and pleasure alone and allows for sexual intercourse to be considered as a cardiovascular and aerobically stimulating form of adult play. Teleological reasoning states that, should we engage in sexual conduct of our own autonomous want and merit, then we are giving our consent to answer to the consequences of our actions. These consequences are namely pleasure, self-expression and gratification—the reason most of us engage in sexual intercourse—as well as sexually transmitted diseases, pregnancy, etc. This openly destroys the idea that if a couple is practicing "safe sex" then they are entitled to use an abortion as a means of opting out of an unwanted pregnancy, since reproduction is the reason for sexual intercourse regardless of whether it was the couple's intent. Ultimately, it is our species' natural and teleological reason for sexual intercourse.

In addition to this argument, I initiate an approach that will effectively level the playing field for all parties involved. As the old adage goes, what is good for the goose is good for the gander. Our society rightfully declares that upon conception of a child, the man and woman are legally and morally responsible for the care of the child in equal parts, 50/50. Our society also agrees, ethically, that if a woman decides to keep the child despite her partner's objections and desire for an abortion, then that man is morally and financially responsible for the wellbeing of the child. In a way, we think of the gentleman as being forced to take on the repercussions (consequences) of his autonomy. Though society has taken a deaf ear to the situation, we must also see as a result of this rule that a woman's carrying (gestation) of the fetus is no more invasive or contrary to her autonomy than that of the position of the man who does not want the child but has a partner who does. This scenario, indirectly supported by both women's advocate groups and directly supported by courts, allows for a universal rule stating that, *when one partner disagrees with having the abortion of a child conceived by consensual sex, then the child must be spared.* In short, life must always be favored when a disagreement over abortion is raised because the autonomies of the two parties in question, namely the man and the woman, are both equal and both have equal investment in the child legally and physically. To destroy this ruling would mean the death knell for many women's advocacy groups due, in part, to their nature of expressing the sexes as being equal in all ways. Should such a group deny a man having a say in whether or not to terminate the pregnancy and decide the fate of the fetus, they would violate his autonomy and lower his equality, a fundamental contradiction in their philosophy. This must be the case for certainly the autonomy of a man and a woman are equal and one cannot negate the other.

Under these lines of thinking, when considering the case study we cannot morally allow the abortion to continue simply because the pregnancy was due to prophylactic failure. Quite to the opposite of what we often hear in regards to abortion, this rule shows that that the woman's autonomy must be minimally abridged in order to preserve both her autonomy and that of her partner. This abridgement is no more a wrong doing than when the man wants the abortion and the woman does not as with both cases it is merely abridging the autonomy of one minimally in order to preserve future autonomy later on a full scale for both parties. It is important to note that this rule *does not* eliminate the autonomy of the woman in favor of the man but instead fights current accepted social views in an effort to equalize them.

One of the most powerful arguments against my proposal is that of philosophers with rigid Kantian backgrounds. A follower of Kant might insist that my argument fails the scrutiny of the categorical imperative. The categorical imperative asks whether a person could universalize their actions or personal maxim. Proponents of Kant might argue that I could not universalize my ruling to cover cases in which the father of the child was unknown, deceased, or out of contact. The categorical imperative also requires me to analyze my actions to determine whether I have taken away the autonomy of any agent, or whether I have degraded any rational agent as a means to an end. Again my ideology would come under fire. The argument to disallow the abortion of the child in this case may be construed as using the woman as a means to an end, treating her as "a mere incubator." In forcing the woman to have a child, it will be insisted, I have used her and violated this principle of the categorical imperative. Some Kantian theorists would go a step further by espousing the idea that a woman's autonomy is her own, and that when the child is being nourished inside her, that child is under her direct control. They would say that a man has no realm of control, nor does he warrant a say in what should happen to the child so long as that child is inside the woman. That person would also say that in any situation that could be devised, the woman's life should come before that of the fetus thereby assuring that an examined life is held above a life yet to be.

In order to combat opponents to my viewpoints, I must point out to my reader that my ideology sidesteps many of the problems that their arguments attempt to exploit. In other words, their arguments attack what could be a legitimate point if my argument had been phrased or approached differently; however, their point of attack is aimed at something that does not exist in my argument. For instance, in the first argument given against my position, the inability to universalize agreement by both parents if the father is unavailable, is unacceptable as an argument to this case or any other. In cases where the father is out of contact for reasons of negligence or death, there would be no need to notify him of the event of the pregnancy. Largely his decision in the matter would be forfeited by his state of absentia. Additionally, when dealing with this case study, we are also informed that this was a very close marriage in which the father was stable, loving, and cared greatly for his wife and children. The argument of my opponents cannot find footing here so their argument is void before it begins.

The second point of attack on my views, my seeming lack of respect for the female autonomy, is a more difficult point to deal with. My argument, basing itself on teleological ends, combats the assault by pointing out that all of us must be responsible for our actions. Responsibility is what makes autonomy different from freedom and this difference must be clearly understood in order to understand that freedom may be attacked or removed while autonomy is untouched. Following this logic, having sexual intercourse is comparative to playing Russian Roulette. There is a bullet in the chamber, so there is always a chance of shooting yourself in the head. Many play but some will not have the chance to play again. Quite contrary to my critics' claims, my argument does not invade the autonomy of the woman's body. In fact, my argument very much asserts a woman's autonomy. No where in my argument do I espouse the idea that a woman cannot smoke, drink, or shoot up with narcotics when she is pregnant. Those choices are hers to make; though I would personally disagree with her decision to do one or more of them, and the consequences of those actions are well documented. She is still free to make up her own mind, to go where she wishes, and to live her life. Furthermore, should we allow the woman to have full say, we are violating the autonomy of the father, a rational agent, and all philosophy agrees that no one has the right to take away the autonomy of a rational being. This authority, at best, is only delegated to a God or Goddess (if indeed they do exist) and is not given into non-divine hands.

The reasoning behind my argument, and explanation of how I see that a woman is not used as a means to an end, lies in the following premise: a woman enters into sexual intercourse with the knowledge that the worst case scenario—barring a troubled pregnancy—will be that she may become pregnant, her body will serve as a home to a child for an average time span of nine months. It is the woman's teleological end, assuming she voluntarily enters into the sexual intercourse, to carry the child of her partner until term. Therefore, the woman has exercised her autonomy by having sex and answering to the consequences. Should we return to the Russian Roulette analogy, she has effectively pulled the trigger on the pistol. Should she find herself having conceived a child, she got the chamber with the live round in it and it is up to her to fulfill her responsibilities and obligations as the host for the child. Not one of us could take the bullet back once the firing pin hit the bullet's primer, and so it is and should be with pregnancy barring a forced sexual encounter or a pregnancy in which the woman's life is above a level of normal risk or death.

Another argument against my own, is the teleological argument that only pleasure is the end result of sexual intercourse and that reproduction itself is a side effect, especially where a prophylactic is concerned. The advent of prophylactics meant that we as a society shifted from the meaning of sexual activity previously held. Those who argue that the use of a prophylactic shows that teleologically sex is for pleasure, are flawed in their judgement when we review that there is always a chance for reproduction (conception) while pleasure is not one hundred percent given. In addition, the effectiveness of prophylactics is not one hundred percent, easily allowing for pregnancy to occur. It is also of importance to note that until means of cloning become significantly more available and reliable, sexual intercourse will be our species' only means of reproduction, thus strengthening the notion that reproduction is the teleological end of sexual activity.

Lesser arguments include the view that a woman who has a child born to her without wanting it would most likely have the child come to that same realization and feel unwanted. They argue further that as a consequence there will be surmountable emotional and even the possibility for physical abuse which would burden the child and decrease the quality of its life. Further, that child, having been exposed to such treatment, would most likely continue the cycle that brought him or her into the world to again start a cycle of misery and abuse. Granted, these pleas are more along the lines of emotional sentiment, but I will readily agree with the seriousness, if not validity, of this issue.

To the remaining argument, my responses are quite simple. The argument dealing with a child feeling 'unwanted' is a consequentialist idea and as such is subject to the same weakness as all others similar to it. That weakness is quite simply that we can never know all the consequences of our actions one hundred percent of the time. The probability of what an opponent would say is going to happen is just as equal as the probability of anything that I could say to dispute them, thus the two sides would negate each other. This is a reason, among several, of why I did not mention in earlier justification that the woman was morally wrong in her decision because she jeopardized her marriage, relationship with her children, and personal health by having the abortion. I could not make this argument because I, myself, would fall victim to this same criticism. The final rebuttal I wish to make of this argument is to deal with the ideology that an abortion should be allowed because an unwanted to child would feel unwanted and start a dreaded cycle of misery. In addition to the faults of consequentialist thought, this argument is dispatched because many children, adopted, planned for, etc. feel that way. In contrast, many unwanted or unplanned pregnancies have ended with a very loving relationship between parents and child. A child's behavior, while definitely reflective in many cases of his or her environment, is not completely determined by it. Take the case of the Menendez brothers. Certainly we would agree that they had the best of everything and did not have to feel insecure in their positions of wealth, yet that was not enough; they wound up killing both of their parents as they watched television on the couch. Therefore, behavior can be a random facet and completely qualitative factor open to the faults of all consequentialist arguments.

To sum up my views, I leave my readers with this rule. It reflects the situation of this case study and I believe that it can be universalized reasonably well. In a case in which a couple finds themselves in a relationship that produces a pregnancy, should there be a disagreement on whether or not to have an abortion and there are no factors that would indicate an above normal chance of health risks for the woman, then the life of the fetus must be spared in order to preserve both parents' rights and autonomy. The qualities of this rule are that it reflects both the autonomy of the man and the woman and above all it preserves a man's right to have a say over his own unborn child. Moreover, this rule effectively eliminates the ability our society has given women to hold the unjust ability and power to deprive a man of his autonomy while allowing for both individuals and their views to be fairly represented.

Michael Alan Payne

REFERENCES

Thomas, John E. and Wilfrid J. Waluchow. *Well and Good: a case study approach to biomedical ethics* (3rd edition). Orchard Park, NY: Broadview Press, 1998.

"Teleology." *Microsoft Encarta Encyclopedia*, 1998 ed.

POLITICAL NOISE AND VOCIFEROUS SILENCE: HEIDEGGER AND NAZISM

Tamara Johnson

Binghamton University

This paper addresses the main controversies surrounding the career of Martin Heidegger: his involvement with the Nazi party and the silence he maintained regarding that involvement. One may, with some justification, expect of a philosopher a higher standard of ethics and therefore feel especially appalled by Heidegger's relation to one of history's most nefarious evils. How could a philosopher, of all people, subscribe to such a heinous ideology? This is a exigent question to be asked as post-modernism, a movement with roots in Heidegger's writing, becomes one of the most dominant philosophies of our culture. If the relativism in Heidegger's existentialism allowed for genocide, what about the relativism that so permeates contemporary thought? I attempt to explain how it came about that Heidegger made such despicable choices by relating his philosophy of anxious authenticity and historicity to the philosophy of Hitler, hoping to thereby point out some of the strengths and weaknesses of Heidegger's thought.

How is it that Martin Heidegger, the philosopher of individuation and solitary authenticity, was able not only to condone, but actively support the Nazi movement, history's favorite exemplar of the dangers of blind acceptance of *de facto* herd ideologies? What does his involvement with Hitler's party signify about his philosophy? Must it be considered defunct, irrevocably discredited? Was Heidegger nothing more than a philosophical Tartuffe, willing to write, propound, and profess anything for the sake of his career? And what is to be made of the infamous silence he refused to break about his politics?

Was he a coward, ashamed, arrogant, evil? There have been many attempts made to explain away the Heidegger conundrum, and many approaches to the explanations. Some simply dismiss Heidegger's contributions to philosophy entirely. Others deny his sincere commitment to Nazism. There are still others who posit an absolute schism between Heidegger's life and his writing (Haber 4). All of these, however, seem erroneously simplistic and evasive. It would seem that the most exigent question to be asked has not yet been adequately addressed, namely: "How is the man reconcilable with the philosophy?" The following discourse will attempt to articulate a space in which a chiasm is possible between the two.

The most conspicuous part of Heidegger's career spanned two basic periods: the time during which he enjoyed the favor of the Nazi party and the time after his estrangement. During the first period he enthusiastically endorsed Hitler and National Socialism, committing several anti-Semitic acts himself. During the second, he steadfastly abstained from recanting any of his actions. All of these choices seem abominable, and also undeniable. They ought to be investigated and understood. This paper will examine each period through the perspective of the thesis: Heidegger endeavored to live his life in harmony with his philosophy of authenticity. His agreement with Hitler was the result of over-zealousness with regard to that essay, and his silence was a resolute realization of, and response to, his mistakes. Obviously, it is not possible to prove any hypothesis concerning this query, since the subject is dead (and would probably offer only a continued reticence in avail if he were still alive). However, the law of Occam's Razor would seem to vindicate the stance taken in this explanation of the Heidegger controversy, as would even a small measure of faith in the philosopher. And it is the intention of this paper to show that he deserves at least the benefit of the doubt.

Heidegger's philosophy resembles an exsanguinated Buddhism written from within the confines of a sterilized ivory tower. In *Being and Time*, his "non-prescriptive" findings are parallel to the satori of Siddhartha. Buddhism teaches that one must reconcile oneself with Nothingness. Heidegger's existentialism also urges one to authentically resolve oneself to Death, so that meaning falls away and reveals the Nothingness of Being. The key difference is that Buddhism is supposed to be a path away from the pain of life, while Heidegger himself acknowledges that his authenticity has its source in and is the source of angst. He is not concerned much with sparing or rescuing fallen beings from their trivial lives; he is in the service of Being. In "Letter on Humanism" he writes, "the essence of ek-sistence derives existentially-ecstatically from the truth of Being" (Heidegger 2: 272), so "in the determination of the humanity of man as ek-sistence what is essential is not man but Being" (Heidegger 2: 273). These statements are critical in helping to elucidate why Heidegger could have been so attracted by National Socialism.

One might expect of a philosopher a heightened sense of ethics, and thus feel slighted in those expectations when an eminent philosopher such as Heidegger proves susceptible to an ostensible evil like Nazism. However it seems Heidegger did possess an exceptional sense of ethics, so profound that he was actually ossified in his commitment to them. His ethics were simply on a different level than, say, Kantian ethics. Kant proposed that no man ought to be treated as a means to an end, but as an end in himself. Heidegger, on the other hand, felt that all are a means to Being. Being is the highest ideal of Dasein and its proper task.

"Thinking should be directed only toward saying Being in its truth, instead of explaining it as particular being in terms of beings" (Heidegger 2: 238). It is man's role to dwell in the House of Being and to guard its truth. This is Dasein's moral obligation; Heidegger recognized no other.

That being the case, it is not terribly surprising that he would be attracted by a charismatic politician who claimed, "Not only does man live in order to serve higher ideals...these higher ideals also provide the premise for his existence" (Hitler 380). Part of Hitler's agenda was to form a party apodictically unified in its devotion to a higher ideal of itself—to its potentiality for Being, in other words. His promise to the German *Volk* was to bring about a return of Germany's greatness and deliver it over from its mediocrity to the superiority that Germany was destined to attain. He swore to rescue his empire from the politicians who coddled and perpetuated an impotent and ignorant public (Hitler 374). Hitler recapitulated into a political movement the philosophy that Heidegger had promulgated as the individual's mission: achieve one's potentiality through resolute action with general disdain for the lesser "public," which was to be considered as fallen and as something to be transcended.

Hitler wrote,

> The men who want to redeem our German people from its present condition have no need to worry their heads thinking how lovely it would be if this and that did not exist; they must try to ascertain how the given condition can be eliminated. A philosophy filled with infernal intolerance will only be broken by a new idea, driven forward by the same spirit, championed by the same mighty will, and at the same time pure and absolutely genuine in itself. (Hitler 454)

Imagine Heidegger's excitement upon learning he had a doppelganger! The matter of translating an ontological jihad against the "they" into an actual holocaust must have seemed trivial as compared to the possibilities revealed by announcing such a wonderful philosophy into a grandiose movement (which would, admittedly, have to sacrifice beings for the sake of bringing about the restoration of Being). Hitler's appeals echoed Heidegger's with nearly perfect coincidence. The Führer managed to touch upon such issues as thrownness, fallenness, resoluteness, and authentic futural projection. Read through Heidegger-colored glasses, Hitler was offering the historico-repetitive return to Hellenistic Athens and all that that entailed. He saw that the neoteric culture had become lost in a pathetic public mediocrity into which it had been thrown by history. That averageness had to be overcome, and a truer, more primordial state of Being had to be regained. Said becoming had to assume the manifestation of authentically chosen, resolute action dedicated to re-discovering a potentiality that had been leveled down by ambiguity imposed by an ubiquitous and specious they. The philosophy of the "they" was intolerant of authenticity and thus obfuscated Being. The "they" had to be transcended to clear the way for truth. "To the man of this unprecedented will…a three-fold *Seig Heil*!" proclaimed Heidegger (Collins 96).

The marriage seems only natural. The fact that Hitler's itinerary was manifestly hostile to all opposition, whether it took the form of political parties with differing convictions, Judaism, or any human being unworthy of living in his glorious Reich would not have deterred Heidegger, considering the vector of his morals. "Thinking that thinks the truth of Being as the primordial element of man, as one who eksists, is in itself the original ethics" (Heidegger 2: 258). An ethics that rests primarily in thought, as genuine as that thought may be is not capable of considering consequence to life as it is lived. Indeed, Heidegger would have found that average-everyday life unworthy of consideration—unless a meditation on everydayness were going to be used to contribute to a fundamental ontology intended to phenomenologically reveal Being. However, that particular mode of Care conceals a less exalted mode in which the victims of Hitler's movement were assumed to have existed and which presumably did not reveal remote Heideggerian ethics.

But if, in a state of anxiety, all meaning falls away into nullity, where is the justification for the ethnocentrism and racism in this towering new creed? The answer to this, insofar as both Heidegger and Hitler were concerned, lay in Dasein's historical nature. Heidegger, throughout his career, bemoaned the fallenness of civilization from the more primordial era of the pre-Socratic Greeks. It was his thought that the state of Dasein had so degraded due to thrownness into a history of such denigration, a thrownness that is constantly a thrownness into inauthenticity and fleeing-from-Being. However, so long as Dasein is authentic, the potentiality for redemption is also in Dasein's essential Being.

Authentic historicality consists in resolutely choosing a future of repetition. As always already thrown into a past, Dasein finds itself in a situation in which possible futures have been foreclosed, but also disclosed. Authentic Dasein must choose, in the moment of vision, the possibility onto which it will project itself. At every moment, however, Dasein is faced with the onus of ek-statically synthesizing time and is doomed (or blessed) to always have to repeat the moment of vision. The structure of repetition in Heidegger's philosophy is deeper than merely this though; it resonates with Nietzschean eternal recurrence in compelling Dasein to refer always to its past. And, for authentic Dasein, this evokes an eventual reunion with a primordial state of truth and Being.

> The resoluteness which comes back to itself and hands itself down, then becomes the repetition of a possibility of existence that has come down to us. Repeating is handing down explicitly—that is to say, going back into the possibilities of the Dasein that has-been-there [historical Dasein]. The authentic repetition of a possibility of existence that has been— the possibility that Dasein may choose its hero—is grounded existentially in anticipatory resoluteness; for it is in resoluteness that one first chooses the choice which makes one free for the struggle of loyally following in the footsteps of that which can be repeated. (Heidegger 1: 437)

When Dasein does resolutely choose to project itself upon its authentic possibility of repetition, it frees itself for its fate. The authentic historicity of Dasein which is Being-with is destiny.

> But if fateful Dasein, as Being-in-the-world, exists essentially in Being-with Others, its historizing is a co-historizing and is determinative for it as destiny...Our fates have already been guided in advance, in our Being with one another in the same world and in our resoluteness for definite possibilities. Only in communicating and in struggling does the power of destiny become free. Dasein's fateful destiny in and with its 'generation' goes to make up the full authentic historizing of Dasein. (Heidegger 1: 436)

Heidegger betrayed a reverent attitude towards the historicity of Dasein with the language he chose to describe it. Prescribing the words "fate" and "destiny" to Dasein's only authentic course of action assigns religious significance to that mode of Being. It also establishes an ethical imperative to fulfill one's providence which is determined, in a finitely free way, by the possibilities revealed by the past. When that fate is translated to a more universal level and becomes destiny, the past that informs it also becomes more universal; it assumes the character of a pre-fall, pre-nihilism, pre-forgetfulness-towards-Being origin of truth. There could be no more honorable, authentic, resolute, or purposeful choice for a community of Dasein than to choose to realize that primordial heritage.

Heidegger was extremely nationalistic. He believed it was Germany's destiny to begin the true Renaissance, which would ultimately permeate the world with truth. Despite his professed non-religiousness, he was moved to speak of divinity by this oneiric hope for the future of his home:

> "German" is not spoken to the world so that the world might be reformed through the German essence; rather, it is spoken to the Germans so that from a fateful belongingness to the nations they might become world-historical along with them. The homeland of this historical dwelling is nearness to Being. In such nearness, if at all, a decision may be made as to whether and how God and the gods withhold their presence and the night remains, whether and how the day of the holy dawns, whether and how in an upsurgence of the holy an epiphany of God and the gods can begin anew. But the holy, which alone is the essential sphere of divinity, which in turn alone affords a dimension for the gods and God, comes to radiate only when Being itself beforehand and after extensive preparation has been illumined and is experienced in its truth. Only thus does the overcoming of homelessness begin from Being, a homelessness in which not only man but the essence of man stumbles aimlessly about. (Heidegger 2: 242)

This seems to explain why Heidegger was so eager to join Hitler's party. Nazism was seen as the movement that would inaugurate the great era that it was the destiny of his homeland to inherit. Assigning the signification of destiny to Hitler's campaign was something like the equivalent of vying a war in the name of God: Nazism was allowed to take on the character of a holy crusade. It would have been "immoral" to have not supported what, in Heidegger's thinking, was "a humanism in which not man but man's historical essence is at stake in its provenance from the truth of Being" (Heidegger 2: 245).

Heidegger's philosophy of authentic, repetitive historical destiny may also have helped him to justify the flagrant racism in Hitler's philosophy. Considering that Heidegger was greatly influenced by Nietzsche and that, other than the rampant sentencings of the "they," there was really no reason to posit anything but arbitrariness as the meaning of anti-Semitism, it is difficult to understand why Heidegger would have condoned such a prejudice. However, if the Jewish history of persecution and pogroms is taken into account, it becomes less dubious. If destiny is a return to authentic history, then the holocaust could be seen as the authentic historizing that Being was to hand down to the Jewish people.

This all seems to make apprehensible the reasons that Heidegger would have become a Nazi, thus explicating the first period of his questionable prominence. But are the answers here provided too convenient? Is it too improbable that the philosophies of Heidegger and Hitler would be so congruent? One writer makes the assertion that Heidegger manipulated his philosophy to force it to conform to the dogma of the political party into which he was trying to insinuate himself (Collins 97). Is that answer a more viable one?

No, it is not. That hypothesis is too quick to discredit Heidegger. The foundations of Heidegger's philosophy, which led him to adopt National Socialism, had been clearly laid out in *Being and Time*, and the ideas expressed in that manifesto had appeared prior to that in his lectures. The Nazi party was not dominant until 1932, five years after the publication of *Being and Time*. It would have required remarkably sagacious political insight on Heidegger's part to predict the rise of Nazism, and the man was not such an astute statesman.

> He had no experience of political life prior to the period of the Rectorship. Close friends and associates such as Jaspers and Marcuse were surprised by his eruption into the political arena, having understood him to be a man preoccupied with the 'eternal' questions of philosophy rather than the detailed actualities of contemporary life. He was generally agreed to have been—and remained—a political ingenue. (Young 11)

It is highly unlikely that Heidegger had managed to foresee the future of German politics years in advance, and then compromised his philosophy to defend the coming trends.

Further testimony to his authentic commitment to his philosophy is the fact that he remained vested in it even after his falling out with the Nazis. It could be argued, admittedly, that this was only due to obstinacy and arrogance rather than any genuine conviction, but that seems uncalled for. There was a transformation in the parts of his philosophy that Heidegger deemed faulty, so he was not unwilling to admit mistakes. The points that were changed, however, did not affect the theories that allowed him to place faith in Nazism, suggesting that he honestly believed those theories to be sound throughout his life. Heidegger's philosophy metamorphosed in its attitude towards *techne*—not history, not Dasein's temporal structure, not echt *deutsch,* and not destiny (Young 140). Those points remained with him well after the end of his Nazi engagements, finding vociferous expression in "Letter on Humanism." It does not seem at all that that expression was an insincere attempt to vindicate his philosophy; the language in that piece is indicative of an unfeigned piety towards the Being that he perceived to have compelled him to become a Nazi in the 1930's.

The damning biographical item remaining to be addressed is Heidegger's silence about his Nazism. This is often viewed as evidence that he was never sorry for his role in Hitler's success. Indeed, the closest he ever came to apologizing for his actions appeared in the interview "Only a God Can Save Us Now" in which he does not explicitly denounce Nazism (Inwood 6). What is to be thought of this?

If Heidegger did believe in his philosophy, which this paper assumes he did, silence would have been the most authentic apology he could have made.

> Keeping silent is another essential possibility of discourse...In talking with one another, the person who keeps silent can "make one understand" (that is, he can develop an understanding), and he can do so more authentically than the person who is never short of words...Keeping silent authentically is possible only in genuine discoursing. To be able to be silent, Dasein must have something to say—that is, it must have at its disposal an authentic and rich disclosedness of itself. In that case one's reticence makes something manifest, and does away with "idle talk." As a mode of discoursing, reticence gives rise to a potentiality-for-hearing which is genuine, and to a Being-with-one-another which is transparent. (Heidegger 1: 208)

To Heidegger, speaking an authentic recantation would have amounted to concealing its truth, especially considering the public interest in his excuse. Announcing a personal feeling of regret to any kind of public forum, be it an interview to be published or a denazification panel designated to judge one's right to re-enter society, would have been utterly inconsistent with his beliefs. Had he made a public apology, that would have been a better ground for suspecting him of indifference regarding his past. It is also to Heidegger's credit that he had his dedication to Husserl re-instantiated in *Being and Time*. That action coupled with his silence reveals more about his regret than any apology could have.

It is also indicative of precisely what it was for which he was sorry. Heidegger was probably not sorry for his belief in Nazism in general, but for actions he may have eventually come to realize were born of inauthenticity. These actions included his maltreatment of Husserl and the blocking of the academic careers of non-Nazi students during his institution as Rector. Although Heidegger's withdrawal from the position was debatably more the result of an insulted ambition than a fundamental protest of Nazi methods, the fact remains that he did quarrel with the party towards the end of the Rectorship about the anti-Semitic system he was required to follow. He also rekindled friendships with Jewish acquaintances after his resignation (Inwood 4). It seems he did finally come to realize that that aspect of Hitler's philosophy, among others (such as the Nazi obsession with mastery over Being), was not to be honored. Perhaps he knew he had made the mistake of abiding by it due to his own inauthentic attention to the dictates of the loudest "they" of the time.

Tamara Johnson

The fact that a non-repentant Nazi could be so plausibly defended raises an obvious question: What does it portend for the future—or present—that a philosophy intended to return care for Being to an individual could result in a justification of genocide? Are existentialist morals valid as a possible doctrine of life for lives that now find themselves in a world with more than six billion individuals? If Dasein is essentially thrown into the mode of Being-with others, what happens to those others when Dasein, in its authenticity, has no choice but to choose to see those others as null? It would have behooved Heidegger to have addressed such issues, but his conception of Dasein as alone Being-unto-death precluded the possibility of their even being brought to light. Is it possible to appropriate a Heideggerian philosophy of resoluteness and authenticity into a possible authentic mode of Mitsein?

Perhaps if Heidegger had been willing to place Dasein in a body, the body could have become another primordial phenomenon onto which Care is projected. It may have been able to form an ontological basis, commonly shared by every Dasein, for something like a universal respect for the Being ek-sistent in every being. He did not provide Dasein with a phenomenological embodiment, probably because he was too concerned with constructing a fundamental ontology that could transcend one. That made his philosophy inorganic, to the point of deficiency, but it is certainly not irredeemable. There is a great deal to be learned and admired in Heidegger's thought.

In conclusion, Heidegger's Nazism was, if not forgivable, at least comprehensible. He had genuine belief in his philosophy, causing him to place too much faith in Hitler's, which bore a striking resemblance to his own. The similarities between the two thoughts inspired Heidegger to adopt a political regime that he hoped would be able to reveal Germany's destiny. He eventually came to realize that such was not to be and, although he never publicly made amends for his involvement with Nazism, seems to have authentically recognized and answered for his actions. There is an element of incompleteness to a philosophy that can make space for Hitler's specific war for excellence, but taken in its entirety Heidegger's philosophy nevertheless stands out as one of enormous value. If nothing else his contributions to ontology, phenomenology, and existentialism can be said to have revealed the potentiality for a becoming of further revelations, which would have occasioned at least a moment of relief from anxious gravity for Heidegger.

Tamara Johnson

REFERENCES

Collins, Jeff. *Introducing Heidegger*. Ed. Richard Appignanesi. New York: Totem Books, 1998.

Haber, John. "Heidegger and Nazism." 10 November 1999. *http://www.haberarts.com/heidnazi.htm.*

Heidegger, Martin. (1) *Being and Time*. Trans. John Macquarrie and Edward Robinson. New York: Harper and Row, 1962.

_____. (2) "Letter on Humanism." *Basic Writings*. Ed. David Farrell Krell. New York: Harper Collins, 1977.

Hitler, Adolf. *Mein Kampf*. Trans. Ralph Manheim. New York: Houghton Mifflin Company, 1943.

Inwood, Michael. *Heidegger*. Ed. Keith Thomas. Oxford: Oxford University Press, 1997.

Young, Julian. *Heidegger, Philosophy, Nazism*. Cambridge: Cambridge University Press, 1997.

LANGUAGE GAMES

Incommensurability, Normative Vices, and the Comparative Language Game: A Wittgensteinian Model for Comparative Philosophy

Erin Cline

Belmont University

The examination of what might cause one to be "torn away" from a particular worldview is essential to the construction of a Wittgensteinian model for comparative philosophy. In this paper, I discuss the obstacles which plague comparative studies and place Wittgenstein in conversation with other key thinkers on the subject of different worldviews. I give attention to Alasdair MacIntyre's discussion of intertranslatability, Donald Davidson's discussion of incommensurability, and to the normative vices proposed by Martha Nussbaum. I conclude my paper with an examination of a comparative language game, and the manner in which it is a process of refinement with many levels and characteristics.

* * *

> Certain events would put me into a position in which I could not go on with the old language-game any further. In which I was torn away from the sureness of the game. Indeed, doesn't it seem obvious that the possibility of a language-game is conditioned by certain facts?[1]

The examination of what might cause one to be "torn away" from a particular worldview is essential to the construction of a Wittgensteinian model for comparative philosophy. Such an examination requires that we pay attention to his remarks on the plurality of worldviews. In this paper, I intend to place Wittgenstein in conversation with several other key thinkers on the subject of comparative worldviews. The problems of incommensurability discussed by Alasdair MacIntyre and Donald Davidson, in addition to Martha Nussbaum's discussion of the intellectual vices which infect comparative philosophy, present a comprehensive picture of the obstacles which plague this endeavor. Following Wittgenstein's assertion that we may be at some point "torn away from the sureness" of our own language games or cultural systems, I will argue that he believed comparison of worldviews to be a process of refinement and progression towards overcoming the barriers between those of differing traditions.

Before offering my own reading of Wittgenstein's method for doing comparative philosophy, I would first like to provide a brief overview of some of the major models for this enterprise. In his work regarding incommensurability between cultures and traditions, MacIntyre places great weight on the intertranslatability of cultural concepts and ideas. MacIntyre asserts that "There are indeed large parts of every language that are translatable into every other." But he also calls attention to the many concepts for which there is no adequate translation. The problem of untranslatability between languages, and thus between worldviews lies in the fact that "it is precisely those features of languages whose mastery cannot be acquired from phrase books which generate untranslatability."[2] He notes that the individual, "...in deciding to spend his or her life within one linguistic community rather than the other, is also to some substantial degree [choosing between] alternative and incompatible sets of beliefs and ways of life."[3]

The more complex concepts belonging to each culture are the real sources of the incommensurability problem, according to MacIntyre. He writes,

> ...it is not that the beliefs of each such community cannot be represented in any way at all in the language of the other...rather...rendering those beliefs sufficiently intelligible to be evaluated by a member of the other community involves characterizing those beliefs in such a way that they are bound to be rejected.[4]

MacIntyre attributes this rejection to the fact that explanations of concepts which are integral to a particular worldview depend upon reference to socially recognized canonical texts, expressions, and exemplars that are unique to a different culture than that of the interpreter. The ultimate outcome is that without an understanding of the canonical background belonging to a different culture, any comparative endeavor will "necessarily appear contextless and lacking in justification."[5]

Davidson also believes that comparisons between worldviews are ultimately doomed by the problem of incommensurability. Yet, he presents a different approach than that of MacIntyre. According to Davidson, the problem of incommensurability lies in methods of reasoning and justification, not merely in lexical untranslatability. Like MacIntyre, Davidson agrees that the translation of words and concepts of a simplistic nature are possible, but even then, Davidson says that the way in which concepts "anchor language to the world" is incommensurable between worldviews. Davidson claims, "the correct interpretation of what a speaker means is not determined solely by what is in his head; it depends also on the natural history of what is in the head."[6] He goes on to write: "...if we merely know that someone holds a certain sentence to be true, we know neither what he means by the sentence nor what belief his holding it true represents..."[7]

Nussbaum believes that the project of comparative philosophy can overcome the types of incommensurability MacIntyre and Davidson notice. But she does warn us that there are several intellectual vices to be avoided when comparing worldviews. In her work *Cultivating Humanity*, Nussbaum discusses three normative vices that plague comparative philosophy.[8] The first vice, normative chauvinism, is defined as thinking one's culture is best and insofar as other cultures are unlike it, they are inferior. Normative arcadianism is a second vice Nussbaum notices. This occurs, for example, when a non-Western culture and worldview is viewed as full of spiritual and moral richness lacking in the materialistic, corrupt, and aggressive West.

Normative skepticism is the third vice Nussbaum identifies. In normative skepticism, the individual narrates the values and practices of another culture, but suspends all judgment about whether these are coherent, true, or desirable. Typically, normative skepticism parallels a third type of incommensurability, which involves the suspension of evaluation and the idea that "we cannot make a judgment of superiority between our own theory and at least some other theories." This vice is a form of relativism in which individuals have achieved a more balanced perspective than that of either normative chauvinism or arcadianism, but they lack the ability to make an accurate appraisal of the benefits and drawbacks of a worldview.

Normative skepticism is not to be confused with the position taken by David Wong. Wong writes,

> The most interesting and substantial cases for evaluative incommensurability arise, not from our inability to make sense of another people's beliefs, but precisely from those situations in which we understand and see how different their beliefs are from our

> own...because we can understand how they are tied to
> a life that people would want to live.[9]

In the situation Wong is noticing, different traditions are incommensurable but there is no skeptical despair. There is instead the acknowledgement that some different forms of life are just as desirable or acceptable as our own and there is no felt need to decide between them.

In addition to the normative vices mentioned above, Nussbaum calls attention to the vice of descriptive chauvinism. This vice occurs whenever interpreters adopt the position that apparently differing worldviews are all saying essentially the same thing. MacIntyre describes this vice too. He says:

> ...our culture has been far too hospitable to the all too plainly self-interested belief that whenever we succeed in discovering the rationality of other and alien cultures and traditions...what we will also discover is that in essentials they are just like us.[10]

Davidson acknowledges this vice as well, arguing that in order to "gain a foothold" in the translation of other beliefs and practices, we must assume the speaker agrees with our beliefs, and thereby "render them like ourselves."[11]

Now, I would like to turn from describing the way in which the problem of incommensurability is understood to compromise the comparative project, and the various vices into which we might fall in trying to conduct comparisons between worldviews, towards offering a constructive model for comparative philosophy. In so doing, I wish to draw on the work of Wittgenstein. A Wittgensteinian model for comparative philosophy entails the placement of both the discipline and its framework into his conception of a language game. In other words, we should describe what it is we do when we compare worldviews in ways that avoid the vices Nussbaum notices. What we are describing then might be called the language game of comparative philosophy.

Wittgenstein once commented on the project of comparative worldviews in a fairly direct way. Of the work of Otto Spengler in this area he wrote,

> Spengler could be better understood if he said: I am comparing different cultural epochs with the lives of families; within a family there is a family resemblance, though you will also find a resemblance between members of different families...[12]

The resemblance Wittgenstein has in mind is appropriately illustrated by those characteristics, which are shared between cultures, or worldviews. This reveals that a Wittgensteinian approach to comparative philosophy supports the view that differing worldviews can be compared successfully and intelligibly, because there is a resemblance between cultures, just as between members of different families. The Wittgensteinian concept of family resemblance can be used by the comparative philosopher to deflect the stronger versions of incommensurability found in MacIntyre and Davidson.

Though incommensurability theories point to the difficulties inherent in trying to explain concepts in different languages and the manner in which they are tied to forms of life, Wittgenstein's idea of how language games are learned relies not on explanation, but on example and behavior. He repeatedly stressed the importance of moving past explanation, even referring to our desire to explain (linguistically) as a disease.[13] In the Wittgensteinian understanding of a language game, the rules of any game must be learned by example. He wrote:

> For doesn't the technique (the possibility) of training someone else in following it [the language game] belong to the following of a rule? To be sure, by means of examples...How do you follow the rule? — "I do it like this;..." and now there follow general explanations and examples [of what is done and said].[14]

Wittgenstein wrote the following about the process of teaching a language game: "I shall teach him to use the words by means of examples...I do it, he does it after me; and I influence him by expressions of agreement, rejection, expectation, encouragement."[15]

Engagement in the comparative language game moves the individual beyond normative skepticism, eliminating the inability to evaluate, while at the same time maintaining the ability to see value in both perspectives. For Wittgenstein, this is a descriptive comment, based on the learning of the game. It is participation in this game by example and word which leads to the rejection of the notion that all forms of life are equally good. But it also gives birth to the recognition that there is more than one desirable form of life. Wittgenstein stresses that participation in the language game of comparative worldviews yields no general rule for choosing the desirability of one view over another, yet neither does participation lead us to skepticism or relativism. Wong illustrates this particularly Wittgensteinian insight in his example of a woman trying to decide between the life of a musician and the life of a philosopher. He writes:

> We want to say in this case that the rationality of her accepting one or the other "form of life" essentially depends upon factors such as her temperament, her most important desires, her talents, and her circumstances. We would be most reluctant to say that one or the other form was generally superior. We do not think that our inability to prescribe a general choice is evidence for skepticism about value judgments.[16]

One way of thinking about participation in the comparative language game is well illustrated by Roger Ames. Ames says that those engaging in comparative philosophy most effectively "dim the lights" on their own worldview. He has used the analogy of standing in a lighted room, looking out through a glass door at night. In this situation, instead of clearly seeing a person on the other side of the glass, one sees only his own reflection, because the light inside is too intense. Normative chauvinism, arcadianism, and skepticism are all caused at least in part by the inability to see another worldview clearly. They are all in one way or another traceable to the situation Ames is describing. In order to successfully observe another culture, one must "dim the lights" on his own background and experience. Indeed, this might be understood in Wittgensteinian language as a rule for the comparative language game.

Still, to follow Ames' analogy further, to open the door and walk outside to converse with the other person is to go beyond mere description of the other, and to reach toward understanding. What gets created in this new engagement is what Wittgenstein has in mind as the language game of comparative philosophy. S. L. Hurley supports this Wittgensteinian approach. He writes:

> ...it is possible to have the relevant concepts and to understand what someone believes or desires, for purposes of intelligibility, even if one does not understand everything about what it is like for him or her to have that belief or desire.[17]

There is substantial support for the assertion that the comparative language game in the Wittgensteinian model is under construction in ways most other language games are not. In *Culture and Value* Wittgenstein writes, "The origin and the primitive form of the language game is a reaction;

only from this can more complicated forms develop. Language—I want to say—is a refinement."[18] The comparative game is a game in continual refinement, defined by consistently engaging oneself in the process of encountering persons of other cultures and conceptual beliefs. It is in this encounter that the problems associated with incommensurability and comparative vices are overcome.

It is also in this process that we may be "torn away" from the sureness of our own cultural beliefs and worldviews. The primitive form of a language game, Wittgenstein says, is a reaction, and in the comparative game that reaction is the process of being "torn away." This is also a rule of the game. But Wittgenstein does not mean to imply that a destruction of our own worldview must occur. Instead, he says, "Not all corrections of views are on the same level."[19] The problems of incommensurability, normative chauvinism, normative arcadianism, and normative skepticism can be understood as dead end corrections because each in its own way derails the conversation between worldviews.

When we think of corrections to our worldviews, we can describe a few. First, as we listen to another worldview we find that we wish to reform our own. This may be because we come to consider our worldview incorrect, or less desirable. Wittgenstein says, "certain events would put me into a position in which I could not go on with the old language game [my old worldview.]"[20] Or perhaps we find that our view is satisfying but the other view does not seem to be in any need of reform or change. This is certainly a different kind of correction, but it is a correction nonetheless. It is not the correcting of our own worldview, but the correcting of our understanding of the other view. We may also experience correction at another level, when we find that a belief we thought was true in another worldview is in fact not held (such as thinking that Catholics worship Mary and finding out they do not). The point here is that corrections occur at many levels and in many ways. There is no complete catalog of them.

Ultimately, the Wittgensteinian model for comparative philosophy is conducive to producing the type of individual termed "the 150% man" in Malcolm McFee's study of Blackfeet acculturation. Certain individuals in this study showed the continuum principle of cultural loss and replacement to be inaccurate due to post-assimilatory retention of traditional culture. Instead of scoring the typical cultural percentage ratio of 75-25, these individuals scored from 60 to 90 percent on both scales. McFee wrote that the study's surprising discovery that individuals could become acculturated in both knowledge and usage of such areas as language, religious beliefs, and artistic expression indicates that "a man is more than a culture container."[21] For the field of comparative philosophy, such studies serve as a reminder that in the midst of even the most well-developed theories, there is much to learn, and the work of philosophers such as Wittgenstein can contribute significantly to our endeavors in understanding other worldviews.

NOTES

1   *On Certainty*, par. 617. Hereafter cited as *OC*.

2   MacIntyre, *Relativism,* 187.

3   *Ibid.* 186.

4   *Ibid.* 186.

5   *Ibid.* 188.

6   Davidson, "*The Myth of the Subjective*," 164.

7   Davidson, "*On The Very Idea of a Conceptual Scheme*," 77.

8   Nussbaum 130-39.

9   Wong 156.

10   MacIntyre, *Relativism*, 201.

11   Wong 142, 144.

12   Wittgenstein, *Culture and Value*, 14. Hereafter cited as *CV*.

13   Wittgenstein, *Remarks on the Foundations of Mathematics*, 333. Hereafter cited as *RFM*.

14   *RFM* 418.

15   Wittgenstein, *Philosophical Investigations*, 3rd par. 208. Hereafter cited as *PI*.

16   Wong, *Three Kinds*, 154-155.

17   Hurley 90.

18   *CV* 31.

19   *OC* par. 300.

20   *Ibid.* par. 616

21   McFee 1096-1107.

REFERENCES

Davidson, Donald. "On The Very Idea of a Conceptual Scheme," in *Relativism: Cognitive and Moral*. Ed. Jack W. Meiland and Michael Krausz. Notre Dame: University of Notre Dame Press, 1982.

_____. "The Myth of the Subjective," in *Relativism: Interpretation and Confrontation*. Ed. Michael Krausz. Notre Dame: University of Notre Dame Press, 1989.

Hurley, S.L. "Intelligibility, Imperialism, and Conceptual Scheme," in *Midwest Studies in Philosophy vol. XVII: The Wittgenstein Legacy*. Ed. Peter A. French, Theodore E. Uehling, Jr., and Howard K. Wettstein. Notre Dame: University of Notre Dame Press, 1992.

McFee, Malcolm. "The 150% Man, a Product of Blackfeet Acculturation." *American Anthropologist* 70, no. 6, 1968.

MacIntyre, Alasdair. "Relativism, Power, and Philosophy," in *Relativism: Interpretation and Confrontation*. Ed. Michael Krausz. Notre Dame: University of Notre Dame Press, 1989.

Nussbaum, Martha C. *Cultivating Humanity.* Cambridge: Harvard UP, 1997.

Wittgenstein, Ludwig. *On Certainty.* Ed. G.E.M. Anscombe and G.H. von Wright. Trans. Denis Paul and G.E.M. Anscombe. New York: Harper Torchbooks, 1972.

_____. *Culture and Value.* Ed. G.H. von Wright. Trans. Peter Winch. Chicago: University of Chicago Press, 1984.

_____. *Remarks on the Foundations of Mathematics*, revised edition. Ed. G.H. von Wright, R. Rhees, and G.E.M. Anscombe. Trans. G.E.M. Anscombe. Cambridge: MIT Press, 1994.

_____. *Philosophical Investigations*, 3rd edition. Trans. G.E.M. Anscombe. Englewood Cliffs: Prentice-Hall.

Wong, David B. "Three Kinds of Incommensurability," in *Relativism: Interpretation and Confrontation*. Ed. Michael Krausz. Notre Dame: University of Notre Dame Press, 1989.

WITTGENSTEIN AND NATURALISM

Zachary Haines

Macalester College

Recently, philosophical texts have been based more and more on a naturalistic approach to philosophy. One author who instills the belief that philosophy should be concerned with the way things *are* done, not with how they ought to ideally be done, is Ludwig Wittgenstein. His *Philosophical Investigations* is not only a shift in philosophy of language methodology, but symbolic of the change occurring across the field of all philosophy. Philosophical inquiry is receiving more credibility with the layman because exploring the nature of things through empirical observation is done in place of normative, theoretical ideologies that would otherwise be produced. This is not to say that there is no place for theorizing about what should or could be done, but this is to come after what actually is done is examined.

The sub-disciplines of philosophy seem to be sharing a common thread in the late twentieth century. Epistemology, philosophy of language, ethics… most writings in these fields seem to be shifting from being primarily prescriptive to focusing on descriptive under the skeptic's microscope. Wittgenstein was a major contributor during this shift, taking a naturalistic approach to language and epistemology in general. Wittgenstein rejected foundationalism and, in doing so, he rejected normativity as well. In lieu of skepticism, he developed a holistic approach that was naturalistic, at least in the sense that naturalism is relevant to philosophical exploration. This is known as the relevance theory of naturalism, as opposed to replacement theory naturalism.

Naturalism

It would be difficult to explain what naturalism is without invoking the language of Quine. Quine, in his now famous essay, "Epistemology Naturalized," said that epistemology should be "naturalized." This was in 1969 and was one of the earliest urgings of naturalization in the Wittgensteinian discipline. What brought this on? Quine thought that we should leave traditional epistemology behind for a new epistemology that was essentially empirical psychology. Why would he give up traditional epistemology for a psychological approach? Quine reasoned that skepticism was doomed to failure, and that we should stop trying to hold epistemology under the skeptic's scrutiny. Instead, we should be "scientifically investigating man's acquisition of science" or knowledge. Thus, the shift from prescription to description began.[1]

What is the difference between these two methods? Prescriptive philosophy attempts to prescribe how one ought to do things, such as how one ought to know things (prescriptive epistemology). Descriptive philosophy attempts to describe how one really does things, such as how we come to know things (descriptive epistemology). It becomes readily apparent that the descriptive philosophers rely much more on empirical data or observations.

Quine's naturalism provides a well-laid out plan for tackling how we come to know things—an epistemological blueprint if you will. He bases his naturalistic agenda on three central doctrines:

1. the *mandatory use* doctrine: epistemology must make use of empirical data;
2. the *exclusive use* doctrine: no data other than empirical data may be used in epistemology —

there is no first philosophy, no transcendent standpoint, no *a priori* truth;

3. the *free use* doctrine: the free use of empirical data about the formation of belief is unproblematic.[2]

The change from prescription to description is very noticeable in Quine's doctrines, as they all require empirical data. The requirement of empirical support for philosophical claims was very important to Quine in philosophical inquiry. This characterizes the difference between traditional and naturalistic epistemology in philosophy.

Quine had the desire to build a descriptive foundation of science that would have a predictive value to it. He wanted to practice discovery instead of justification of epistemological beliefs. Quine wanted a naturalistic philosophy to replace the skeptic's meaningless quest to find how the world is vs. how it appears. He sets out to form a theory of the world based on sensory, empirical, data. This would later evolve into his "web of belief."[3] This web was a system of beliefs about the world that based on the rejection of two distinctions: *a priori/a posteriori* and analytic/synthetic.

A characteristic of the web of belief that seems common in naturalism is that it is holistic. In Quine's theory of beliefs about the world, there are stronger beliefs and weaker beliefs. The weaker, auxiliary beliefs, when contradicted, are easier to change than the stronger, center beliefs. When a center belief is contradicted, one can choose to change, in a major way, one's theory of beliefs or one can reject the contradiction.[4]

Philosophy in naturalized epistemology does differ from cognitive psychology. In naturalized epistemology we can use the information gained to predict future occurrences involving epistemology with more accuracy. It is as if one uses the descriptive naturalized philosophy in order to come up with some prescriptions about epistemology in general or the future of epistemology.

Wittgenstein rejects skepticism and in doing so, he rejects foundationalism. The rejection of foundationalism follows from the Wittgensteinian rejection of skepticism because foundational approaches generally lead to skepticism. In rejecting foundationalism, Wittgenstein accepts holism and in holism, naturalism works well. Wittgenstein's philosophy of language holism can be seen as early as the 1960's in the *Blue and Brown Books*, "Understanding a sentence means understanding a language."[5] Now that we have a clearer idea of what it means to have a naturalistic approach to a philosophical discipline, namely epistemology, what does it mean to have a naturalistic approach to language, as Wittgenstein did?

The replacement sense of naturalism says that naturalized epistemology renders traditional epistemology unnecessary and thereby replaces any previous uses of traditional epistemology. The relevance sense of naturalism is making claims that empirical facts are relevant to traditional epistemology or epistemology in general. Psychology does not hope or need to replace epistemology. There are two different arguments one can make about Wittgenstein's naturalism. The first is that he is a naturalist in the sense of replacement theory of naturalism, and the second is that he is a naturalist in the relevance theory of naturalism. I will argue that Wittgenstein was a naturalist in the relevance sense of naturalism.

Zachary Haines

Traditional Philosophy of Language and Wittgenstein

The traditional idea of language has a logical atomistic feel. In the logical atomist's view of language, words stand for things. This occurs in Wittgenstein's *Tractatus Logico-Philosophicus* where he claims that the foundation of language is atomistic.

Another idea that goes with the traditional view of language, later dropped by Wittgenstein, is that there is a logically perfect language that is prescriptive and has a direct word/object relationship throughout. In the *Tractatus* he argues that there must be a fixed correlation between names and objects, and that the meaning of a word is the thing to which it refers.[6] Based upon this, one could have language in categories with clearly specified boundaries and a set of defining characteristics necessary and sufficient for membership in the category. In this language, sentences are determinably true, false, or meaningless because the meaningfulness of a sentence cannot be separated from the true/false possibilities of a sentence. If words had ostensive definitions relating to objects in the world then it should be possible (given omniscience) to determine the truth-value of the sentences in which they occur; otherwise these sentences are meaningless. This idea of determining truth-value for all meaningful sentences is known as the determinacy theory. However, "determinate" is not equal to "being able to be determined (by use)." Determinacy theory relies on a fixed, definite foundation for beliefs and knowledge. This ties in to the traditional epistemological notion of identifying the criteria for justified belief and examining the possibility of knowledge by these criteria, epistemological foundationalism. This was the skeptic's challenge.[7]

In the *Philosophical Investigations*, Wittgenstein claims that the skeptic's question is unanswerable and that it is impossible for language or epistemology to stand up to the skeptic's demands. The skeptical question is meaningless to him because the language of the skeptical question is useless. The main idea underlying Wittgenstein's later conception of language is that words derive their meaning from use. Words have meaning by the way that they enter into discourse. The meaning of language is only secured by using a word according to rules. Simply put, a word's meaning is its general use, and there can be no meaning found outside of a particular use. If there is no use, the language has no meaning. There is, as a necessity, agreement in expressions and reactions of language. Rhees puts it, "Because there is this agreement we can understand one another. And since we understand one another we have rules."[8] Hence, skeptical questions are useless.

Why is meaning derivative of use? In the *Philosophical Investigations*, comment 244, Wittgenstein says "…words are connected with the primitive, the natural, expressions of the sensation and used in their place… [T]he verbal expression of pain replaces crying and does not describe it."[9] McGinn interprets this, and I agree, as making the requirement that language must find meaning in that which can be publicly verified.[10] How else would anyone know what the word(s) mean, including the speaker? How could I say I was incorrectly following the meaning of the words I use when I can look to no place in order to determine how the words are used?[11]

The language user must have some place to look in order to verify correct language use. Wittgenstein explains this point; "[It] is not that others must see what my words refer to. It is just that if my words are to refer to anything they must be understood."[12] This is what Wittgenstein means when he says that words have meaning, and understanding, in their use.[13] Simply going through the motions of chess is not understanding the rule-guided nature of chess, just as going through the motions of language does not mean rules are being followed. Language is not contained in the models of mathematics or logic but is "...a game, an activity embedded within a background of human practice."[14]

In order for me to make meaningful use of expressions of language, I must understand what they mean. For me to understand their meaning I have to know how they are used, and to know this I must have experienced their use in context. From somewhere I must acquire the training of how to use the language. This is both acquired and constantly up for revision. Many times one may think one knows how to use a word and someone says "No that's not what it means" or "No, that's not how you use that word." In the context, the rules naturally occur. In use, naturally agreed upon rules develop or form. The naturalistic or descriptive qualities of Wittgenstein's language begin to be more readily apparent. He is relying on observable instances for the foundation of the meaning of language. The meaning is not fixed or definite, as the use is alterable.

Wittgenstein and Naturalistic Inquiry

Is Wittgenstein really engaging in naturalistic inquiry or is he simply a semi-behaviorist or psychologist in a philosophical disguise? He claims in his *Tractatus Logico-Philosophicus*, "Psychology is no nearer related to philosophy, than is any other natural science. The theory of knowledge is the philosophy of psychology."[15] The point that Wittgenstein makes is that psychology is related to philosophy, but so are other natural sciences. The philosophical development of a theory of knowledge is the philosophy of psychology but this does not imply that one does psychology, rather than philosophy, when exploring epistemology. Descriptive epistemology does certainly edge much closer to a form of psychology, and the rest of natural science, than the traditional prescriptive forms of philosophy. This is because naturalized epistemology, as so well set forth by Quine, relies solely on empirical data.

This is a stark contrast to the traditional transcendental philosophical approach to epistemology or language. No longer do we sit on high and decide *a priori* how the world works and why. The new trend is to take a down-to-earth approach, which seems to make much more sense. Why not discover why we do certain actions and how we acquire knowledge by observation, rather than formulate postulates or foundations that prescribe what we should do and how we should know? Wittgenstein says that prescribing what one should do is what the psychologist does. The psychologist is studying behavior of man and different characteristics of this behavior.[16] Psychology describes and then makes normative claims based on the descriptions or observations. (So the question is where does Wittgenstein, as a philosopher, make normative claims based on descriptions?) The psychological or behavioral influence only makes sense in the naturalistic approach to philosophy. As Fogelin says, Wittgenstein's *Philosophical Investigations* are a kind of philosophical psychology.[17] He is writing down thoughts that are products of his observations. The observations of linguistic expression become a psychology of sorts because through the observation of behavior one can philosophize about the psychological processes being implemented. The psychologist may explore the processes but this is not Wittgenstein's concern, it is merely a consequence of the method of investigation Wittgenstein uses. It does, however, provide an explanation of how and why Wittgenstein's naturalistic philosophy bleeds into the natural sciences as it explores our language.

However, natural scientist or just plain philosopher, Wittgenstein is in the philosophical camp of naturalists. He writes, in the *Philosophical Investigations*, of the training required in the acquisition of language. This idea of training rather than deciding on an *a priori* explanation of language demonstrates Wittgenstein's naturalistic approach to philosophy. Contrary to prescriptive language theories, it is through teaching that we learn language. Wittgenstein eventually makes prescriptive claims but these are based upon the descriptions he has made throughout his philosophical exploration. He gives up on trying to please the skeptic and takes the sensible path from there. Skepticism is irrefutable, meaningless, and cannot be answered. Wittgenstein wants to observe and describe how we do what we do and maybe then he can suggest ought or why. If we try to prescribe before we describe, we slip into the kind of philosophy of which Wittgenstein was most critical. Shatz writes, "[Strawson] also quotes with approval Wittgenstein's naturalism as it emerges in *On Certainty*, paraphrasing as follows:

> To attempt to confront the professional skeptical doubt with arguments in support of these beliefs, with rational justification, is simply to show a total misunderstanding of the role they actually play in our belief-systems. The correct way with the professional skeptical doubt is not to attempt to rebut it with argument, but to point out that it is idle, unreal, a pretense; and then the rebutting arguments will appear as equally idle...there is no such thing as *the reasons for which we hold* these beliefs.[18]

Wittgenstein and Naturalism

To clarify, Wittgenstein says there is no skeptic-proof way to answer the question of what qualifies as knowledge. Quine considers this Wittgenstein's therapy for philosophers. He cures philosophers of the delusion that there are epistemological problems. Epistemology answers to the natural sciences, which in turn answer to epistemology.[19] Again, epistemology is normative of psychology, and Quine would argue that psychology is normative of epistemology. The wave of naturalism, upon which Wittgenstein is a force, sweeps epistemology, and maybe philosophy or philosophical inquiry itself, into the natural sciences.

Zachary Haines

NOTES

[1] Wagner, Steven J. and Richard Warner. *Naturalism: A Critical Appraisal*. David Shatz. "Skepticism and Naturalized Epistemology." Notre Dame, IN: University of Notre Dame Press, 1993. Page 117.

[2] *Ibid.* Page 119.

[3] Quine, W. V. *Word & Object*. Cambridge, MA: The MIT Press, 1960. Pages 76-77.

[4] Quine, W. V. and J. S. Ullian. *The Web of Belief*. New York, NY: Random House, 1978. Pages 9-19.

[5] Wittgenstein, Ludwig. *Preliminary Studies for the "Philosophical Investigations" Generally Known as "The Blue and Brown Books."* New York, NY: Barnes & Noble, 1969. Page 5.

[6] Wittgenstein, Ludwig. *Tractatus Logico-Philosophicus*. New York, NY: Routledge & Kegan Paul, 1992. Pages 31-43 (2-2.225).

[7] Kornblith, Hilary. *Naturalizing Epistemology*. Richard Nisbett and Lee Ross. "Judgmental Heuristics and Knowledge Structures." London: The MIT Press, 1997. Page 278.

[8] Rhees, Rush. *Discussions of Wittgenstein*. New York, NY: Schocken Books, 1970. Page 57.

[9] *Ibid.* Page 89.

[10] McGinn, Colin. *Wittgenstein on Meaning*. New York, NY: Basil Blackwell, 1987. Page 49.

[11] Rhees, Rush. *Discussions of Wittgenstein*. New York, NY: Schocken Books, 1970. Page 58.

[12] *Ibid.* Page 61.

[13] Wittgenstein, Ludwig. *Preliminary Studies for the "Philosophical Investigations" Generally Known as "The Blue and Brown Books."* New York, NY: Barnes & Noble, 1969. Page 72.

[14] Stern, David G. *Wittgenstein on Mind and Language*. New York, NY: Oxford University Press, 1995. Page 103.

[15] Wittgenstein, Ludwig. *Tractatus Logico-Philosophicus*. New York, NY: Routledge & Kegan Paul, 1992. Page 77 (4.1121).

[16] *Ibid.* Page 179 (II:v).

[17] Fogelin, Robert J. *The Arguments of Philosophers: Wittgenstein*. London: Routledge & Kegan Paul, 1976. Page 172.

18   Wagner, Steven J. and Richard Warner. *Naturalism: A Critical Appraisal*. David Shatz. "Skepticism and Naturalized Epistemology." Notre Dame, IN: University of Notre Dame Press, 1993. Pages 125-126.

19   Quine, W. V. *Ontological Relativity and Other Essays*. "Epistemology Naturalized." New York, NY: Columbia University Press, 1969. Pages 69-90.

REFERENCES

Fogelin, Robert J. *The Arguments of Philosophers: Wittgenstein*. London: Routledge & Kegan Paul, 1976.

Kornblith, Hilary. *Naturalizing Epistemology*. Richard Nisbett and Lee Ross. "Judgmental Heuristics and Knowledge Structures." London: The MIT Press, 1997.

McGinn, Colin. *Wittgenstein on Meaning*. New York, NY: Basil Blackwell, 1987.

Quine, W. V. *Word & Object*. Cambridge, MA: The MIT Press, 1960.

_____. *Ontological Relativity and Other Essays*. "Epistemology Naturalized." New York, NY: Columbia University Press, 1969.

Quine, W. V. and J. S. Ullian. *The Web of Belief*. New York, NY: Random House, 1978.

Rhees, Rush. *Discussions of Wittgenstein*. New York, NY: Schocken Books, 1970.

Stern, David G. *Wittgenstein on Mind and Language*. New York, NY: Oxford University Press, 1995.

Wagner, Steven J. and Richard Warner. *Naturalism: A Critical Appraisal*. Notre Dame, IN: University of Notre Dame Press, 1993.

Wittgenstein, Ludwig. *On Certainty*. New York, NY: Harper & Row, 1972.

_____. *Philosophical Investigations*. Englewood Cliffs, NJ: Prentice-Hall, 1958.

_____. *Preliminary Studies for the "Philosophical Investigations" Generally Known as "The Blue and Brown Books."* New York, NY: Barnes & Noble, 1969.

_____. *Tractatus Logico-Philosophicus.* New York, NY: Routledge & Kegan Paul, 1992.

THE MASK UNMASKED: THE ROLE OF HYPOCRISY IN THE DIALECTIC OF *THUS SPOKE ZARATHUSTRA*

John Kaag

Penn State University

This paper examines the implicit lessons that lie beneath the surface of Zarathustra's teachings in Nietzsche's philosophical and literary masterpiece. We must consider not only *what* is said, but *how* it is said, dissolving the hypocritical mask of Nietzsche's fictive "sage." The echo, the eternal return of his words "all is empty," turns the violent stroke of Zarathustra back on himself. His mask gives way, not to a substantial reality, but to a "man-ness" lacking *all* substance. Nietzsche's critical reader slowly catches sight of himself falling, mirroring the proverbial free-fall of Zarathustra. His ears are deaf to the guiding words of those who wish to control his thoughts and feelings. He does not hear the church, the state, nor Zarathustra himself.

In the structural and thematic development of *Thus Spoke Zarathustra*, Friedrich Nietzsche abandons the perspective of the traditional philosopher, the traditional author, quickly adopting the stance of the poet, of the Hellenistic playwright. He introduces a single actor bearing a single mask, a mask that bears marked similarity to those employed in the Bacchanalian festivals of ancient Greece. This work *is* Nietzsche's Dionysian celebration; Zarathustra is the playwright's seasoned thespian. The acting "prophet" wears the grinning face of "the dancing god"—the *semblance* of Dionysius himself. The costumed Zarathustra stands as both actor *and* man; he stands as both doctrine *and* essence of the overman. During the traditional dance, however, the "man-ness" of the Athenian player was masked as the character of the "actor" emerged. The truth of the player's existence and the *essential* determinant of the play were suspended for a time, yet were realized once again at the end of the ceremony. The actors shed their mock identities, reassuming this essential "man-ness." It is worth noting that these acts were self-perpetuating. The script, the content, of the players brings the play closer to a theatrical resolution. The action, the method prescribed by the playwright, similarly exists solely for its own destruction, a destruction embodied in the applause at the conclusion of the play. Each step of each player does its part in finding and insisting upon the dance's terminus.

The movement of *Zarathustra* is reminiscent of this classical content of the stage. The true essence of Nietzsche's ideal man is shrouded in the doctrine espoused by the acting vehicle of this ideal, the *teachings* of the acting "sage" (227). Nietzsche assumes the position of the skilled choreographer. His "dance," the action and dialogue of Zarathustra, heralds its own destruction; the curtain must close on this act as well. The juxtaposition of atheistic sentiment and theistic method draws *Zarathustra* to an explicit dénouement grounded in hypocrisy. The "playwright's" hypocritical blunder draws this curtain closed and strips the primary actor of his costume. The blunder, however, lies not in the process of the author, but rather in the eyes of an impatient audience. The life of the actor, the vitality of Zarathustra's teachings, fades, yet the overman is not destroyed by this unmasking. Man, once an actor, is "naked" (93), without costume or pretense. Nietzsche's reader is also robbed of his role as the passive student. The novel lends little to rely upon; it is an empty vessel that this active pupil must fill. It is, in fact, the essence of the Overman himself, in the reader himself, which is revealed.

The stimulus that drives the "dance" of *Thus Spoke Zarathustra* is the inescapable conflict between the will of the commune and that of the individual, the tension between free will and conformity. Zarathustra does not present a synthesis of these two opposing poles, but rather foretells the death of the communal "herd" (61) and the birth of a new strain of independent man. "Behold I teach you the overman" (13). These brief words establish the masks which Nietzsche's subject will carry throughout the work, the masks of "instructor" and "prophet." The last word in this declaration establishes the character's vision of the ideal being. It is crucial to examine the dialogue in regard to both the implicit characterization and explicit message of Zarathustra.

This explicit message is the one of the overman. This "man" is "a first movement," "a self-propelled wheel" (62), "the meaning of the earth" (13). These metaphorical definitions fill the pages of *Thus Spoke Zarathustra*, yet lend room at times for more articulate explanations of the Nietzschean ideal. He is the consummate existential hero, a man who comes to know his individual state as one of initial nothingness. This void can only be filled by his hands, his will. The overman wills himself beyond the hellish confines of Sartrean inter-subjectivity, creating a nirvana that is the joy of being in and for-oneself. In doing so, this *Ubermensch* leaves the realm of societal norms and domineering institutions that threatens the absolute freedom of his existence. In Sartrean terms, this true individual "carries the weight of the whole world on his shoulders; he is responsible for the world and for himself as a way of being" (Sartre 52).

This proverbial Atlas is not imbued with the strength of the socialized mind of the adult; it is the prankish mentality of the child that gives this character such awe-inspiring power. In "On the Three Metamorphoses," Zarathustra notes:

> The child is innocence and forgetting, a new beginning...a sacred "Yes." For the game of creation, my brothers, a sacred "Yes" is needed: the spirit now wills his own will, and he who had been lost to the world now conquers his own world. (27)

The child maintains the conception of self that Nietzsche proclaims for his overman. The "yes" that the toddler murmurs is a response purely for-itself; the young individual has yet to be trained to produce the empathetic response of the community. It has yet to be conditioned to pose the "yes" for-another. The overman ought to remain fixated in this "premoral" stage of development, in a position that elevates the importance of "self" beyond that of the "common good." The greed of a youngster "who knows no better" is excusable. The egoism of the Nietzschean hero is excusable for he has come to *know* that there is no motive better than his own. In a return to the natural origin of morality, the Nietzschean ideal can be considered "a first movement."

This radical egoism transforms the traditional standards of virtue and law. It posits itself as the single determinacy of virtue, thus failing to recognize the external determinacies of "justice." Zarathustra insists that this overman must be a "self-conqueror," "a commander of senses," and "a master of virtues" (69). This mentality breeds a kind of Machiavellian mantra in which *personal* ends justify *any* means.

The German author forces his character to echo the Italian's general theme in the section entitled "On the Virtuous:"

> (I am) Weary of saying: what makes an act good is that it is unselfish...Oh, my friends, that your self be in your deed as the mother is in her child—let that be *your* word concerning virtue. (96)

Characters such as Camus' Meursault and Dostoyevsky's Raskolnikov reflect this Nietzschean perspective. The overman, the consummate *raskolnik*, the consummate schismatic, will surpass the wanderer of the beach and the student of disillusionment, *succeeding* his quest to become "his own judge and avenger of his own law" (63).

Zarathustra comments that to be such a judge is to be truly alone, yet loneliness is the state of all noble beasts. Man must reclaim the title of the noble beast. The "sage" is sure to qualify this statement; beasts of burden (those of bovine and ovine dispositions) have no claim to the overman. It is Zarathustra's eagle and serpent, the two companions of *his* "isolation," that one must emulate. Emulate the beast whose back carries nothing but himself, whose life carries nothing but his Darwinistic will, whose existence resembles nothing but a "self-propelled wheel."

In presenting babe and beast as forerunners of his "super-man," the author questions the mores of traditional meta-physics. Neither of these models respects the Epicurean stance that regards the soul as a transcendent entity external *to* the body. The soul of the child holds no place in the "af-ter-worldly" (133) of the traditional Christian sense, but rather dwells in the immediacy of life. Zarathustra insists that "the awakened and knowing say: body am I entirely, and nothing else; the soul is only a word for something about the body" (34). The Nietzschean conception of spirit does not manifest itself in the vision of the cross or the practice of the Eucharist. Instead, this soul lives in the cry, in the laugh, and in the dance; it lives in the *natural* expressions of a singular subjectivity's unbounded power.

The corporeal nature of Zarathustra's vision of spiritual life does not, according the words of the prophet, compromise the validity of his conception of the soul. The soul maintains a certain omnipotent infinitude. Once moved, dancing feet and laughing tongues cannot be stifled. It is interesting to note that the author maintains the Platonic conception of virtue. It is still the movement of the mind toward the soul. This movement, however, holds a very different connotation when viewed from the German's position. Hellenistic virtue carried the mind from the body, drawn by abstract Forms and divine superstition of the *after-life*. Similarly, the Christian faith willed and wished an external heaven into existence for which all should strive; the object of life was to become other than life. Zarathustra's teachings stand in marked contrast. He attempts to perpetuate the mind's "eternal return" to the body, employing the blessed hedonism of *this life* as the catalyst of movement. He implies that he does not wish for the divine, for he states: "Will nothing beyond your capacity: there is wicked falseness among those who will beyond their capacity" (289). This "capacity" to which he refers is existence in its most immediate sense. The overman's will must foster a living utopia in *this* life, giving meaning to *this* world, becoming "the meaning of the earth" which is *his* alone.

As the Zarathustrian hero learns the "founding words," learns the freedom of saying, "Thus I will it" (139), he must come to know the power of negation, the power in saying, "Thus I will it not." This *Ubermensch* is the creator and defender of personal destiny. This defender, however, is not one of passivity; he is girded with a "courage which attacks" (157). "Whoever must be a creator always annihilates" (59). Zarathustra, the teacher, the preacher, insists that one must destroy the institutions and individuals that threaten the sacred autonomy of the single man. According to the doctrine advocated by the prophet, this new breed of man has no use for the herd mentality of present-day society. The affirmation predicated by group dynamics is "superfluous" to one whose singularity poses as a universality. In "On Free Death," the sage refers to the "superfluous" rabble, to the all-to-many, saying: "Would that they had never been born!" (71). Unfortunately, however, these "sheep" live—and live in mass—the slaughter must begin. Zarathustra challenges his pupils: "Are you capable of this—to be murderers?" (63). The fatalistic shades of Zamiatin, Dostoyevsky, and Camus once again grace this Nietzschean landscape.

The initial victim of the teacher's murderous words is the modern church of Christianity. The noble substance of this institution, God himself, has been killed by the very institution that he sought to support. In dissolving the importance of *human* spirit, the clergy has stripped its congregation of the Holy Spirit. In its move toward "gravity" and "repentance," the church has silenced the gay soul that feeds a "dancing god" (197). "Church-goers" have "knees that adore and their hands are hymns to virtue, but their heart knows nothing about it" (95). In its appeal to unqualified commandments and static idols, religion has alienated itself, failing to associate itself with living selves. Zarathustra comments:

The Mask Unmasked

> We are presented with grave word and values almost
> from the cradle...And therefore one suffers little chil-
> dren to come unto one—in order to forbid them be-
> times to love themselves thus the spirit of gravity or-
> ders it. (193)

This puritanical stance has its culminating point in the belief of original sin. The advent of a new life, in the strictly
religious sense, is equated with an inescapable sin from
which all must be absolved in the waters of divinity. This
purifying water seems absurdly superstitious to the
Nietzschean subject; a new life is purity in and for-itself.

The Nietzschean teacher notes that the dogmatic foundations of Christianity are still grounded in redemption, yet is
quick to expose the paradox inherent in this new salvation.
The pious are not saved from death, but rather life. These
"learned" individuals of the church maintain the conven-
tional mind-set of the traditional scholar that Zarathustra
berates at the end of Part II. "They want to be mere spectators (of life), and are beware of sitting where the sun burns
on the steps" (125: parentheses mine). They die a slow living death, ignoring the pleasure of the basic, oftentimes
bestial, elements of being human—ignoring the glory of the
overman. The sage responds to the repression which such
men of piety breed: "I love freedom and the air over the
fresh earth; rather would I sleep on ox hides than on their
decorums and respectabilities" (125). In "On the Priests,"
Zarathustra articulates and assumes the role of man's re-
deemer from the prison of *this* redemption.

The original "jailer" of these religious cells, the Savior
himself, must lead his followers to the slaughterhouse of
Zarathustra's words; he is the first to feel the blade of this
Anti-Christ. Both Nietzsche and his fictional mouthpiece

recognize the overman-like potentiality of such an individual, yet condemn this potentiality for failing to realize actuality. For forty days and forty nights, Christ grasped the concept of the Nietzschean hero. In the barrenness of his desert, in the renunciation of his followers, he became his own god. Zarathustra laments: "Would that he had remained in the wilderness far from the good and the just! Perhaps he would have learned to live and to love the earth—and laughter too" (73). Jesus, however, implicitly succumbs to the third temptation of the devil: "honor." His singularity is unable to honor itself as meaning and substance of the earth; he must return to his flock, to his particular role as leader of the flock, in an attempt to regain a sense of identity. In his return to the recognition of his dutiful followers, of his faithful sheep, the "shepherd," in the natural vein of Hegelian recognition, grows fleecy wool and is fattened for the butcher's cleaver. In *The Will to Power* (1887), Nietzsche echoes these sentiments: "And it is all one whether he preaches current morality or uses his ideal for a critique of current morality: he belongs to the herd—even if it be as the herd's supreme requirement, its leader" (879).

In the closing sections of Part I, a frustrated Zarathustra speaks to his students: "All names of good and evil are parables: they do not define, they merely hint. A fool is he who wants knowledge of them!" (75). This obvious allusion to the teachings of Christ exposes Nietzsche's contempt for the *objectification* of such subjective accounts of morality. The parable is based on a certain immediacy gleaned by means of a first-person perspective; the story is sacred only in the sanctity of the single author's word. The institution that Zarathustra exposes is one that has dissolved the definite action of a proud and noble man in an ambiguous universal medium. The creation of general maxims attenuates the essence of Man beyond the point of recognition. It is only the self-deception of "bad faith" which allows one to believe that he alone embodies these *alien* commandments. At first glance, "time" seems wholly responsible for the stagnation of Christ's existence mentioned above. "AD," however, has no meaning without a determinant point of reference. Ultimately, Christ himself is the determinant of this stagnation; he is solely responsible for being *known* by the populace. To be *known* is to be objectified, in existential terms, to lose the unquantifiable power of the subject. To be well *known* is to be sucked, as an object, into a mythology whose destiny is rooted in stagnation.

Nietzsche's reader reaches the final section of *Thus Spoke Zarathustra* with a clear understanding of *what* has been spoken by the author's primary character: the man of convention and dogma must be "overcome;" a new man of autonomy and will must be born (15). The author's audience, however, must not accept the "face-value" expression of Zarathustra's teachings as the thematic and conceptual goal of the "playwright's" creation. *What* the player has said is merely the explicit half of Nietzsche's dialectical equation. *How* the player has said this *what* constitutes an implicit variable that the critical reader must evaluate. Such an evaluation dissolves the superficial mask of the fictional rhetor, unveiling the profound aim of Nietzsche's philosophical work.

In a critical reflection which delves deeper than the cursory reading, the lack of continuity between Zarathustra's method, the *how*, and Zarathustra's purpose, the *what,* becomes apparent. The content of his purpose, what he proposes, is the death of teachers and preachers, the engines of convention and groupthink. The initial stanzas of the work, however, establish the focal character as one of teaching and preaching. A reader must remember the opening proclamation: "Behold, I *teach* you the overman" (13). He maintains *his* pulpit with *his* static virtue. He sustains *his* congregation with *his* mechanical prayers. A traditional religious atmosphere, the very object of his deadly resentment, is unmistakable. The mechanical hymns, the not-so-new idols, and mindless followers which he propagates stand as monuments to his hypocrisy. The reverent "Thus spoke Zarathustra" replaces the reverent "Amen" which ends this preacher's every sermon. He disdains the lifeless symbol of Christ, the caretaker of the "flock," yet is overjoyed when given this symbol, the shepherd's staff (74).

The prophet heralds the death of objective law and the repressive doctrine of the herd, yet gives these entities new life. His singular subjectivity fails to resemble that of the overman for it is not for-itself, but rather for-another, for his audience. He implies that the creation of the overman stands as an unconditionally "good." In entering the arena of the "common good," subjectivity takes on the appearance of unquestioned objectivity. He urges his pupils to further objectify his pseudo-subjectivity by writing these "new values on new tablets" (24). In Part III, he seems to retract this request, deeming the will of his followers too weak for such a task. He shoulders the onus *for them*, creating thirty alien commandments to replace the ten of Moses, which he promises to destroy. This actor's *actions* fail to suggest an end to the inter-dependence between the singularity of man and the particularity of the group. He merely proposes a shift in institutions: from one of traditional *morality* to that of traditional *amorality*. These are insignificant changes. An uncritical pedagogy, the antithesis of the overman, is preserved in either case.

The subsidiary characters of *Zarathustra* highlight the player's authoritative stance that proves to be incongruent with the content of his teaching itself; it is strictly the teacher's lack of self-reflection that grants him the ability to *preach* the overman. In the opening of Part II, a lonely child commands Zarathustra, saying, "look at yourself in the mirror" (83). The reflection, however, is not his own; the "player" is confronted with the image of a laughing devil. A hasty interpretation of the event is made—the prophet must return to the people to clarify the distorted reflection of his doctrine. This premise presupposes a flaw in the mirror, in the populace to which he has spoken. The devilish grimace, however, is not governed by the *reflection* of the face but rather by the *face itself* that Zarathustra wears. The reflection *is* his own; he *is* his own devil, a devil which tries to eliminate the foundations of the *status quo*, yet accomplishes this end by establishing a masked universal—just another *status quo*.

The magician sees Zarathustra in the light of truth and exposes the fraudulence of the teacher: "I know him; I know this monster whom I love against my will, this Zarathustra: he himself sometimes seems to me like a mask of a saint" (297). Indeed, he has become the "monster" of the domineering state which he earlier condemns to death, a state which rapes the single man of his independence (148). Indeed, in his defense of the Ubermensch as a pure vision to be accepted by all, he has become a "pure perceiver" who he himself criticizes for adopting the masks of "saints and dead gods" (123).

Like the dead god of modern Christianity, this new divinity must be affirmed in an asinine celebration of the herd. Zarathustra receives this affirmation in "The Ass Festival" near the end of the work. The facade of pro-activity crumbles; the "actor" is identified with the passivity of a needy beast. The mentality of this beast is a far cry from the nobility of the eagle or independence of the serpent, which are originally lauded as the defining characteristics of the Nietzschean superman.

The soothsayer provides Nietzsche's reader insight into the dialectical self-destruction inherent in the being of Zarathustra. He accurately quotes the teacher of the overman, saying, "All is empty, all is the same, all has been" (133). This statement is the deadly stroke meant to kill the convention of modern-day society. This claim, in terms of the *essence* of the overman, however, is not aimed strictly at the conformity of the *present*, but conformity in *general*. In this respect, the proclamation reverberates through the corridors of eternity; the seer continues: "from the hills it echoes: 'All is empty, all is the same, all has been'" (133). The echo, the eternal return of these words, turns the violent stroke of Zarathustra back on himself. Zarathustra is included in the set of "All." The words of a seemingly profound authority, the symbols of *Thus Spoke Zarathustra*, are quickly drained of meaning; they too are empty.

Nietzsche's "play" comes to an end. The acting doctrine of the overman is silenced by the "playing out" of his character's acting method and acting purpose. The pomp and circumstance of Zarathustra's hypocritical mask is removed.

This unmasking, however, does not reveal a substantial reality, a "man-ness" essential to the Hellenistic playwright. Instead, the mask gives way to a nihilistic void, a "man-ness" lacking *all* substance. In simpler terms, the actor of the stage, when stripped of his dialogue, when stripped of his play, falls back upon the flesh and bone of reality. The "actor" of a literary work, when stripped of his words, when stripped of his text, falls back upon "nothing." Nietzsche's critical reader slowly catches sight of himself falling, mirroring the proverbial free-fall of Zarathustra. If Zarathustra's word is to be taken as true, particular groups, which the reader relies upon to validate his identity, carry no substantial merit. The truth of the character's word, however, negates the truth of *his* own being—a being that attempts to create another privileged high-ground. The "play" of *Thus Spoke Zarathustra* proves to be devoid of any prop or actor that could break the absurd monotony of its barren "stage."

This "empty" stage, cleared by the implicit contradiction of Nietzsche's subject, is considered by many to be the author's greatest failure; no one character is able to approach the ideal of the *Ubermensch*. Those, however, who desire a written explication of *Ubermenschlichkeit* have ignored the thinker's primary aim. The author's ideal is not embodied in a documented account of an idealized character. It *lives* in *life*, in the *free* life of Nietzsche's reader. This "empty" nothingness, the remnants of a self-destructing plot, *is* the ultimate determinant and essence of the overman. The Nietzschean superman, the reflective reader, is absolutely alone on the deserted stage of *Thus Spoke Zarathustra*, on the deserted stage of life. He is absolutely free.

In the deconstruction of his own work, the philosopher establishes a nihilistic arena in which the singular reader, in the glory of his subjectivity, is forced to take center stage. This individual is the only subject of the "play." No superfluous props clutter the set, restricting the reader's free dance; no external actor enters the scene to restrict the reader's free will. The reader has listened to the words of Zarathustra and has taken his advice—he listens to no one. His ears are deaf to the guiding words of those who wish to control his thoughts and feelings. He does not hear the church, the state, nor Zarathustra himself. He has shed all alien thoughts, all foreign feelings, and has looked beneath his own mask. He has remembered Nietzsche's words: "Behind your thoughts and feelings, my brother, there stands a mighty ruler, an unknown sage—whose name is self" (34). The reader has become conscious of this "sage," has become *self*-conscious of this "sage." He has become this "sage," this "self," this overman. Thus spoke Zarathustra.

REFERENCES

Nietzsche, Friedrich. *Thus Spoke Zarathustra.* New York: Penguin Books, 1978.

Nietzsche, Friedrich. *The Will to Power.* Boston: Hamilton Press, 1982.

Sartre, Jean Paul. *Existentialism and Human Emotions.* New York: Citadel Press, 1957.

TRUTH AND BEAUTY

The Experience and Expression of Truth

Justin C. Maaia
Suffolk University

Truth cannot be expressed. It can only be experienced. The first part of this paper examines the experiential nature of truth as expressed in the *Upanishads* and the *Bhagavad Gita*, by Greek Philosophers such as Pythagoras, Heraclitus, Parmenides, Socrates, Plato, and Aristotle, as well as by Jesus and the authors of the *Tao Te Ching*. The zenith of this belief about the nature of Truth is found is Zen Buddhism. Accordingly, the second half of the paper is devoted to developing a better understanding of how the Zen practice of meditation can lead a person to the realization of Truth.

On Sunday, I received a package from a graduate school in the Boston area. As I flipped through the pages of the course description, I was fascinated by the program that was offered at this school. I began reading about the faculty, the concentrations offered in the field, and the requirements for the degree. These requirements seemed impressive and quite challenging to me—that is, until I read the last item on the list. This was the section regarding the dissertation, and it described the scope of a paper of "no more than three hundred pages." This seemed to me to be the easiest requisite for the degree: After all, who couldn't ramble on for about 250 pages on a particular research topic, whether he or she really knows anything about it or not?

There isn't any subject about which I would want to write three hundred pages. In fact, there isn't any subject worth writing three hundred pages about. Even if there were a subject worth that much verbiage, such as Love or God, three hundred pages would not do it any more justice than one page would. Or one word, if it was the right word and said in the right manner. This is because words are inadequate for expressing the Truth. This is characteristic of all forms of expression. While a word, a picture, or a song may act as a catalyst for another person to seek out the Truth, the medium itself cannot imbue someone with the understanding that the Truth itself can instill. This is why the only way to understand the Truth, or any other concept, is through direct experience. Any means of expressing it should be tailored to the purpose of inspiration. In this way can another person be convinced to seek out the Truth. Attempting to capture its essence through some medium other than itself is futile. The Truth cannot be communicated. It can only be experienced.

This "Truth" is the truth or reality that is inherent in any particular subject. There is a truth in music, and one cannot experience it by reading a review in the Boston Globe. One must hear the music for oneself. There is a truth in art that cannot be absorbed, except by looking at the piece of art itself. There is also a truth inherent in childbirth, but only someone who gives birth can know it. These truths cannot be known through any amount of discursive thinking or reading about their subjects. Just like these three examples, so too is there a truth in each thing. And there is a collective Truth that can be thought of, a Truth underlying Reality—a Reality that is a sum of all of these things and yet perhaps more profound than their sum.

This collective Truth, or Ultimate Reality, is the world as it really exists. It is the universe as seen objectively, stripped of the layers of subjectivity that each person applies to his/her life. It is like the case of two students. One student,

Justin C. Maaia

David, retires to bed late at night, after going out drinking
with his friends. He sleeps through his alarm and wakes up
late for class on the next day. After throwing on some
clothes and skipping breakfast, he runs to class and takes
the last available seat in the corner of the classroom. David
is consumed by his exhaustion, dehydration, and anxiety.
Catching his breath, he looks around the room and mutters,
"Why the hell is it so hot in here?" A second student in the
class, Linda, had a different reaction to the same situation.
She had gone to bed early the night before, after having a
cup of herbal tea. Having had a good night's sleep, Linda
woke up, took a relaxing shower, and ate breakfast. She
took her time getting to class and when she got there, she
was able to sit next to her friend. After taking a deep
breath, she turned to her friend and asked, "How was your
night last night?"

Here are two completely different reactions to the same
situation, the fact that it was seventy degrees Fahrenheit in
the room. One student's subjectivity caused him to react to
the situation in a hostile way. The other student, con-
versely, did not even notice the temperature of the room.
Neither of them realized the Truth. David was affected by
his mood and disposition, while Linda was distracted by
how perfectly her night and morning had gone (although
Linda did come closer to the Truth by accepting the room
the way it was). An enlightened person would not have
been annoyed by the temperature, nor would she/he have
been oblivious to it. Enlightenment is realizing that the
room is neither hot nor cold, but that it is seventy degrees.
Nay, enlightenment is even more than that. The enlightened
person walks into a room, sees the beads of sweat on his
hand, or the goose bumps on her arm, and realizes that
he/she is alive. This is the Truth, the Ultimate Reality.

The Experience and Expression of Truth

In order to study this primary Truth, it may be helpful to examine instead a particular component of Reality. This example would have to be one that is somewhat elusive, like the concept of Truth, but more tangible. Some examples are concepts such as Love or God or Enlightenment. Each may be found to be a part of the Ultimate Reality, and to express some of its qualities. The case of Love is a valuable one to study. This is not because it is necessarily more important than any of the other concepts (that is the topic for another paper), but because it is a universally thought-of concept. Some philosophers would choose a different case to examine, but philosophers and non-philosophers alike devote time to the subject of Love, and so by studying such a universally pondered example, perhaps something can be learned about the case of Truth in general.

First, consider the search for Love. It is much like the search for Ultimate Reality. One can walk the streets of the world, running up to people and asking them, "Are you the 'love of my life?' Are you my soul-mate?" However, it is not any more likely that one would find her or his soul-mate in this fashion than if one simply walked around, twiddling one's thumbs, and bumped into someone. That is actually how it happens much of the time. Of course, it does help to be open to the idea of finding a soul-mate in order for it to occur. This is the same with Ultimate Reality: Having an open heart might allow one to more easily experience Ultimate Reality, but no amount of searching will help one to see it. It will spontaneously happen, just like Love. This is certainly what must have been meant by John Coltrane, a great saxophonist and very spiritual man, when he said,

> I am [Christian] by birth; my parents were and my early teachings were Christian. But as I look upon the world, I feel all men know the truth. If a man was a

Christian, he could know the truth and he could not.
The truth itself does not have any name on it. And
each man has to find it for himself, I think.[1]

To extend this case, one should think of a time when he or she fell in love, if one can recall or imagine a time. When one falls in love, he or she does so without any communicable reason. Yes, there may be many reasons why a person loves another person, but there is a part of love that appears at first sight, even before any of the communicable reasons are identified. It is this initial Love that is like Reality, while the communicable reasons for loving a person are like the attributes identified with Reality. For example, a lover could try to explain his/her love to a third party. The lover could relate how beautiful the beloved is, how he or she has gorgeous hair and breathtaking eyes, and a wonderful personality. The third person can understand these reasons. He or she may even agree that the beloved has all of these qualities. However, understanding those reasons and even agreeing with them will not make that person love the beloved as the lover does.

It is the same with Truth. Truth is something that can only be experienced. Someone who knows the Truth can talk about it, and another person can understand it intellectually. However, doing that will not make that person enlightened. One "falls into" enlightenment much like one "falls in love." One must be open to it, but no amount of effort will help one to find it—both enlightenment and one's soulmate. The Truth has an intellectual aspect, but its essence is something that can be known only through one's mind, body, and soul. One can understand the intellectual aspects of the Truth, but that does not mean that one is enlightened.

Many of the world's greatest thinkers knew and expressed this quality of the Truth. Some talked about the Truth more than others did, but almost all of them knew that this communication could not instill enlightenment in another person. That person would have to experience it for her- or himself. The thinkers who have expressed this condition for knowing Truth are found throughout the world and throughout history.

The sages of ancient India make one of the earliest claims that knowledge can only be attained experientially. The *Upanishads*, for instance, were written by those who were afflicted by "the hunger of the mystic for direct vision and the philosopher's ceaseless quest for truth."[2] All of the inspiring passages contained within the *Upanishads* could only have been written by sages who "spoke out of the fullness of their illumined experience." The *Upanishads* do not offer any systematic course of reasoning to support its claims about Truth. While there is some philosophical reasoning, the main purpose of the *Upanishads* is to provide inspiration and practical advice for someone who would search for the Truth for her- or himself.

> The real which is at the heart of the universe is reflected in the infinite depths of the self. Brahman (the ultimate as discovered objectively) is Atman (the ultimate as discovered introspectively). *Tat tvam asi* (That art thou). Truth is within us.[3]

"When we realize the universal Self in us, when and what may anybody fear or worship?"[4] The word that is emphasized in these passages is "realize." One must realize the Truth for oneself; it cannot be known through someone else's teachings.

Likewise, the *Bhagavad-Gita* in the Hindu tradition emphasizes each individual's need to practice in order to realize the Truth. In this epic, different disciplines and their value in helping one to realize Ultimate Reality are offered. Some passages are dedicated efforts to describe Ultimate Reality, but the better part of the epic is devoted to illustrating the three "ways" of discipline. These are *jnana-yoga* (the way of knowledge), *bhakti-yoga* (the way of devotion), and *karma-yoga* (the way of action).[5] Three different ways of knowing Reality are offered because of the diversity of people. One may not be predisposed to the way of knowledge, but may be able to apply her- or himself to the way of action. Some people can apply themselves to reading scripture, while others are more comfortable with a physical practice such as that contained in yoga postures. In this way, the all-important notion of practice is made available to everyone who seeks the Truth.

In the same proximity of time to these Indian sages, a group of Greek thinkers were making similar revelations about the nature of Truth. One of these was Pythagoras, who lived in ancient Greece from about 570 to about 495 BC. He, too, stressed the importance of practice. In his belief system, it is the practice of purification that is necessary for one's soul to experience Ultimate Reality. It is known that the rituals associated with this purification were extensive, but little else is known about them. This obscurity is due to Pythagoras' realization that the Truth cannot be expressed: The only people allowed to know of his prescription for realizing the Truth were those initiated into his religious order. Pythagoras obviously knew that making his idea of Truth public would only result in its bastardization. Because the Truth cannot be expressed, any attempt at expression can result in a misinterpretation. Consequently, Pythagoras knew that he could speak of the Truth only with those who at least were initiated into his way of thinking.

Other Greek thinkers realized this same characteristic of Truth. Heraclitus (540-480 BC) alluded to his conception of

The Experience and Expression of Truth

Reality through aphorisms and obscure sayings. The reason for this obscurity is his pessimistic view "about the ability of people to grasp the truth even when they hear it stated."[6] About his conception of Objective Reality, called the "logos," Heraclitus himself stated in Fragment 1 of his work,

> Though this logos is always so, men never understand it, neither before nor after they have heard it. For although all things happen in accordance with this logos, it is as if other men had no experience of it when they meet those words and acts which I set forth, distinguishing each according to its nature and saying how it is.[7]

Heraclitus tries to explain the Truth of Reality, but those around him obviously do not understand it, either on their own or with his help.

Parmenides, too, admits this shortcoming of humankind. In his poem in which he sets forth the only true way of thinking, he also states, "It is proper for you to learn all things: both the unchanging heart of complete truth and also how things seem to mortals, in which there is no truth."[8] The goddess in Parmenides' poem teaches him not only the Truth, but also the false ways of thinking. She does this because the false ways are so widespread that he also needs to be aware of them. Parmenides realizes that Objective Reality is not seen by the majority of people.

Socrates was also aware both of the Truth and of the Truth's reluctance to being expressed. For this reason, he never wrote anything. Socrates knew that, as Plato recalls in *Phaedrus*,

> ...when [true words] have been once written down they are tumbled about anywhere among those who may or may not understand them...and if they are maltreated or abused, they have no parent to protect them; and they cannot protect or defend themselves.[9]

It is for this reason that Socrates stressed the act of "knowing thyself." Human beings are a part of Reality, and so by looking inwardly the Truth may be known. For Socrates, the Truth could only be known experientially, not through rhetoric, or writing, or someone else's words.

Plato was not so harsh in his treatment of expression of Truth. However, his description of Reality as containing a world of perfect Forms that parallels the world of matter says something of his characterization of Truth. Plato held that there is a perfect Idea or Form that corresponds to the multitude of beings here on earth. He said that the human soul was of the realm of Forms and therefore could know of perfect Reality. The way to accomplish this was through contemplation of the Forms, something that can only be done individually. No amount of description of their likeness can enlighten one to their nature.

One more Greek philosopher who claimed that the Truth could not be expressed but only experienced was Aristotle. He wrote on a great variety of subjects, and one of his writings was devoted to the art of music and poetry. In his *Poetics*, Aristotle analyzes these arts and prescribes the formula for their success. But he also states the limitations of such a book. "No man, so soon as he knowest this or reads it, shall be able to write the better; but as he is adapted to it by nature, he shall grow the perfecter Writer."[10] Here, Aristotle refutes the importance of *techne*, or technical knowledge, in favor of real knowledge of the Truth.

Moving forward in time and towards the East in direction, we have the teachings of Jesus of Nazareth. Jesus, like Socrates, did not write anything; what we know of his teaching is to be found in the writings of his disciples. There is an observation concerning Jesus' teachings that has been put forth by more than one scholar: "Jesus never taught morality, only mystery."[11] Perhaps the reason underlying the focus of Jesus' teachings can be found in the nature of Truth. Jesus, aware of the Truth of Reality, could have passed on moral codes of conduct for the masses. However, he knew that people would have the choice either to follow these codes or to dismiss them. Even those who would follow them could potentially debase the codes by following their "letter" rather than their "spirit." There is an infinite range of circumstances surrounding each action. Consequently, strict moral codes can guide a person only most of the time. Rather than preach such codes, Jesus instead chose to teach mystery. He knew that spiritual mystery could ignite the spark of inspiration in someone. After experiencing that initial curiosity, a person will be eager to unveil the mystery for her- or himself. To do this, the person will have to live his or her life in the manner that Jesus did. By living in this way, a person is inherently living a morally good life. Therefore, by teaching mystery, Jesus was able to inspire people to seek the Truth and also to live morally good lives.

Expressing this sentiment further to the East are the mystics who contributed to the *Tao Te Ching*. Traditionally attributed to Lao Tzu, this collection of poems was probably written by a number of mystics who wanted to remain anonymous. They claimed to have discovered "Something for which there was no word or name. A name for it is 'Way'; pressed for designation, I call it Great."[12] The mysticism underlying the words of the *Tao Te Ching* is of a tradition that is at least two hundred years older than the text. Here it is obvious that these writers were reluctant to commit their observations of Reality to paper. They knew that something would be lost in the process, but they wished to preserve the teachings of the old masters so that new students could contemplate this wisdom.

The zenith of this belief about the nature of Truth is also found in the East. It is the Zen Buddhists who are most wary of their use of both the spoken and written word. They continually emphasize the inadequacy of words to express the Truth. Their faith lies in a personal experience of Reality. They do not only defend this concept, but offer a practice whereby one may encounter Reality. This practice involves two applications of meditation, that of living mindfully and of sitting meditation.[13]

The Truth cannot be communicated. It can only be known through direct experience. This experience is divided into the two aspects of sitting meditation and mindfulness because of where the Truth is to be found. The Truth is contained in all things, but is not limited to what can be seen, felt and touched. By living each moment in a mindful way, one is able to appreciate the Truth that is present in all things—in actions, in events, in living beings, in objects. This is the immanent Truth. Because each person is a part of this immanent Truth, the Truth can also be known by looking inwards. This is done through sitting meditation. The practice of meditation serves two purposes: to help one to see the Truth immanent in oneself, and also to experience the transcendent Truth. The transcendent Truth is truth in its purest form. It is unaffected by the perceptions of a person. Nor is it obscured by the layers of subjectivity created by the selfishness of one's ego. Through meditation, one can scrape oneself clean of these layers and experience the unaffected, Objective Reality. A balance is sought between experiencing the unaffected, pure Truth and seeing that the immanent, "affected" Truth is also divine.[14]

The validity of these two Buddhist practices can only be proven by the individual. Each person needs to commit her- or himself to these practices and will then be convinced of their effectiveness. It is not known precisely what makes a person take up these practices, as no amount of discourse on their validity can capture what it is that happens during sitting meditation and mindful living. This is again due to the impossibility of expressing the Truth. Perhaps mindfulness can be more easily understood than meditation.

The object of mindfulness is to keep one's mind focused on the moment at hand. This is because the present moment is the only "Real" moment. This is true if it is considered that the past exists only in one's memory, and the future in one's imagination. Cluttering the present moment with the hopes, fears and disappointments of the past and the future will prevent one from making the most of that present moment. By being mindful of that moment, one can focus all of one's energy on it. Each moment can be made a masterpiece. By stringing together enough of these moments, one's life can achieve a sort of perfection.[15] This may in some small way explain mindfulness. The task of explaining the effectiveness of meditation is somewhat more involved. It is best to start at the beginning.[16]

Truth cannot be expressed. It can only be experienced. As was stated before, this experience of Ultimate Reality can be attained through living mindfully and through meditation, in the Zen Buddhist sense. To try and explain the meditation aspect, it is helpful to begin with the thoughts of a Greek thinker, but one whose ideas were in the same spirit as that of the Buddha.

As Parmenides stated, the cosmos could never have come-to-be from a state of non-being. This is because the very definition of non-being implies that a state of non-being could never exist. That the universe came from non-being is a dualistic notion that can be proven false.

A state of non-being is something that cannot be talked about because if it is non-being, then it never existed. One may argue that non-being could have existed using the following two examples. One may say that an extinct animal, like the Dodo bird, does not exist any longer, but that it can still be conceived of. This is true because the bird did exist at one time. However, non-being by its definition has never been, and so has never existed. One may also say that the mythological unicorn has never existed, but that a discussion about unicorns could still take place. This is true because the idea of a unicorn is a product of one's imagination and so it exists in that form. The idea of a unicorn is real, but the unicorn itself is not. Likewise, the idea of non-being can be thought of, but non-being itself cannot exist. It is an empty notion; the careless stringing together of a word with a prefix that does not belong.

This argument defends the idea of the infinite nature of the cosmos. It has always been. More importantly, it is at every moment in time. It exists right now as these words are being read...and now...and now...and now. Furthermore, if one continues in this fashion backwards, stating that the cosmos existed a moment ago, and another moment ago, and another, one will realize that there could never have been a moment in which the universe was not in existence. It changes ever so slightly from moment to moment, but there never could have been, or never will be, a moment where there is non-existence. That is non-being, and non-being simply cannot be. Even if, at one time, the universe did not exist as we know it because it came from some almost incomprehensible dimension or state of being, it still did not come from non-being. It would have come from something, namely the original form of the same universe with which we are familiar.

The Experience and Expression of Truth

What is this original form? In order to determine that, one should look to the beginning of oneself, for the workings of the atoms in the body mirror the operation of the cells, which mirror the operation of the body as a whole, which in turn reflects the operation of the different classes of beings in nature. This operation again mirrors the operation of the earth as a whole, and also the solar system, the galaxy, and, finally, the universe.[17] So, it is to the beginning of one's life that one might go to infer the origin of the universe.

A human being is made up of many cells in its adult state, but at one time it was but one cell. This one cell, located in the mother's womb, is made up of two smaller half-cells, called gametes. These two, the sperm and the egg, each come from corresponding processes in the man and woman. It is sometimes said, in a romantic way, that the true beginning of a person is as "a thought in the minds of the mother and father." This is much truer than one may think, as can be seen by tracing the origin of these two gametes. Their paths are identical, and following that path will help in determining the origin of the universe.

The reproductive cells are produced by the reproductive organs. This is where the search begins. By determining the absolute origin of each of these half-cells, perhaps a clue will arise as to the origin of the universe. So, one may ask, "Why is the gamete produced in the reproductive organs?" It is produced here because the brain sends impulses to a certain gland that secretes hormones. These hormones eventually trigger the production of such cells by the reproductive organs. The next logical question would be "Why does the brain send these impulses?" Within the answer to this question lies the truth to the statement that a person has his or her origin as a thought in the minds of his or her parents.

It is a thought that triggers the brain to send an impulse to the body to produce gametes. This thought is not the conscious thought of a cute little baby boy or baby girl. It is an instinctive, intuitive Thought. It is the type of thought that comes from the part of the mind that thinks without consciously thinking. It is the part of the mind that knows the necessity of breathing, eating, and loving. It knows these necessities without having to reason-out their importance. This Thought is of a higher level of thinking than we are accustomed to recognizing. It is at this point, when a Thought becomes an electrical impulse of the brain, that a person has his or her physical origin.

One cannot ignore this Thought, however intangible it may be. It cannot be dismissed, just as scientists cannot ignore the fact that a person's emotions begin as Thought and end up as tangible hormones in the body. Experiments have been done that show that a person feels an emotion—happy, sad, depressed—at precisely the same moment that the physical substances related to that emotion are detected in the brain. The conclusion that this experiment implies is that abstract Thought has a counterpart that is seen as physical, tangible reality. It can be seen, touched, measured, and felt, but it is also recognized as what may be called Thought. This is akin to the statement that a child was once "a thought in the mind" of his/her parents.[18]

So, is it to be said that the cosmos began as a Thought? This is conceivable if one remembers that Thought has Matter as its counterpart, or rather its other aspect. Now the question is, "Who's Thought was it?" Well, since humans are of the class of physical bodies that occupy the cosmos, then it must have been our Thought that became the universe. And, since animals and plants are also present here, then it must have been their thoughts, too. The same must be true of each object in existence, both animate and in-animate, as all Matter must have this Thought aspect to it, however hidden it may be.

The world as it is known is not the first generation, if you will, that has been in existence. There have been people and plants and animals and rocks that have precluded what is present right now. Each generation begets the next through the type of profound thought that was spoken of earlier. One should now go back, then, to the original generation of the universe. Whatever beings and forms were present then must have come from somewhere—some Thought, to be specific.

The variety of the cosmos is like a pyramid. The cosmos as we know it has a myriad of different beings in it. Each generation of beings would necessarily have had less variety than the one after it. Therefore, the first generation must have had but a few beings in existence (whatever they might have looked like or been classified as), going all the way back to the beginning of the universe and its origin as Hydrogen and other elements. This type of consolidation of variety as one looks to the past—coupled with the idea that all physical things begin as profound Thoughts—necessarily means that the existence of the universe had not only Matter, but also Thought at its origin. One single, profound Thought coming from where? Coming from the same place that each person receives his or her profound Thoughts to reproduce, to breath, to love—from the divine mind of what may be called Truth, or God, or the Undifferentiated, or a myriad of names corresponding to the myriad of beings that have come from and still share that same Mind.

This foundation of Thought makes perfect sense from simple observations of the world. Some philosophers may

Justin C. Maaia

think that there only exists the world of matter that we know through our five senses. How can it be true that there is only this world? Yes, there is a world of matter, but why does it move? Scientists may explain this movement through a series of chemical reactions. However, even these chemicals are matter, and something must underlie their interaction. Maybe there was a Big Bang, but what caused it? There must be a principle that causes and underlies movement. It is the spiritual aspect of Matter, its Thought.

It is impossible to deny the existence of the spiritual. The beliefs of a materialist—in the general usage of the term— are absurd. After examining both monistic and dualistic belief systems, this fact can be realized. There are only two choices as to what exists. The first is the idea of a dualistic universe, one in which the material and the spiritual are separate and yet interact in the reality that we observe. The second choice is the monistic one. This claims that there is only one substance, but that it has both Matter and Spirit.

Many philosophers agree that there are, potentially, two aspects to all beings. These dual aspects represent the physical and the nonphysical qualities of which everything is comprised. There is a physical part, namely the body, and a nonphysical part, referred to as the spirit, soul, consciousness, or mind. The monist (by "monist" and "dualist" I am referring to those people who prescribe to a fundamental monism or dualism with regard to the true nature of the universe) believes that one of these aspects can actually be reduced to the other. The dualist, in opposition to the monist, argues that reducing one aspect to the other brings its own set of problems with it.

The monist claims that everything is ultimately either physical or nonphysical. In the latter case he/she tries to prove that what we know as the physical world is actually some sort of projection of our minds or an incarnation of our spirit. Oppositely, the other type of monist believes that everything that we know as nonphysical—thoughts, feelings, emotions, even consciousness itself—is merely the intricate arrangement of molecules, atoms and electrical impulses. Hence, the definition of a "materialist." However, I could just as easily reduce the material world to nothing. I can appeal to the scientific discovery that the subatomic particles that compose neutrons, protons, and electrons actually have no mass. Does this mean that nothing exists? This "nothing" could be possible, but for now it can at least be said that the "mental" exists or does not exist at least as much as the physical does or does not exist. This suggests that the physical and non-physical go hand-in-hand.

The dualist makes a claim to this concept, and refutes both of the monist beliefs as wrong. While each may in some way be possible, neither is probable. To believe that everything physical can be reduced to something mental is to completely deny the physical world around us, claiming that it is some kind of illusion. Likewise, to say that the mental aspect of existence is nothing more than an arrangement of matter and physical forces is equally absurd. One may argue that even if someone were to map all of the molecules and electrical impulses of the brain, that person would not be able to see the thoughts or feel the emotions of the subject.

While these are all good arguments against monistic beliefs, I claim that the dualists themselves actually subscribe to their own forms of monism. Some of them claim that, at death, there is an end to consciousness, an end to the non-physical. They believe that a person dies, becomes a part of the earth, and that is it. This belief is actually a reduction of the dual aspects of life to one substance; hence it is a form of monism. Other dualists claim that, at death, every part of our being survives in the form of the spirit. This is another form of monism, and so is subject to the same arguments that these so-called dualists used against the belief in monism. While it is possible that everything is ultimately physical or spiritual at death, it is not probable.

Therefore, if there truly is a physical and a nonphysical nature to us, then they must remain two and it is most probable that they continue to be two after death. If you believe that there is a dual aspect to every being, and you believe that at death the physical body goes into the ground and decomposes, then you must also believe that the nonphysical goes somewhere. If it mirrors its physical counterpart, then it must lose its identity in some great store of consciousness. This is just a speculation, but it must be agreed upon that it goes somewhere.

There is one other option, however, and it is a true monism. This monism cannot be like one of the two types mentioned above. Instead, one could believe that everything is of one nature and that it remains one substance. The only way that this is possible is if the physical can be reconciled with the nonphysical. To do this is to say that the one cannot be without the other. They must arise at the same time into what we know as beings and things. They must also expire at the same time, not going out of existence but instead retiring to some form of impersonal substance. This substance would be neither all physical nor all spiritual. It can be only a combination of the two, forever joined and without a fine line of distinction. Just as the leaf of a tree cannot live without the root, nor the root without the leaf, so this substance cannot live without both of its parts. Furthermore, what we classify as parts cannot be considered separate at all, but part of one Being, just as the root and the leaf are nothing more and nothing less than a tree.

After reading this, it should be evident that to deny material existence is absurd, but that it is likewise absurd to deny the existence of the spirit. One could believe that all that there is is Matter, but that person must also alter their definition of Matter to include the words "Spirit," "Mind," or "Consciousness." There are only two possibilities from which to choose: The first is to believe that there is a physical realm and a spiritual realm which are separate and yet miraculously interact in the reality that we normally observe. At death, the material body returns to great store of matter we know as the universe. Likewise, the spiritual must return to some spiritual realm. The second choice proposes that all that exists is what we see as Matter. However, the spiritual aspect that we observe in things is part of this Matter, an inseparable attribute of it. We see this spiritual aspect in everything. We see it most readily in ourselves, while in other things it is less evident (i.e. rocks, water, air). To recognize that everything has this one nature with two aspects is to see an Ultimate Reality

Throughout the life of a human being, there is an evolution in the capacity to think. This is true both of each individual human being and of the human race as a whole. Does this not imply that sentient beings are progressing toward a realization of their Thought-aspect? This idea can be coupled with the theory that the material universe is moving toward a sort of "Heat death." The law of entropy suggests that the energy of the universe is being transformed from dynamic, useful forms to less useful forms. For example, areas of heat—according to the Second Law of Thermodynamics—naturally and necessarily flow into areas of cold. This reduces the ability of energy to perform work, reducing the dynamism of the universe. With this in mind, and the idea that beings are evolving toward and realizing their Thought-aspect, suggests that perhaps the universe has a *telos*, a final cause, or that it will be in a perfect state of Thought/Energy/Matter to start another cycle or life of the universe.

The question that now arises is "Why would either of these options take place?" A particular answer cannot be proposed to this question, except that there must be a reason. This necessity is evident because of the nature of Thought. For why would something known as pure Thought do anything without an all-encompassing Reason? Thought must manifest itself as matter for some purpose, or number of purposes, which contribute to a final Reason.

This is where the practice of meditation may make sense in the attempt to experience Ultimate Reality.[19] Through meditation, one is able—hopefully—to quiet the multitude of discursive and random thoughts that rule the mind each day. By observing these thoughts, one is able to be more aware of the Thought that is Matter and that is at the center of each person. Whenever one is able to experience this Thought—the Thought aspect that most people neglect—one is able and compelled to fulfill one's purpose here on Earth. This fulfillment is furthered through meditation because it allows one to be aware of Thought- and Matter-aspects at the same time. Having a material aspect allows one to interact with others while fulfilling one's purpose.

Part of this purpose is certainly to help others realize their purpose. There are many ways that a person may be able to make others aware of the Thought in them. In the end, though, every person must experience it for themselves, as the Truth cannot be explained, but only known.

The Experience and Expression of Truth

This explanation also shows why many people who do not meditate or think about such things are able to fulfill their purpose. One reason is that each person may have a meditation that is not known as such. For some it is music, for others it is cooking or cleaning, still others athletics, etceteras. Although focusing on nothing may be ideal, concentration on one thing is still a form of meditation. A second reason is that there are people who, while they do not think about the act of meditation, similarly do not analyze any other thing that they do. When these people act without rationally examining the action, they are able to fulfill their purpose. This is what children often do. They do not let discursive thought or reasoning get in the way of the purpose for which they are here.[20] Therefore, they are able to act toward this purpose.

This is an attempt to offer a reasonable explanation for why one can experience Reality through sitting meditation, or the practices of other traditions. The Zen Buddhists have faith that one can experience the Truth through this practice and through living mindfully. It cannot be known in any other way. This entire paper was written with inspiration from Zen and its emphasis on the simplicity of Truth, the necessity of practice, and the futility of words. However, the spirit of Zen has been lost merely in the act of writing such a paper. Perhaps the Zen saying, "That stone Buddha deserves all the birdshit it gets," applies to this situation. Words, like the stone Buddha, are representative of the Truth and may help one to focus on it. However, words are not the Truth. They do not even come close to describing it, just as worshipping a stone Buddha will in no way bring one closer to Ultimate Reality.

Is then all written and spoken word futile? What of the arguments put forth by the various philosophers mentioned earlier? Are they to be ignored because the arguments themselves are verbal? The answer to this question is, of course, "No." It must be remembered that the Truth is immanent in everything. The stone out of which the Buddha was sculpted does contain an element of immanent Reality and so it is not totally devoid of Truth. There is Thought as well as Matter in everything that exists. Therefore, even people are a part of the Truth of Ultimate Reality. Because this Truth is something we already have, a sort of memory of it can be aroused. A famous Zen master was quoted as saying, "The Buddha's smile can only be a result of his realization that he spent his whole life looking for something he already had." Words are not spoken or written in vain. They can act as a catalyst to make someone realize their part in the Truth, or to put someone on the path towards it. Words cannot express the Truth, words cannot teach the Truth, and words cannot imbue the Truth. And, while they can be distorted and their message deviated from, words can serve a purpose. They can inspire someone to begin the quest for Truth, a journey that must be made by each individual. For the Truth cannot be communicated. It can only be experienced.

NOTES

1   *Grolier's Multimedia Encyclopedia*, 1995.

2   Sarvepalli Radhakrishnan and Charles A. Moore, eds. *A Source Book in Indian Philosophy* (Princeton: Princeton University Press, 1957) 37.

3   Radhakrishnan and Moore, 38.

4   *Mundaka Upanishad* III.ii.4.

5   Radhakkrishnan, S., *The Bhagavadgita, with an Introductory Essay, Sanskrit Text, English Translation and Notes* (New York: Harper and Bros., 1948).

6   Merrill Ring, *Beginning with the Pre-Socratics* (Mountain View, CA: Mayfield Publishing Co., 2000) 62.

7   Ring 62.

8   Ring 84.

9   Irwin Edman, ed., *The Works of Plato* (New York: Simon and Schuster, Inc., 1928) 324.

10 Aristotle, *On the Art of Poetry with a Supplement on Music*, trans. S. H. Butcher, Milton C. Nahm, ed. (Indianapolis, New York: The Bobbs-Merrill Co., Inc., 1956) x.

11 David G. Hackett, *The Silent Dialogue: Zen Letters to a Trappist Abbott* (Chiron Publishing) 176.

12 Lao Tzu, *The Way of Life*, trans. R.B. Blakney (New York: Penguin Books U.S.A Inc., 1983) 77.

13 Each tradition has its own practice that facilitates an experience of Truth, for example, the practice of "Centering Prayer" or "Contemplative Prayer" in Christianity. I have chosen to speak about Zen meditation only because of Zen's emphasis on the experience of Truth versus the expression of it.

14 To use our example of the classroom again: One must be able to see that the room is actually 70 degrees. However, it is equally important that one be attuned to the fact that other people's perceptions of hot and cold are "real" too. Their perceptions are caused by their life experiences. When a person realizes both of these aspects of the Truth, he/she is enlightened. An enlightened person experiences Ultimate Reality, but also understands how other people can see things

in the way that they do. Because of this understanding, he/she can have compassion for all beings.

15 Taisen Deshimaru and Nancy Amphoux, *Questions to a Zen Master* (Arkana, 1991) 66.

16 I would like to preface this next part of the paper where I explain the benefits of meditation.

You see, here I am very close to making metaphysical assumptions, something that strays from the teachings of the Buddha. However, I am trying to illustrate why the Zen Buddhists emphasize direct experience in the form of meditation in place of the spoken or written word. To do so, I need to offer an explanation of meditation that remains true to the Buddhist practice, but which can be understood by all, including myself.

If someone had asked the Buddha, "Why should I meditate?" the Buddha would have probably answered, "You should meditate to meditate," or "You should meditate for the sake of meditation." Now, this answer may be the best answer, and it may be quite appealing to some people. However, it seems to me that the vagueness of this answer will be quite troubling, especially to people who are not familiar with Buddhist thought. Consequently, I am offering an explanation of meditation. I have tried to illustrate how it may offer a direct experience with Objective, Ultimate reality. This is Reality as different from the subjective reality that each individual perceives because of their likes, dislikes, dispositions, and prejudices. By examining and explaining meditation in this way, I feel that a greater number of people may be able to intellectually see its value. They may even be prompted to try it.

The only true way of knowing the value of meditation is to practice it. Even then, its vast impact can probably never be known. Hence I offer my explanation of it only in the hopes that it may make the practice seem logically beneficial. (It should be kept in mind that this explanation does not apply exclusively to Zen Buddhist meditation.)

17 By "operation", I am referring to the generation, growth, function, movement, decay, and death of all of the parts of each of the above-mentioned systems.

18 Keep in mind that this thought is not a fleeting, changeable thought like those that we consciously think of and construct, but a pro-

found Thought that one does not *think* as much as one *knows* without thinking.

[19] By now, you have probably forgotten what this paper is actually about!

[20] Reason can be a helpful tool, but it relies on the examination of circumstances. Since the human brain can only be conscious of a small fraction of the circumstances of Reality, it cannot always properly assess a situation. Using reason is like trying to put together a puzzle when half of its pieces are missing (and most of those pieces can only be found somewhere in the future or the forgotten past).

REFERENCES

Aristotle. *On the Art of Poetry with a Supplement on Music*, trans. S. H. Butcher, Milton C. Nahm, ed. Indianapolis, New York: The Bobbs-Merrill Co., Inc., 1956.

Deshimaru, Taisen and Nancy Amphoux. *Questions to a Zen Master.* Arkana, 1991.

Edman, Irwin, ed. *The Works of Plato.* New York: Simon and Schuster, Inc., 1928.

Grolier's Multimedia Encyclopedia, 1995.

Hackett, David G. *The Silent Dialogue: Zen Letters to a Trappist Abbott.* Chiron Publishing, 1991.

Lao Tzu. *The Way of Life.* Trans. R.B. Blakney. New York: Penguin Books U.S.A Inc., 1983.

Radharkrishnan, S. *The Bhagavadgita, with an Introductory Essay, Sanskrit Text, English Translation and Notes.* New York: Harper and Bros., 1948.

Radhakrishnan, Sarvepalli and Charles A. Moore, eds. *A Source Book in Indian Philosophy.* Princeton: Princeton University Press, 1957.

Ring, Merrill. *Beginning with the Pre-Socratics.* Mountain View, CA: Mayfield Publishing Co., 2000.

On the Event of Truth:
A Discussion of Art, Truth and The Primal Conflict in Heidegger's "The Origin of the Work of Art"

Iain Tucker Brown

St. Mary's College of Maryland

This paper explores two highly significant yet extraordinarily difficult sections of Heidegger's work, "The Origin of the Work of Art." Key points of inquiry include concealedness, unconcealedness, and truth in the work of art. My intention is to illustrate, with the philosophical genius of Heidegger's aesthetic reflections, the function of art, not as a mere mechanism for the causal interpretation of thoughts and feelings that stand in relation to the aesthetic response or the artwork at hand, but rather as the impetus for a meaningful reconciliation between two dialectically opposed states of existence in the form of the event of truth. Art will be explored as a sort of story in which we, as characters, interact with ourselves and the world in order to resolve what Heidegger terms the *primal conflict*.

Art is obscure. Truth, too, is equally obscure. But what if the two, art and truth, were brought together? What is meant by the enigmatic phrase, *art as truth*? In what follows I shall put into question Heidegger's work, "The Origin of the Work of Art." My exploration into the text will attempt to bring to light three questions:

1) "What is *concealedness*?"
2) "What is truth as *unconcealedness*?" and
3) "How do we attain toward truth in the work of art?"

On the Event of Truth

Through his rendering of art as truth, Heidegger offers a valuable paradigm, which, if understood properly, affords the opportunity to resolve what he terms the *primal conflict*. As I interpret it, the *primal conflict* is the most fundamental yet mysterious state of existence where we, as beings that experience the world (in one sense) as a sum of *others*, must come to terms with our, equally as fundamental and seemingly contradictory, existential state as *beings-with*. I will attempt to show that art, which unfolds truth as unconcealedness, is the impetus for a sort of self-realization that enables us to resolve, if only for a moment, this primal conflict.

What is concealedness?

Heidegger advances his notion of *concealedness* by founding, or at least clarifying, two fundamental grounds of being, by which we encounter the world. He mentions, "things are, and human beings, gifts, and sacrifices are, animals and plants are, equipment and works are" (OWA 52-53). Firstly, what meaning may be derived from this obscure reference to 'things'?

As I read him, Heidegger is bringing forth one of two fundamental ways in which we, as beings that dwell, live and exist among other beings, encounter the world. If we look at the way in which we experience the world, that is to say, if we give attention to and meditate on our experience at work, at home, and in nature, we see, at one level, a world that consists as a sum of 'things.' While sitting in a lecture hall, we see chairs, a podium, a speaker, and many individual people. In a leisurely stroll through the forest, we see trees, rocks, and broken stumps that jump forth from the mossy earth. We see, in all these situations, many beings, many wholly *other* 'things,' a series of them in fact, for we could, it seems, list them as they appear before us.

Think, for a moment, about the sensation of entering a large gathering of people. The word 'many' comes to mind, and we feel this 'many,' these 'many people,' before us. They are, in one sense, a collection of *others*, and by sensing this *otherness*, we, in turn, affirm ourselves as others too. Heidegger implies that, in one way of encountering the world, all beings are other, singular entities that stand in their own obscurity. In our experience of them we encounter them in their otherness, and this too re-affirms a sense of otherness in us. Here, a demarcation, so to speak, outlines for us the separation between ourselves and the objects that we experience.

Heidegger, in attempting to realize the magnitude and significance of this way of encountering the world, asserts:

> What is, is never of our making or even merely the product of our minds, as it might all too easily seem. When we contemplate this whole as one, then we apprehend, so it appears, all that is—though we grasp it crudely enough. (OWA 53)

In this elementary way of encountering the world as a sum of others, we do, as I have attempted to show, experience a sort of singularity in being, both in ourselves and in the others that manifest themselves in the world. That is to say, we feel that the world is an obscure and mysterious world of others, where we, too, are another singular other in a long list of other, particular beings.

The way we experience things, at this level, further affirms for us a sense of otherness. But for Heidegger, this does not mean that we are at war with the world in conquest of the other, for as he contends, "through being there passes a veiled destiny that is ordained between the godly and the counter-godly. There is much in being that man cannot master" (OWA 53). Otherness and other, as both our experience and felt-perception of things imply, are not to be understood as alien, impenetrable. "Other" is but the designation that beings are different, obscure, unique and uncontrollable, and ultimately and eternally irrepressible. At one of two levels, at the ground of how we encounter the world, we experience and feel things to be other, ourselves included.

In another sense, apart from otherness, we encounter the world with-us; namely, we encounter the world as a *being-with*. Heidegger expounds, "and yet—beyond what is, not away from it but before it, there is still something else that happens. In the midst of beings as a whole an open place occurs" (OWA 53). What is this open place, and how does it differ from our experience of beings as *other*?

If we bring ourselves before a mountain setting, we encounter the world quite uniquely. The sky is a dark shade of blue, which further reminds us, in one perceptive mode, of the cold and beating wind that hardens our skin and waters our eyes. The wind, too, echoes off the surrounding rock, creating a powerful vocal whirl that taunts our ears. At the summit, the depth of the earth below, its rock-abyss, brings us into the scene where we dwell with the wind, with the resonating noise of the powerful whirl of air, with the impenetrable mountain wall. Here, we encounter the world, not as a collection of others, but rather as a being-with. The mountain, in the mountain-scene, is no longer a separable entity in the mix of others that we experience. The wind, the echoes, the feeling that the rock-abyss inspires, become one with us, as we are one with them. We encounter this scene as an indistinguishable whole. The mountain, the wind, and the cold unite into our experience in an unrecognizable way. Heidegger asserts:

> There is a clearing, lighting. Thought of in reference to what is, to beings, this clearing is in a greater degree than are beings. This open center is therefore not surrounded by what is, rather, the lighting center itself encircles all that is, like the Nothing which we scarcely know. (OWA 53)

This open, where the lighting occurs, is the metaphysical space in which, when we encounter the world as such, objects do not become distinguishable in their otherness. Rather, we are with world, and in this second fundamental mode of world-perception the singularity of beings in their otherness is at one with our being. This is, for Heidegger, the making of the *clearing* in which we, simultaneously with others, present ourselves before each other and with each other.

As Heidegger further contends, "that which is can only be, as being, if it stands within and stands out within what is lighted in this clearing" (OWA 53). In this sense, a being is understood as wholly other, as something that is both inextricably bound with and intrinsically connected to the world. There exists a constant duality at play where we, at one level, encounter the world as an indistinguishable whole, and in another sense as a collection, albeit an ultimately indeterminable one, of wholly other others, where we, too, are an equally integral component. This, then, becomes the stage upon which we interact with the world, and with others in the world.

The two fundamental ways in which we encounter the world are either as a collection of distinguishable others, or as an indistinguishable whole of beings-with. Our experiences, too, support these two opposed yet unifying modes of *self-world* relational understanding. I have attempted to show how we, in several senses, encounter the world and our standing therein as either an otherness or as a being-with. Now, in clarifying Heidegger's notion of *concealed-ness*, I will explore how these modes of perception conceal themselves, in a twofold way, from our ability to experience the world truthfully.

Because 'things' are, in one sense, quite other, they *refuse* us in our attempts to conceive of them in any ultimately definable way. The constitution of otherness maintains that, because something is wholly distinct from us, beings must escape our ability to conceptually assimilate them into some sort of ultimately definitive framework, for, in fact, they are beyond us and therefore not within our singularly-felt realm of experience. Heidegger asserts, "concealment as refusal is not simply and only the limit of knowledge in any given circumstance, but the beginning of the clearing of what is lighted" (OWA 53-54). Because beings refuse us in their otherness they, too, equally open for us and initiate a drive to unfold the mystery of their being. And similarly, because beings are, in this sense, encountered as quite other, they do not escape mutual interaction entirely, leaving us idle without any relational ground upon which to stand. Rather, the very fact that beings are, in this sense, wholly other impels us to seek after the other, to search in a positive way for a deepened understanding of the other.

Concealing as refusal is a claim upon us that speaks to a longing for the other. It is both mystical and ultimately transforming, only if we choose to accept it, to meet and respond to its call. I wish to bring us, here, before Van Gogh's masterful rendering of a seemingly simple pair of peasant boots.

The dark and scuffed black of the leather against the earth-tone background, the boots, worn and weathered, speak to us in their otherness, indeed the image demands a response in the form of a calling, for even to engage in the painting is to be pulled by something extra-ordinary, to be claimed, so to speak, by the presence of the work. We imagine the boots and their wearer; we awaken a world in which the boots live amid the occupations and hardships of a laborer. We are brought inward, pulled forth to explore the mystery that stands forth in color and stroke on the canvas. As Heidegger visualizes Van Gogh's masterpiece, "this painting spoke. In the vicinity of the work we were suddenly somewhere else than we usually tend to be" (OWA 35). The painting, the other, as *refusal, pulls*. Refusal is the feeling of this claim, this 'pulling.' Recognizing this pull and its origin is realizing the otherness of the other, the obscurity and uncertainty of that which is before us. This realizing is the beginning of the journey into the clearing of the world, based on encountering the world as a sum of wholly other *others*.

Being-with, too, as a mode of encountering, conceals us in its own way as well. Heidegger states, "but concealment, though of another sort, to be sure, at the same time also occurs within what is lighted" (OWA 54). This lighting, as I previously stated, is the open space in which we encounter beings as being-with. Furthermore, as Heidegger contends, "this concealment is dissembling" (OWA 54). Dissembling, by definition, means to disguise, to mask or to cover up. So what then, is disguising, as concealing, when we encounter the world in being-with?

As a being that is with the world, we are subject to and in congruence with what Heidegger terms, *das Man*. The term describes the sort of societal structure into which we, as beings-with, are thrown. *Das Man* is the public voice, the influential and guiding hand of society as a whole that shapes and interprets both our thoughts and actions. It is important to explain that being-with is never just a *letting-be*, which is to say that we never just sit, passively, and gape fixedly at *another*. Rather, in every instance, we are always in tune with the orientation of *das Man*, and this in turn manifests itself when, in being-with, we approach and encounter the world. *Das Man* informs us how to read the world and consequently the role therein of others and ourselves too. In this way, being-with is not only a being-with something, but also always, and more specifically, a being-with *das Man*. Here, as dissembling, *das Man* conceals our being-with in many ways. Heidegger informs us of this by asserting,

> if one did not simulate another, we could not make mistakes or act mistakenly in regard to beings; we could not go astray and transgress, and especially could never overreach ourselves. (OWA 54)

Das Man transposes the appearance of one with another and forces others into conceptual boxes of its own creation. In the intimately sewn fabric of relational encountering in being-with, *das Man* both enables and shapes our understanding, but it also obscures our ability to respond to those beings, with whom we engage in a sort of reciprocal exchange.

We encounter the otherness of others, ourselves included, and are refused permission to unfold the other, with the understanding that the other is, in fact, quite other and as such 'pulls' or 'compels' us to seek after it. Refusal is a mode of concealing in a positive sense: to recognize the world as an indefinite sum or as a whole of 'many beings' is to affirm the otherness of the other, to affirm its refusal (which, in another way, is to enable an ethical understanding among beings in the world). To encounter the world as other, as a whole of others, is to say that the others claim each other in a way that is both obscure and indefinable. It is to say, equally, that the other is in itself also obscure and ultimately beyond description. In this encounter, as refusal, the other conceals itself yet pulls us up toward it to seek after its murky presence which is, according to Heidegger, "the beginning of the clearing of what is lighted;" that is, the beginning of being-with.

Being-with, too, is a positive way of encountering the world, but whereas *das Man* asserts its incessant presence, being-with conceals as a sort of disguise or mask placed over our perceptive lenses. As being-with, the world is obscured. Similar to the thickly entrenched fog that slumbers upon the rolling meadows, *das Man* clouds our interactive being-with in such a way as to conceal by covering-up, by laying a superficial gloss over our ability to encounter the world, truthfully.

Concealing, in the sense of refusal, seems to be an essential quality of how we encounter the world. Regardless of the experience, when we approach the world as other we will always feel the upward pull of the other, positively, in the form of refusal, which, encouragingly, sets us forth to seek after the other. However, the presence of *das Man* in being-with, as dissembling, is something less essential to the proper group of beings and more affixed to our experience. Concealing, as dissembling, is a process, which implies, on account of its vexatious nature, that a counter-process can occur, that unconcealedness can take place. This then brings us to my next question; what is truth as *unconcealedness*?

On the Event of Truth

What is truth as unconcealedness?

We often think of truth as a claim that hovers above our consciousness, an infallible and divine explanation of the order of the cosmos. For many, truth is placeable: it exists, in a certain way, as something fixed. Truth, in this sense, is a sort of static representation or proclamation to which everything else must conform. We search for truth, in purity, with a final purpose in mind. Truth is the glory of ultimate discovery in that, for some, it discloses all that is and should be known. This way of reasoning, according to Heidegger, is problematic.

In light of the examination of how the world that we encounter conceals itself from us in a twofold way, which is in accordance with the twofold way by which we fundamentally encounter the world, Heidegger contends, "the clearing *happens* only as this double concealment. The unconcealedness of beings—this is never a merely existent state, but a happening" (OWA 54). Here unconcealedness is manifested not as an attainable fact, but rather as a process of clearing, of being 'pulled' upward by the otherness of the world while, at the same time, sorting-through the disguise that *das Man*, in being-with, places upon the possibility of our encountering the world truthfully. It is a happening, an occurring progression of constant clearing, where we realize, simultaneously, the pull of the other and the mask before us in being-with. This, then, becomes the ground in which truth is set forth as *unconcealedness*.

However, something still lurks in the realm of the clearing. Heidegger asserts, "we believe we are at home in the immediate circle of beings" (OWA 54). Through unconcealedness we begin the clearing to attain to truth, but truth is not that which, upon our discovery of it, rests above all in eternity. In the aforementioned excerpt, Heidegger is suggesting that what is, for us, ordinarily "true" is that which we are usually accustomed to or familiar with. Truth is the general everyday way in which we take the world and simplify it according to our formulated structures. Truth, thus taken, is found in agreement and thus becomes "ordinary." But as Heidegger further contends, "the ordinary is not ordinary; it is extra-ordinary, uncanny" (OWA 54). Therefore, our formulaic way of living-in and with the world is not essential to world, or to truth, but rather remains as an imposition upon world, upon truth. Moreover, "the nature of truth, that is, of unconcealedness, is dominated throughout by denial" (OWA 54).

By unconcealing the world, in accepting the 'pulling-refusal' of the other, and by sorting-out the guise of *das Man*, truth denies us, not in the pejorative sense of the word (where we would never come to any true realizations), but rather in a positive sense, in that truth is always changing and transforming itself. This, consequently, demands even more so that we strive for understanding: namely, seek out and sort-through the complexities of the other as an other, and as a being-with.

Truth, then, consists, in part, in the two ways by which we encounter the world. In our seeing the world as a sum of distinguishable others we are, in this sense, concealed by the refusal of the other as an*other*; but in another sense, we are also pulled forth to unfold the other's mystery as a being that stands outside of us. In seeing the world as an indistinguishable whole, as a being-with, things are concealed by the disguise of *das Man*. Thus we must sort-through the sway of societal pressures to attempt, at the very least, to reach the being with which we are a being-with. And this process, this happening, as unconcealedness, is always maintained by a denial, which is to say that truth never becomes something permanent in the presence of our encountering the world. Rather, truth is in constant flux, fitting-in here and erupting there. Truth as unconcealedness is the perpetual pursuit, the unceasing attempt, to unfold the partial mystery of the world that we may know. Truth is constantly revealing and obscuring itself as we attempt to disclose it; thus we are always in conflict, in a twofold struggle, that continues *ad infinitum*.

In Heidegger's concluding remarks on truth as unconcealedness, he contends "truth is, in itself, the opposition of the primal conflict in which that open center is won within which what is, stands, and from which it sets itself back into itself" (OWA 54). It is my point, now, to explore what this primal conflict is and to put into question the question, "How do we attain toward truth in the work of art?"

How do we attain toward truth in the work of art?

When I began our discussion of concealedness, I attempted to bring forth two fundamental ways by which we encounter the world. In one sense we see the world, fundamentally, as a sum of separate and distinguishable others. In another way, the world appears, for us, to be a whole, and we, in this respect, are a being-with. In making these claims, I am passing over many structures and substructures that Heidegger puts forth amid the vast collection of his invaluable works. Concepts such as *ownmost possibility, being-in-the-world,* and *facticity* are being left at my discretion for later evaluation. Here, where our concern is truth and art and the meaning that both can have, I want to focus explicitly on these two modes of encountering the world, and portray as well their relationship with the primal conflict. Before this endeavor is undertaken, however, the road must first be marked accordingly: we must unfold the

particular inextricable quality of the primal conflict—
namely, the tension between earth and world, the eruption
of the rawness of being through the inadequate conceptual
constructions of humankind—to bring together art, truth,
and the primal conflict with the possibility of our own self-
reconciliation. Heidegger states:

> Rather, the world is the clearing of the paths of the
> essential guiding directions with which all decision
> complies. Every decision, however, bases itself on
> something that not mastered, something concealed,
> confusing; else it would never be a decision. The
> earth is not simply the Closed but rather that which
> rises up as self-closing. World and earth are always
> intrinsically and essentially in conflict, belligerent by
> nature. Only as such do they enter into the conflict of
> the clearing and concealing. (OWA 55)

The earth, the obscure and reverberating grandeur that sustains all life, the powerful and cosmic body of being, is the
inextricable *other*, the godly element of existence. The
world, also an obscure entity, is the fabricated rendering of
the earth, incomplete, inadequate, confusing, and vexatious.
In this manner the two are joined in an essential conflict.
Amid this conflict, wrapped in each other's being, the earth
erupts, exploding the world's constructions of thought and
revealing its own spectacular profundity. This tension, at a
microcosmic level, is the primal conflict of our being, the
demand of earth for us to truthfully clear for the unfolding
of our twofold relational constitution in world, as other and
as being-with, to prepare the world for an authentic union
with earth in the form of the event of truth. The calling of
earth and world, the primal conflict, is the essential command to reconcile our two fundamental states of existence.
This claim, as shall now be explored, becomes manifest as
truth in the work of art.

On the Event of Truth

In being there exists this tension between the world that we encounter as other with the world that we encounter as with, a tension drawn from the eruption of earth through world, from the pulling-refusal of earth as other with respect to our conceptual frameworks of world, from the call to bind together in thought and construction, as being-with, the mysterious reverberation of the godly qualities of existence. In being, this tension is a rupture within our sense of self, a contradiction that is opened from the time we are set forth into the world and thus claimed by the earth-world primal conflict. In truth, this conflict is won through unconcealedness, through the continual clearing and unfolding that is perpetuated by our encountering the world as other, and sorted-out by our encountering the world as being-with. As Heidegger states, "art then is the becoming and happening of truth" (OWA 71). Art, in itself, is this unconcealing process; it is the story of how we come to terms with the primal conflict.

If art is truth as unconcealedness, and if this unconcealedness is a rendering of the primal conflict, then we can, through art, come to terms with the tension that exists between our two opposing existential states: wholly other beings, and beings-with. The meaning of art, in a unique way, is this self-realization, or the momentary reconciliation of a self as a singular self that stands in the world among others with whom the self is always and intrinsically a being-with.

In dwelling with an artistic masterpiece, there is much that is revealed, but also a great deal hidden, obscured, and concealed. Van Gogh's work brings to light this conflict: the painting, in its otherness, pulls as refusal and simultaneously binds as a being-with; it opens up a world for exploration into the grandeur of existence, into the earth-world conflict, as earth stands, erupting through world. The painting, and any masterful art piece for that matter, is the story of this conflict, a bringing together of humankind's struggle to compose an authentic representation of the relationship shared between a fabricated world that rests upon a cosmic and godly earth. This conflict between earth and world is the existential story of the demand upon us, by this conflict, to reconcile our seemingly opposite states of being as singular entities and as beings-with. If we turn to Heidegger we can see, once again, that art, as truth, is the story of our lives, the rendering of our primal conflict. In referring to Van Gogh's painting of two peasant boots and a poem of a Roman fountain, Heidegger asserts:

> The picture that shows the peasant shoes, the poem that says the Roman fountain, do not just make manifest what this isolated being as such is—if indeed they manifest anything at all; rather, they make unconcealedness as such happen in regard to what is as a whole. (OWA 56)

Though more is at work here in terms of the entirety of Heidegger's philosophical paradigm, these works of art do manifest truth, in that they bring forth the basic diametric tension between *otherness* and *being-with*. This being the case, I believe that if we respond to this tension to reveal truth in the work of art, we can similarly reveal the tension in our own self, as singular beings that exist with others in a being-with. And if truth can be revealed in the work, so too can it be realized within us. Art as truth as unconcealedness brings to resolution the *primal conflict*, our primal conflict.

REFERENCES

Heidegger, Martin. *Poetry, Language, Thought*. Trans. Albert Hofstadter. New York: Harper & Row, 1971.

Towards a Processean Aesthetics Within a Whiteheadian Metaphysics

Scott M. Gleason

SUNY Potsdam/Crane School of Music

Many philosophers engage in discussions of art and such considerations are, obviously, founded upon their metaphysical principles. Consequently, a vast and rich body of aesthetic investigation has risen, however, mostly within the static, dualistic ontologies characteristic of these philosophers. The work of Alfred North Whitehead (1861-1947) offers a decisive and rewarding framework with which to conceive of the nature of art and music, accepting many of the former principles of aesthetics, while at the same time challenging and revising them.

Whitehead's metaphysical notions, so unique and compelling in their own right, abound with aesthetic implications and significance. However, Whitehead's discussions of art are fairly limited and beg for further investigation. To this end, this paper explores some notions regarding aesthetic experience that are latent in Whitehead's process metaphysics, as well as some of his more salient notions of art and its function. It is the central aim of this paper, then, to show that Alfred North Whitehead's metaphysics can be adventurously conceived of as a Processean Aesthetics.

The metaphysics of Alfred North Whitehead (1861-1947) offer a unique and important view of reality and the reality of change. Comprising his "philosophy of organism" are the notions of process, creativity, novelty, becoming, satisfaction, perishing, feeling, and purpose, each used in a technical sense. One purpose of this discussion is to show that these terms may be applied to music and art in equally important ways. Indeed, one can consider Whitehead's metaphysics to be an "aesthetic metaphysics." This is a literal interpretation: the Greek origin of the word "aesthetic" means "sense perception," and by extension the term has come to mean "relating to feeling." This interpretation is validated when Whitehead discusses his notion of the essential ontological act in terms of becoming as an act of "...feeling the feeling in another and feeling conformally with another" (PR 162). He further states that "the basis of experience is emotional" (AI 176). The problem is that Whitehead only partially ventures into the realm of aesthetics proper as an area of philosophical inquiry. The more common aesthetic notions and the related terms above are never discussed in the sense of a specific philosophy of music, and only briefly in relation to art generally. It is the dipolar aim of this paper to discuss a Whiteheadian aesthetic ontology and a Whiteheadian aesthetics of music.

Whitehead, in *Adventures of Ideas* and in *Process and Reality*, offers what seems to be an adaptation of Platonic artistic representationalism. "Art has essentially to do with perfections attainable by purposeful adaptation of appearance" (AI 268). "The speech, for the theatre audience, is purely theoretical, a mere lure for feeling" (PR 185). However, he does not extend any of his complex metaphysical notions to arrive at an explicit, unique conception of the fine arts or, specifically, music. Whitehead makes reference to art and does offer a general aesthetics of art, but does not give the reader an aesthetics of music or other specific arts. This is surprising given what I believe to be the "artistic" character of his metaphysics. The emphasis on feeling, creativity and satisfaction alone give his writings the quality of an aesthetics of reality. There is a fecundity latent in Whitehead's cosmological notions that will benefit from exploration within an aesthetic realm, and this is the goal of my discussion.

Scott M. Gleason

For Whitehead, the principle of "creativity" is the principle or "rule" by which every actual entity comprising the universe acts. "Actual entities—also termed 'actual occasions'—are the final real things of which the world is made up. There is no going behind actual entities to find anything more real" (PR 18). They are not substances in the traditional sense of having a subject-predicate formation and only non-physical reality. They are "feeling" and "prehending" processes of existence.

> 'Creativity'… is the pure notion of the activity conditioned by the objective immortality of the actual world – a world which is never the same twice… Creativity is without a character of its own… It is that ultimate notion of the highest generality at the base of actuality. It cannot be characterized, because all characters are more special than itself. But creativity is always found under conditions, and described as conditioned. (PR 31)

This quotation illustrates Whitehead's empiricism. Creativity has no being merely as a principle. It only "attains" reality when it is found at work in an actual occasion. It is in actual, concrete experience that we come to behold creativity at work. "The creativity is the actualization of potentiality, and the process of actualization is an occasion of experiencing" (AI 179). When one takes part in a musical experience, that person is experiencing the reality of this creative principle in a concrete, particular, and therefore "fully actual" sense. The artistic or musical work, and its performance, are the set of "conditions" under which creativity is found. The score—i.e. the written or notated music—is "ingressed" in a performance: the actual entity functioning as a subject. "The term 'ingression' refers to the particular mode in which the potentiality of an eternal object is realized in a particular actual entity, contributing to the definiteness of that actual entity" (PR 23). In this way, then, the music "absorbs" its definiteness from the score. The performance is only fully actual by virtue of the score. Additionally, as Whitehead states in *Adventure of Ideas*, music can act as an eternal object that serves as a catalyst for the growth of the person, functioning as an actual entity and in the growth of the larger society.

The standard literature on aesthetics is acute at analyzing the various meanings that are signified by the terms, "creation" and "creativity." However, these traditionally relate to the artistic or creative process whereby a work is brought into existence: the composer's "creative urge" or inspiration to create a piece of music and the actual process of composition. Additionally, they usually assume a creation *ex nihilo*, which is contrary to Whitehead's metaphysics. This will be explained in detail later.

First, Whitehead's ontologically creative process shall be explored. It then can be expanded into what I believe to be a satisfactory aesthetic theory. We must first understand what an artistic work is on the ontological level. From that, Whitehead's broader aesthetic and cultural notions will follow. "Creativity," "concrescence," "satisfaction," and "novelty" play important roles in Whitehead's ontology of process. It is important to note that these notions work together; nothing exists in a vacuum for Whitehead.

> The human being is inseparable from its environment in each occasion of its existence. The environment which the occasion inherits is immanent in it, and conversely it is immanent in the environment which it helps to transmit. (AI 63)

When achieved through actual entities, as in a musical performance, creativity works in a very specific manner. "Creativity... is that ultimate principle by which the many, which are the universe disjunctively, become the one actual occasion, which is the universe conjunctively" (PR 21). Creativity takes what was in multiplicity and transforms it into what is in unity. Creativity has this special quality, when working through concrescence, of actually unifying what was with what is. Although seemingly obvious, creativity does not have the opposite function; it does not take what was in unity and result in multiplicity. "In the organic philosophy an actual entity has 'perished' when it is complete" (PR 81-82). This completeness is the wholeness of the entity.

At this point, we must explain Whitehead's term, "concrescence." Concrescence can be thought of as the aesthetic and artistic process *par excellence*. It is inherently a "relational activity." These last two words are important, for, as stated earlier, no entity can exist solely by itself, so it must therefore be related to things external to itself. "...The process, or concrescence, of any one actual entity involves the other actual entities among its components" (PR 7). The specific actual entity maintains its own "being," but "borrows" part of the other's "being," during its process of becoming.[1] In this way, it maintains its identity as a separate "being," but is altered by external entities. Concrescence is also an activity because for Whitehead an entity cannot cease to act. "Being" is really a progression of acts of becoming. Even non-being is being; being is the concrescent process of becoming and perishing. More specifically, when an actual entity is discussed as a subject—as an actor, agent, the "subjectivity," as the effect—it combines itself with an eternal object—a motive, the "objectivity," potency, or cause—in a process of becoming. This is concrescence: the creative striving of an entity towards completion, borrowing part of its "being" by feeling that which exists in the past, and eventually perishing.

> In this process the creativity, universal throughout ac-
> tuality, is characterized by the datum from the past;
> and it meets this dead datum—universalized into a
> character of creativity—by the vivifying novelty of
> subjective form selected from the multiplicity of pure
> potentiality. In the process, the old meets the new,
> and this meeting constitutes the satisfaction of an
> immediate particular individual. (PR 164)

The creativity acting in an actual entity "absorbs" the
"data" from the past to create something new. Whitehead
then uses the word "vivifying": life giving. This process is
the creative process; it gives life to an entity by offering its
objectivity. "The old meets the new" because the subject is
acting in the present, absorbing the objectivity of the object. "...It is what the occasion feels for itself, as derived
from the past and as merging into the future" (PR 163).

Whitehead terms this act of experiencing the objectivity of
another "feeling." "Here 'feeling' is used for the basic ge-
neric operation of passing from the objectivity of the data
to the subjectivity of the actual entity in question" (PR 40).
Again, it is an aesthetic process. I (as subject) feel the feeling of another (as object) when I take part in it. The subject
is "concerned" with the object. Many have literally considered this to be the defining moment of the aesthetic experience. Philosophers and musicians from at least Schopen-
hauer to Bruno Walter have accepted this quasi-religious
possibility of music and many have considered it the goal
of music. The concept of "ecstasy," of literally "stepping
outside of oneself," coupled with a "loss of being or self"
has been the paradigm from which Western Aestheticians
have thought of the "climax" of the musical and artistic experience. Mystics and those who interpret the aesthetic experience mystically usually state that it is a complete union
of being. By becoming one with another, I lose myself and

become the other during that moment when time seems to cease—or so the prevailing thought goes.

> ...An actual fact is a fact of aesthetic experience. All aesthetic experience is feeling arising out of the realization of contrast under identity. (PR 280)

Likely without being aware of it, Whitehead has in these two sentences offered a summation of an entire philosophy of music. The concrete, real fact of existence is an aesthetic experience, which is understood as feeling arising out of realization. This realization is of variety, contrast, or many influencing unity, togetherness, or "the one." This dynamic is played out in music and art representationally and actually. Representationally, all musical parameters contribute to this process of concrescence in the musical work. In actuality, all parameters of music *are* concrescencing entities. This, then, is a Whiteheadian ontology of music. What is a musical work? It is a community of actual entities prehending, concrescing, and perishing under the principle of creativity.

We can now discuss a uniquely Whiteheadian interpretation of the height of the musical experience. It is not a loss of the self; it is a borrowing of another in the process of concrescence, which creates the self anew, even if only partially. The feeling of an eternal object "ingressing" in a subject may be interpreted by that subject as a form of ecstasy: stepping outside of itself, but it is only partial. The actual entity takes part in another and therefore "loses" itself, if for only a brief moment and even if only partially. I interpret Whitehead to mean that the two cannot meld completely, for if they could, no identity would be maintained; the two would become one. This line of thinking is entirely contrary to Whitehead's notion of identity. Because concrescence applies to all entities in the universe, if entities could meld with one another, there would be literally one being: a Block Universe. All one need do is look around her surroundings to see that there is not one; there are many. Experience tells us that there is a multiplicity in the universe governed by one system.

In the ontological-aesthetic experience, the moment of "satisfaction" is a completion of the gaining of a subject's identity: the creation of a novel entity. Whitehead calls this "the final phase in the process of concrescence, constituting an actual entity, [and it] is one complex, fully determinate feeling" (PR 25-26). "The ultimate attainment is 'satisfaction'" (PR 166).

> The occasion has become less of a detail and more of
> a totality, so far as its subjective experience is con-
> cerned. The feeling of this width, with its enhance-
> ment of permanence, takes the form of blind zest...
> (PR 163)

This sensation of "width" with an air of "permanence" is what has been considered the "sublime" or "spiritual" experience in art and music for centuries. Often it has been thought of as an "ecstatic" experience; however, as argued earlier, this is not what I would interpret Whitehead to mean. It seems that at this stage in the process, self-identity is achieved ("a novel togetherness"). This perfect self-knowledge is acknowledged as being *the* aesthetic satisfaction. "The 'satisfaction' is the culmination of the concrescence into a completely determinate matter of fact" (PR 212).

There is a flip side to the process of concrescence: the actual entity perishes. Each moment and each act of experiencing perish because no thing is repeated completely; genuine change exists. It holds true to my experience that repetitions in life are not exact. Time and becoming are "serial" processes because each specific occurrence does not reoccur precisely. Its subjectivity perishes into objectivity, immortal objectivity. As has been stated, this produces a "one" which is an actual novelty. This process of creation results in a new entity. "The ancient doctrine that 'no one crosses the same river twice' is extended. No thinker thinks twice; and, to put the matter more generally, no subject experiences twice" (PR 29). However, this new entity is not completely new, because it does borrow some of its being from the objectivity of the past. "Of course no novelty is wholly novel" (AI 8).

Coming back to the notion of creation, one must now see it as a principle applying to real events in the actual world which cannot arrive out of nothingness. Creation is a form, potentially in a very intense and profound way, of combination. And creation is not *ex nihilo* because entities are responsible for part of their being to other beings. The entities created combine with those of the past in order to further themselves. A quote of T.S. Eliot serves to illuminate these notions specifically in terms of art.

> The existing order is complete before the new work arrives; for order to persist after the supervention of novelty, the whole existing order must be, if ever so slightly, altered; and so the relations, proportions, values of each work of art toward the whole are readjusted; and this is conformity between the old and the new... the past should be altered by the present as much as the present is directed by the past. (TIT 50)

Their thoughts are strikingly similar, and while a comparison of Eliot's aesthetics and Whitehead's metaphysics must be saved for another time, the similarities between the two are remarkable and intuitive. Although the majority of this quotation is in line with Whitehead's thinking, some of it contradicts Whitehead's metaphysics. Ontologically, the past cannot be altered by the present. Time moves serially for Whitehead, as does the transfer of feeling from object to subject.

Another issue in interpreting Whitehead's metaphysics as an aesthetics is the role of the creator. On a cosmological level, Whitehead abandons the notion of God the Creator. God is not, for Whitehead, a Prime Mover or efficient cause; rather, he acts as a kind of lure for concrescence by being the first instance thereof.

> [This] is apt to be misleading by its suggestion that the ultimate creativity of the universe is to be ascribed to God's volition. The true metaphysical position is that God is the aboriginal instance of this creativity, and is therefore the aboriginal condition which qualifies its action. (PR 225)

The artistic creator, then, is not a kind of "God as efficient cause," as traditional aesthetics would have it, but rather is an entity who "offers" the best plan of combination to the elements of an artistic work by himself being their first instance. His experiences, knowledge of reality, life, and relationships are represented in the artwork. This runs in contradistinction to expressionist theories of art. Each actual entity comprising a work of art has its own "subjective aim" and it is merely the painter, composer or sculptor's role to offer the best possible solution to achieve "Truthful Beauty," what Whitehead considers the proper or highest aim of art and therefore artistic representation (AI 267). The composer combines what he knows of the past—his past emotions, the past styles of composition as handed down in the musical tradition—absorbs them in the present, and alters them, creating anew for the future. "Art neglects the safety of the future for the gain of the present" (AI 269). This is the concrescent process realized as an artistic process. The composer is the God-like aboriginal feeler of the emotions that will be represented in the work of art. He is the aboriginal conceptualizer of the possibility of the work of music. He therefore acts with mental and physical poles, composing on the edge of being without a safety net, always pushing forward.

In what has come to be known as the "Common Practice Period" of Western European Classical music, there are two major areas of artistic creation: the creation of music as a score and the creation of music in a performance. Given what has been said about the nature of reality, that it is a process of concrescence on every level, both the musical score and the musical performance must be considered to be exemplifications of the process of reality. However, the performance seems to have a primacy to it. In terms of representing past experiences, which is essential to art and to society, the performance is more perfect because it goes through the process of concrescence while being experienced. It becomes, attains and perishes every measure, right before our very ears. It is here, during the performance, that music's true social function takes place. It reaches out to people, effecting a sense of community. Musical performance is therefore the highest representation of the ultimate nature of reality.

One question remains unanswered: does a Whiteheadian aesthetics make all experience aesthetic experience? In my interpretation, the answer is yes, but this does not corrupt the role of aesthetic experience in art. Far from it. Art is still given special worth because of its social duty, and its push for mentality.

> Art has a curative function in human experience when it reveals as in a flash intimate, absolute Truth regarding the Nature of Things. This service of Art is even hindered by trivial truths of detail. Such petty

> conformations place in the foreground the superfici-
> alities of sense-experience. Art performing this great
> service belongs to the essence of civilization. By the
> growth of such Art the adventure of mentality gains
> upon the physical basis of existence. (AI 272)

Finally, it is art that can allow us to realize our full poten-
tials as human beings and as a human society.

> ...Art heightens the sense of humanity. It gives an ela-
> tion of feeling which is supernatural. A sunset is glo-
> rious, but it dwarfs humanity and belongs to the gen-
> eral flow of nature. A million sunsets will not spur on
> men towards civilization. It requires Art to evoke into
> consciousness the finite perfections which lie ready
> for human achievement. (AI 271)

Scott M. Gleason

NOTES

---

[1] I realize the inaccuracies of using the static notions of "being" and the Aristotelian formation of a subject with qualities of becoming; however, it is difficult to express these ideas in a less ontologically and linguistically "static" manner, so please forgive me.

REFERENCES

Eliot, T.S. "Tradition and the Individual Talent," *The Sacred Wood: Essays on Poetry and Criticism.* New York: Alfred A. Knopf, Inc., 1930.

Whitehead, Alfred North. *Adventures of Ideas.* New York: The Macmillan Company, 1967.

_____. *Process and Reality: An Essay in Cosmology.* Ed. David Ray Griffin & Donald W. Sherburne. New York: The Free Press, 1978.

KEYNOTE ADDRESSES

PRAGMATISM AND THE FUTURE OF CONFUCIANISM IN CHINA

Joanna Crosby

Morgan State University

This essay examines the possibility that Pragmatism and Confucianism, both philosophies that emphasize practice over theory and actuality over metaphysics, can help heal the damage done to Chinese culture by the Cultural Revolution. It is argued that life on the streets of China is more complex than many scholars seem to acknowledge. Specific points of discussion include the following: (1) Chinese culture retains strong Confucian influence, though it is often unidentified as such and may involve a characteristic but paradoxical pragmatism; (2) Chinese popular culture closely resembles American popular culture; and (3) while the Cultural Revolution ended officially in 1975, there are aspects, suspicions, and practices that remain and hinder interaction between east and west, as well as the growth of academic communities and intellectual exchange. In the midst of this legacy, it may be easier to infuse Confucian thought into a western way of thinking than to reintroduce it to a Chinese way of thinking.

I want to thank Professor Shrader for inviting me to participate in this conference. I am very honored to be one of your keynote speakers, particularly to be included in such venerable company. The presentation I will make this evening is not a typical philosophy essay; I spent four months in China recently, October 1999 to January 2000, and I am in the midst of processing that experience. I am a very slow processor, so I expect to be doing that for a while, and welcome any assistance I can get. My thoughts tonight are part of that processing, so I look forward to your comments and reflections on what I have to say. My thoughts are in three different stages: the arguments I spell out in this presentation, the arguments I presuppose and gloss in this presentation, and the arguments that are still works in progress and where I particularly welcome your questions and comments.

I want to start with a controversial claim: China is different from the United States.

Shocking isn't it?

Okay, I am being a bit facetious. What's the point? We *are* two very different cultures; we have very different languages, very different perceptions of the world and how it should be, very different ways of being in the world. One might conclude that these differences are so vast, so mighty, that they seriously threaten our ability to talk to or understand one another. China is so different, one might say, we shouldn't even try to comprehend 'those people.' Or, one might conclude that the differences really aren't that important, that the Western values of truth, justice, democracy, altruism, and individualism, conflicting though they may be, are universal values. We can evaluate any system according to these values and understand exactly what is right with it or what is wrong with it. Both of these views represent at worst a kind of racism, at best a shortsightedness or ethnocentrism that lacks a fundamental *respect* for things that are different.

So how do we navigate those two extremes and carve out a position that is more respectful of a culture at least as complex as our own, and several thousand years older? One way to do this begins by recognizing that when we read Chinese texts and when we examine Chinese culture, we do so through Western lenses. Generally, this means that we look for a good argument, one that follows the rules of logic and the common sense that has been instilled in us by our parents and teachers. We have been taught what it means to 'make sense' and we apply those criteria to everything around us.

We are unable to see through Chinese eyes. So, out of respect for the difference between China and the United States, perhaps we should forego making pronouncements about what China should think or do, and look at what Chinese texts and Chinese culture can tell us about ourselves, our culture, and our way of life. In this way, we are able to take China seriously, and yet not suppose that we are right to evaluate China according to a set of values foreign to it. In other words, rather than relying solely on criticism based on values external to a system, we can learn a lot about China through a criticism that evaluates to what degree China upholds its stated values.

This, if I have understood correctly, is the approach that my esteemed and learned teachers, including Professor Rosemont, have taken. In terms of responsible scholarship, I fully support this method. Physicians take an oath to do no harm: in other words, to show respect for human life and individual bodies. Likewise, I think that people in the humanities and the sciences have a similar obligation to do no harm: in other words, to consider the context within which we work and live, and to the extent possible, mitigate the malicious harm our methods and conclusions might cause.

This ethical commitment leads me to question a sometimes uncritical view of China in some works, often taken in order to make China, Chinese texts and culture intriguing, exciting, attractive and worthy of study to those who are being introduced to the area. Thus I am suspicious of anyone who gives a rosy view of post Cultural Revolution China. The claim that Confucianism, Taoism, and Buddhism are alive and well, working hand in hand to enrich the day-to-day lives of the Chinese people doesn't correctly describe the situation I encountered. My students, admittedly a small sample of 220 with whom I communicated in very unscientific ways, on the whole have taken their teachings under communism to heart and belittle religious commitment. However, their curiosity remains high, and they express interest in participating in some religious ceremonies, particularly the exotic rituals we practice in the west like 'going to church' and 'midnight mass.'

Confucianism in particular has traveled a rough road in the past fifty years, having been subjected to a cycle of condemnation and rehabilitation, having been seen as a tool of bourgeois oppressors, partially rehabilitated through Mao's careful use of particular analects, only to be condemned again with the death of Zhou Enlai. Before I move on, let me give a brief summary of Confucianism.

In *The Analects of Confucius*,[1] I find two questions raised again and again. One asks: what do I do to be a filial child? The other: what do I do to be a magnanimous ruler? The first question concerns relations where I benefit from others; as a child, as a student, as a citizen, I benefit from my parents, my teachers, and my rulers. The second question concerns relations where I am the benefactor to others; as parent, as teacher, as ruler I improve the lives of my children, my students, and my citizens. Thus I agree with people like Professor Rosemont that *The Analects* concerns benefactor-beneficiary relationships.

The primary problems with these relationships are located in a different area for *The Analects* than they are for us in the West. We are concerned largely with abuse of power and ways to mitigate that abuse through institutionalized controls, such as a balance of power, oversight committees, and laws. The focus here is on what is being done to me, the individual, and I would describe this as inwardly focused. *The Analects*, in contrast, can be described as an advice book; appropriate action rather than self-protection takes center stage. The question is not how to avoid power, but what is the appropriate use of power. Thus I would say that the focus in *The Analects* is on what I do to others, and I would describe this as outwardly focused.

The Analects can be usefully compared to Epictetus' *Enchiridion*; both explore the actions and attitudes appropriate to achieving particular, albeit different, kinds of life. Appropriate action within benefactor-beneficiary relationships depends upon who I am, those with whom I interact, and the context of our interaction. This is not to say that such action is hopelessly or viciously relative, rather that appropriate action is dependent upon knowledge of complex hierarchies and etiquette. The complexity and contextuality of appropriate action are what make *The Analects* so attractive to me.

So let's try to answer these three questions: "Who am I?" "Who do I interact with?" and "Where does our interaction occur?" First, who am I? To illustrate the different answers to this question, I want to compare two images, a peach and an onion. The Western self is like a peach, soft and fuzzy on the outside, gushy on the inside, with a solid, permanent, unchanging pit at the center, hidden from public view and serving as the core of our being. The pit is the inviolable core of the self, the seat of inalienable rights the immortal soul, and the source of who we are. To know who I am, to find my 'true' self, I need to discover my pit. This often entails wading through, even eliminating all the inessential (read: products of enculturation and socialization) stuff on the outside in order to interrogate the core.

The Confucian self is like an onion, layer upon layer of relationships make me who I am: daughter, sister, teacher, colleague, neighbor, wife, and friend. In playing these roles, and I use the word 'play' in a Wittgensteinian rather than a Milton-Bradley sort of way, a person is established, animated, and brought to life. Who I am is constituted through relationships; take away the relationships, and like pealing away the layers of an onion, nothing remains of me. Thus we can see the consequence of benefactor-beneficiary relationships; they are constitutive of people, and their care and maintenance are of absolute importance.

Who I interact with determines whether I am benefactor or beneficiary, and gives an initial indication of appropriate deportment. I must know with whom I interact if I have any hope of behaving appropriately. Knowing this, however, does not exhaustively determine every aspect of the interaction. The roles of benefactor and beneficiary are not static; a good example of this is the relation between parent and child. The child begins life as a beneficiary and the parent is the benefactor, but often at the end of the parent's life the child has become the benefactor and the parent the beneficiary. Circumstances can quickly lead to the reversal of a seemingly established benefactor-beneficiary relationship.

Thus, I must also know the context of my interaction with another, and be able to harmonize what is appropriate with the variety of things that may occur during our interaction. An example of this in *The Analects* comes from the responses Confucius gives to the same question asked by different students. Three different people ask the same question, what does it mean to be filial? Each one is given a different answer. These answers are not contradictory, rather they are tailored to the needs of the particular student, who Confucius recognizes are on different places along the path of learning. While the relationship is the same, teacher to student, that does not mean that the appropriate response will be the same regardless of the student.

The key, then, to Confucian ethics is learning how to answer the question, "What is the appropriate act for me with respect to this person in this context?" in such a way that harmony between people will be achieved.

Today, as China attempts to re-establish relations, political and cultural, with Hong Kong, Confucian values are back in favor. Editors of Chinese English-language newspapers tend to group stories thematically, so that there is often a message not only in the stories, but in the organization of the stories within the paper. In the October 13th edition of *21st Century*, there are three stories about Confucius and the values of Confucianism. At the top of the page is the headline, "Confucius still China's icon" followed by a story describing a recent celebration of the birthday of 'China's most famous sage,' a brief history of his time, the campaign against him in the 1970's, a student's reaction against a stereotypic misreading of Confucius, and a concern over whether 'Confucius thought' continues to be valuable at the dawn of a new century. The longest article on the page, "Villagers save for house, education," is ostensibly about current policy to increase rural income and spending, but primarily tells the story of a grandmother who lives in a house dug in the side of a hill with her daughter and granddaughter. The grandmother, Song Liying, saves part of her pension, 60 Yuan (approximately $8) per month, for her granddaughter's education. Song Liying and others in her village put off moving to new houses in order to save for the education of their grandchildren. Most savings go to either housing or education, according to the article, rather than consumption.

The third story, only half a column long, concerns Hong Kong's aging population, but with a spin: "Hong Kong losing filial values." While many people have found financial success in the colony, they have not been able to instill the traditional Chinese values of filiality. One man complains that neither his wife, his ten children, nor his eleven grandchildren ever come to visit him. This is an increasing worry for Hong Kong, as its lack of certain social services may leave elderly citizens without means of support, and unable to rely on the traditional safety net: the family. Comparing the treatment of parents and elders on the mainland with Hong Kong, needless to say, the mainland comes out looking better than Hong Kong. We can read several messages in this: first, financial success does not promise happiness and despite Hong Kong's flourishing, life is not perfect, and old people are neglected; second, beware of adopting too much of western culture or your children may abandon you in your old age; third, there is an implied warning to Hong Kong that it better begin to take up some of the older values if its return to China is to continue on its successful course.

Confucianism, like political correctness, can be used as a big stick to beat people with, but also like political correctness, it is not exhausted in this usage. Obviously, there are messages for people living in areas that are coming back to China, but there are also signs of a continuing conversation about the status of Confucius thought. Teachers are worried about its loss; young people wonder what it has to say to them, and about the contradictions between traditional China and the new open China. Of course actually reading *The Analects* may help, although they would have to be translated into modern Chinese, rather than relying on what Mao said about Confucius' thought. My students, many of whom were reading Confucius for the first time and in English, were surprised by what they found there. It is too early to know what Confucius' thought might bring to China in the next century.

To return to my main point, my worry in developing an understanding of China is how to strike a balance among the totalitarian China our press and government suggest is such a threat to our continued well being, the particularities of Chinese communism which has led the country to take a road very different from Soviet communism, and the illustration of the unflappable Chinese citizen who simply takes every change in stride, seamlessly integrating conflicting aspects of her or his own culture as well as those of our own.

While this may seem contradictory to you, my suspicions drive me to make what seems familiar about China strange and make what is strange about China a bit more familiar. Why make the familiar strange? First, the China we know through the U.S. press corps is filtered through the lens of U.S. foreign policy. The idea that we have now, or have ever had an objective press, is mere fantasy.

Second, what most scholars give us through translations and scholarship is filtered, often all too unreflectively, through the presuppositions of western reason with its particular culturally biased priorities and methodologies. This is our legacy, for better and for worse. It has given us great things like television, space shuttles, Wall Street, and personal computers. But it also has limits which tend to flash like a neon sign when it comes to force a different way of thinking and being in the world through the gears of western reason. We have to use it, but we must also be cognizant of the damage it can do, of the misreadings it can produce, and the ethnocentrism it can lead to.

For these two reasons, I think we are best served when we take what we know of China—and any foreign country, culture, or idea—with a grain of salt. This does not mean that we must disregard what we know, but it does mean that we have a responsibility to reflect on sources, hidden agendas, unrecognized agendas, unintentional agendas, and any other bias on the part of the presenter or ourselves that could make us overlook significant factors in our drive to understand. As I often warn my students about the internet, if we are looking for the full story, access to all of this information only increases our responsibility to know who is saying what and why.

Why make the strange familiar?

First, it is too easy to say "This is completely different from me and my experiences, it is too 'other,' I will never really understand it, so I don't have to consider it." Because the language and the culture are so different, we may want to say that our experience, language, knowledge, and way of knowing are incommensurable with that of the Chinese. This would mean that there is no common standard of comparison, or no way to compare the two, and might lead us to the conclusion that the two are not worthy of comparison. If we do this with China, on any level, we will end up like ostriches with our heads in the sand and our rear ends up in the air waiting to get smacked. China is difficult, but we cannot justify turning away from the hard work of coming to terms with China by saying it is too different. While there may be a point at which our understanding fails, incommensurability in this case is not absolute, but perhaps a matter of degree.

Second, China does not see itself the way we see it. China's view of China is much more like the United States' view of the United States. As a country, China remains closed to much foreign travel, and its leaders are hostile to our leaders, and our way of life. China's name for China is 'Middle Kingdom:' they think themselves at the center of the world, and as superior to anyone with the bad fortune of having been born elsewhere. It is easy to think that if the Chinese are not going to meet us halfway, if they are going to run around doing the superior dance waiting for the rest of the world to come to them, forget it. The U.S. has been in the role of a superpower for about two generations now, and we have been THE superpower since the fall of the Soviet Union; thus when we find another country whose ego is as big as our own we get a bit defensive. China, for all of its problems, has the history, the culture (regardless of the last fifty years), the military, and the nuclear capability to back up their national pride. China has proven very difficult to manipulate with either the carrot of foreign aid and trade relations, or the stick of our military might. Our two countries can act like schoolyard bullies who refuse to talk to each other, circling and flexing, insulting each other's mothers, and talking big about whose dad can kick the other's butt, but I don't think this will get us very far. It might be far more useful to understand what China thinks about itself and why.

For these two reasons, I think we have to strive harder and harder to understand China, both through our own western lenses, but also try to see things from a Chinese point of view.

Let me give you an example of what I mean, using another topic that's been in the news lately. I'm sure we have all been feeling the hike in gas prices. I've heard much commentary about how the evil oil producing nations are holding the U.S. consumer hostage, how dare they try to do this to us, etc., etc. And perhaps, from a very narrow, nationalistic standpoint that is an accurate response. However, consider it from the standpoint of an oil producing nation such as Saudi Arabia, who has borrowed a great deal of money in the last few years and is trying to pay down their national debt (as we have) by increasing the price of the primary natural resource they have in their country. If we apply to them the same values we apply to our own economy— specifically, our intolerance for those who want to tell us what we should charge for any of the goods we produce—it seems like the Saudis have every right to price their goods any way they want. They are acting like the sovereign nation they are, and they have problems far beyond what the gas hike means to you and me. Through a U.S. lens, it is easy to say 'poor me.' Through a Saudi lens, we have to acknowledge the actions of a nation attempting to responsibly plan for its own future.

This does not mean we have to agree with the policies and the positions of the Chinese government, but that we have a responsibility to strive to understand the context within which their decisions are made. We can do this only if we understand Chinese history, values, and culture. We will never understand it like someone raised and enculturated in it, but we can come to see that there are different interpretations of international events, and that the U.S. does not necessarily always hold the moral high ground.

So, it should be clear at this point that my goal in making the familiar strange and the strange familiar is a better understanding and appreciation of China. For the rest of my presentation I want to look at similarities between people in the U.S. and China, but from an odd or unexpected direction. I will talk about how we share with Chinese people some of our more unattractive traits, and suggest that one possible mode of mutual understanding may come through the philosophical school of pragmatism.

First, a look at our shared unattractive traits. I mentioned earlier that what the Chinese call their own country, *Zhong Guo*, means 'Middle Kingdom.' In this usage, 'middle' takes on the connotations of 'center' thus leading to the Chinese perception of themselves at the center of the world. Foreigners will not be asked if they speak Chinese, but simply if they speak. Chinese national pride, as contradictory as it may seem to us based on the level of economic development and quality of life compared to our own, leads to a feeling of superiority over anyone who has suffered the bad fortune of having been born outside of China.

Our own national mythology is based upon the Judeo-Christian call to be an example to others. There is a Bible story that calls upon followers to shine the light of their righteousness from the top of a hill for all to see, rather than hiding it under a bushel where no one can see it. America, the new world, was to serve this same purpose: this newly formed country would provide an example to others of how to create a fair government where all could participate on an equal footing, where moral values would be upheld, and a good life could be earned by the sweat of one's brow rather than acquired through the inheritance of one's family. The idea that earning one's own living was a good and moral thing to do is a product of the 'American Experience;' prior to that, working was seen as an ignoble way to live one's life. To have to toil for daily necessities made impossible things like the pursuit of knowledge and the appreciation of art. Much of our foreign policy has been, however loosely, based on this general sense of serving as an example to the world and has directed our attempts to make other countries embrace our form of democracy and capitalism. Rather than recognizing the hubris in our own sense of superiority we have been driven by our desire to make others over in our own likeness, encouraging them to aspire to our own unsustainable 'high standard of living' and the waste of resources that goes along with it.

So while we share a similarly inflated sense of our own worth, China and the U.S. have acted upon it differently. While we have been working to bring converts into the fold, the Chinese have remained more insular, preferring to improve their own situation and deal with their own problems rather than sticking their noses into everyone else's affairs.[2] In other ways, we have acted upon it in a similar fashion. Racism and class biases are problems in both our countries. If you think that race is not a problem in our own country, I will refer you back to the ostrich example, and encourage you to pull your head out. We have spent 150 years inadequately dealing with the problem of race, and like our overuse of natural resources, we must acknowledge the fact that many of us enjoy privileges received unfairly, and to truly live according to our values we must be willing to forgo those privileges.

Joanna Crosby

In China, it is the Han majority who have discriminated against Chinese ethnic minorities. Let me give you an example from my own experience. I ate regularly at a noodle restaurant operated by a family who were Muslim, a recognized minority in China. An Australian teacher had brought her 12-year-old daughter, Josey, with her for a year in China. Josey and I ate *la mien* three to four times a week and had made friends with the young men who worked there, teaching them phrases like 'welcome' and 'come again.' Josey was attending the Chinese elementary school on the University campus and had made friends with several girls in her class. One afternoon, two of them joined us for a meal of *la mien*. These two girls were perfect examples of the Chinese ideals of beauty: round faces, jet-black hair, smooth skin. Even at the ages of ten and eleven, they carried themselves with the poise and confidence of children who hadn't faced much relative hardship in their lives. (The one child rule has produced many spoilt little princes and princesses.) When our favorite young man who always had a huge smile for us came over to take our order, one of Josey's friends put on an air of superiority and refused to talk to the young man.

Now, you might argue that this was merely a young girl reacting to an older boy whom she did not know, and certainly Chinese culture frowns upon interaction between boys and girls, particularly if they don't know each other. (Cultural inhibition is instilled as part of the one child rule.) I should tell you: I went to China with all of my liberal values, a good bit of anthropological theory, reading in precommunist Chinese history, a sense of Chinese etiquette, and accounts of how the cultural revolution called for the elimination of etiquette. I was determined to try to simply be in the difference that was China. I vowed that to the best of my ability, I would not project my values onto a foreign culture and expect them to conform. I applied the principle of charity to interactions and interpreting what I saw in the most favorable light. Most importantly, I often was in the company of native speakers who expressed their dismay at certain behaviors or explained to me what was being said and the larger social context. What startled me was that I could correctly intuit some tones of voice and some behaviors, particularly when it came to discrimination based on class or race. Communism has not worked to make everyone equal; rather, leaders merely assert that they have established a classless society, that the genders are treated equally, and that racism is not a problem. It's not so much that racism has been eliminated, but that the Han sense of superiority has yet to acknowledge that there is a problem to be solved.

So how did the situation resolve itself? I told the girl that the young man was our friend and that she should be nice to him. Josey, whose Chinese is far superior to mine asked her why she didn't want to talk to him. She replied that he was Muslim and she was afraid of him. Perhaps it was the fact that Josey and I were friendly to him, but the girl politely told the young man what she wanted and we proceeded to have a nice meal.

Another, briefer example: one of my students, her English name was "Cindy," was dating a young man from Cameroon. She came to my apartment one afternoon in December, almost in tears, and told me about the scene her father would make if he knew, and the ostracism she felt at the hands of her classmates, whom I had observed treated her rather coolly. Many students, male with male and female with female, walked around campus with their arms around each other, but I had never seen Cindy included in this behavior. Cindy felt their discrimination as well as incredulity towards their racism. She didn't know what would happen with the relationship: although she said she loved the young man, she had a sense of the relationship's inevitable end. What I came to learn through experiences like these is that we are both a prejudiced people, even though our stated values call us to refrain from bigotry.[3]

The last commonality I will address is not necessarily good or bad, but certainly curious, and a potential point of understanding between us. Last fall, while I was in China, I was working on a book review of *Democracy of the Dead: Dewey, Confucius, and the Hope for Democracy in China* by David Hall and Roger Ames.[4] My work in pragmatism has concerned another seminal figure in that field, William James, and I was happy to have the opportunity to read about John Dewey, his travels to China, and how his conception of a democracy, freed from the constraints of compulsory capitalism and the legacy of people like Locke and Hobbes, provides an alternative model more suited to the traditional values of China.

As I watched people in China, to my surprise, I discovered that we are both pragmatic people. This is not to say that everyone in either culture is solely and completely practical; rather that there is an underlying concern with making things work in everyday activities that can be characterized as pragmatic. In the U.S., to speak in broad generalizations, this stems from a combination of Protestant work ethic and the trade companies that financed our initial colonization; at the heart of the U.S. is a drive to *do* and evaluate according to what that doing brings; thus our tendency to workaholism, and our emphasis on the bottom line. For the Chinese, the pragmatic spirit is a new development, and one I think can be linked to the Cultural Revolution. Historically, Chinese culture emphasized the aesthetic over either the theoretical or the practical. In fact, I think that the aesthetic was a particularly elegant way to bring together why one acts with how one acts. In post-cultural revolution China it seems to me, admittedly still a bit of a novice in this field, that many have responded to the ever-changing domestic policies by retreating to a kind of pragmatism; thus the focus moves from why one does what one does—in fact that becomes a very dangerous question—to simply doing.

In the U.S., this focus on practice is explored in the philosophical school of pragmatism, which was developed by Charles Peirce, William James, and John Dewey at the end of the last century and the beginning of this one. Now, to both its benefit and detriment, pragmatism comes in many different shapes and sizes. Peirce initiated pragmatism as a method that could be applied to intellectual problems and James developed it into a philosophical system, bringing pragmatism to theories of ethics, truth, and religious belief. Pragmatism can be crudely described as a kind of consequentialism: in other words, the significance of a theory or idea comes from what happens when it is brought into practice. How does the theory affect how we act? In this way, pragmatism rejects much of traditional philosophy whose focus is exclusively on theory and is often dismissive or unconcerned with what people actually do.

For James, pragmatism becomes an evaluative tool; theories are evaluated on the difference they make in practice—do they actually produce different practices? He says that if two different theories do not produce a difference in practice, then the difference between them is insignificant. For

Joanna Crosby

James, what is good and what is true is what works; and of course this will differ depending on the system. What works in one won't necessarily work in another. What it means to 'work' is contextual; the evaluation of whether a theory works depends upon the goals and values of a particular system and how the theory and the practices it entails makes progress toward achieving those goals and sustains those values. Pragmatism doesn't provide one with goals or values. In other words, it doesn't tell you where you should want to be, but rather its purpose is to help one get to that pre-established goal through the use of pre-established values. Pragmatism is essentially a form of instrumental reason.[5]

Okay, an example: in the U.S. we have foundational documents (constitution, declaration of independence, federalist papers) that lay out certain goals and values, *viz.*, life, liberty, the pursuit of happiness, democratically elected leaders, separation of church and state, and equality among all people, regardless of race, religion, or gender. If we take policy to represent a theory that is meant to be put into practice, we can imagine a discussion over two policies and how they would work to bring us closer to our goals and sustain our values. So imagine that the discussion is over affirmative action and that one of the policies includes the use of quotas, the other does not. The question a pragmatist will not ask is whether we are justified on principle (read: theory) to include or exclude quotas; the question a pragmatist will ask is what difference it will make in practice: Will the inclusion of quotas increase equality among people, or extend the pursuit of happiness? Will we achieve those goals faster and more effectively? Will quotas work? Of course, arguments can be made on either side of this controversial issue. The pragmatist would require those arguments to address issues concerning practice and effects on practice. The pragmatist would pay less attention to arguments about the inherent fairness of quotas, or lack thereof, favoring instead arguments about how quotas might bring people into jobs from which they had been excluded, or how quotas might create a system of greater inequality.

Another example: I assumed when I went to China that their communist economic system would produce an atmosphere very different from the U.S. capitalist economic system. I assumed that these two different theories would produce very different practices. Well, let me tell you; at least from the perspective of a consumer, there is very little difference. Everything is for sale in China, from Pantene to Pringles, peanut butter to Diet Coke, and even better, if you don't like the price, you can bargain! Except for some western food products in the grocery store, like spices and seasonings, or pretzels and lunchmeat, you can find anything you need and almost everything you want. I would assume that the process of setting up a business, getting permits and the like is different, but from the point of view of a consumer, pragmatically, there is no significant difference between U.S. capitalism and Chinese communism.

I want to emphasize again, though, that pragmatism is a tool for the evaluation of practices based on pre-established goals and values. Pragmatism will not identify which values are better, and which goals we should be working towards. While the Chinese may be in a position to appreciate pragmatism, this is where I think pragmatism, as James conceives it, falls short of fulfilling the current needs of Chinese culture. China is in a transitional period; the economy continues to become more capitalistic and more global (for better or worse) but this has left more people destitute and even begging on the streets (which you won't necessarily see in Shanghai or Beijing, but you will see in cities with less tourist trade). Everything is for sale in China, at every level of the economic spectrum, from the street vendor to the fancy department store, but not every one is reaping the benefits of consumer capitalism. China needs to continue discussion about how to reconcile the values and practices of communism with those of private ownership and individual profit making before pragmatism can play a significant role.

Hall and Ames, though, don't address James, but focus on Dewey who expanded pragmatism further than James, proposing alternative forms of education and democracy he thought were more effective because of their emphasis on practice rather than just theory. Hall and Ames argue, I think rightly, that Dewey's formulation of a democracy based on a 'communicating community' is more suitable to China's history, traditional (Confucian) values, and current needs than what they call 'liberal democracy' which is predicated on the Western conception of an autonomous individual and the rights accorded to that individual, all of which are contrary to the Chinese experience. The emphasis on democracy for the good of the community, and the recognition that capitalism may be more of a stumbling block to democracy rather than its facilitator, lend weight to the authors' claims that Dewey has a role to play in transforming both what China thinks of democracy and what we think of China.

Complicating the work engaging the Chinese is increasing globalization, a nice way to say "encroaching westernization." As the Chinese work to resolve traditional, communist, and western values, Western culture rushes to fill the void left by the cultural revolution. One shop I saw epitomized this situation. Two big posters were positioned outside the shop's door, sampling what could be found inside. The first poster was an idealized picture of a young, trim, passionate Mao Tse-Dung; above it was the familiar face of Michael Jordan.

At Hubei University I taught a class called "Language and Culture" to fifty students, in whom I saw firsthand the conflict between old and new values. They recognized the importance of caring for their parents and doing their filial duty, but they also expressed familiar frustrations about meddling parents and parental encroachment on their increasing social freedom. In a way very similar to how we might repeat the dogma of democracy and capitalism, my students would repeat the dogma of communism, acknowledging the difficulty they may have getting a job, yet equally aware of the significant scientific and cultural advances made by pre-communist China. When asked to describe their values, they talked about how duty to parents and to the community had priority over the desires and impulses of the individual, but thought of Confucianism as primarily theoretical and detached from everyday life. When I gave them readings from *The Analects*, which only one or two had ever read, they were quite surprised to find very little theory and much practical advice.

In a certain way, Chinese high school and college students are much like their U.S. counterparts in the 1950's when the word 'teenager' came into popularity and the market began to recognize them as a powerful consumer group. They retain an innocence and an openness that Chinese in their 30's and older lost long ago. My students dressed in western clothing; Levi, Tommy Hilfiger, Nike, Adidas, and Calvin Klein were all familiar names. They preferred blue jeans and khakis, vaguely 70's looking shirts and sweaters, platform tennis shoes, short skirts and dresses, expressing a definite sense of fashion, including the often totalitarian rules that come with fashion. Most were so conscious of these rules that they refused to wear hats or bulky coats when the weather got cold because such clothing was not cool. Cell phones are rampant in China, as it can take up to six months to have a phone installed in your home. Some students also have beepers that can tell them the weather, give them sports scores, and news headlines. Internet access is increasing, somewhat slow, but very inexpensive; you can spend an hour surfing the web for about sixty cents.

On the streets, the influence of U.S. pop music and movies is impossible to ignore. Chinese music videos could have come straight off MTV, VH-1, the Box, or BET; they are slick, colorful, and make full use of the available video technology. Many clothing and music stores have huge speakers on the street blaring the latest songs, both Chinese and western. I think this is meant to attract shoppers, but it just made me wish for earplugs. In the music stores, you can also purchase VCDs, or video CDs, of western movies—often the ones that have just been theatrically released in the U.S. These are like DVDs, only the resolution is not so good; they are often pirated from DVDs or screener videos that go out to distributors, or the result of someone in a movie theater with a camcorder. They can be rented for about a dime, or purchased for under two dollars. I taught a class on western movies while I was there, and I was concerned about the level of violence in many of our movies and the effect it might have on an audience not used to it. I quickly discovered that this was not an issue.

Pragmatism and the Future of Confucianism in China

Between these movies and what the Chinese government says about us, my students have some odd conceptions of what we are like. These include stereotypes about violence, neglect of parents, the use of profanity, lack of community responsibility, and a general self-centered and self-indulgent attitude. On the one hand, this suggests that Chinese consume media in a way very similar to their Western counterparts. On the other hand, the work of building understanding and empathy between people in China and the U.S. is that much more difficult.

What we as a nation need to be more cognizant of and take some responsibility for is the replacement of Chinese culture with western culture. It's not that I want to deprive the Chinese people of Nike and Levi, Michael Jordan and Celine Dion, but it is important that we do what we can in our trade policies to not have our cultural icons act like kudzu, a kind of ivy that is taking over the south, pushing out native species of plants and trees. In four major cities I tried to find a Chinese doll for my mother-in-law, only to be told time and again by shop owners that Chinese dolls were ugly, and that blonde, blue-eyed dolls in western dresses were beautiful. The only shops that carried Chinese dolls were state owned 'Friendship Stores,' patronized almost exclusively by foreigners. It's not just Chinese culture that will be diminished if traditional Chinese arts, such as paper cutting, embroidery, or mask painting are replaced with fast food, video games, and channel surfing.

The coming century is said to be the Chinese century, and understanding China beyond the official propaganda of either Chinese or U.S. origin is becoming paramount. We need to know what Confucianism can do to mitigate the excesses of western culture, and we also need to explore what we may be able to offer to the Chinese to assist them in thinking through their issues. This may include a post- or non-Marxist account of Confucianism, as well as the Pragmatism of people like James and Dewey.

China is different from the U.S. I suggest we want to keep it different—not to deny the Chinese things like good living conditions, adequate food supply, equality before the law, environmental safety, as well as consumer goods—but not to demand that in modernizing they further lose the vast and wonderful cultural heritage that is threatened by increasing globalization.

NOTES

[1] Roger Ames and Henry Rosemont, Jr., translators, *The Analects of Confucius: A Philosophical Translation*. NY: Ballantine Books, 1998.

[2] Taiwan, Macao, Hong Kong, and Tibet are not signs of Chinese expansionism, but rather a desire on the part of the Chinese to re-establish what the government sees as its historical boundaries. Of course, the methods the government takes to achieve its ends and the results achieved are sites of ongoing controversy.

[3] In the discussion following the paper, it was suggested that Chinese policy in Tibet could be another example of Chinese racism. In the West, we see this as an invasion and oppressive occupation, as a blemish on the Chinese government, and a move indicative of Chinese disregard for individual rights. The Chinese see it as liberation on several levels—from a mystical and unscientific religion, from medieval feudalism, and from mismanagement of domestic resources. While I do know that the Chinese presence in Tibet resembles the worst aspects of English colonialism, I do not know enough about the Chinese treatment of the Tibetan people to say that the former's treatment of the later is based on racism. It is difficult for me to separate the events in Tibet from the passionate response of people in the U.S. to those events and to way the Dalai Lama has been unquestioningly and uncritically embraced. I wonder if Buddhism were not so popular, would our rhetoric be less shrill and would the complexities of the situation become more clear. I do not want to suggest that the Chinese are above criticism, merely that the story may not be as simple as we are led to believe.

[4] David Hall and Roger Ames, *Democracy of the Dead: Dewey, Confucius, and the Hope for Democracy in China*. Chicago: Open Court, 2000.

[5] For a more extensive look at James' views see William James, *Pragmatism*. Bruce Kuklick, editor. Indianapolis: Hackett, 1981.

REFERENCES

Ames, Roger and Henry Rosemont, Jr., translators. *The Analects of Confucius: A Philosophical Translation.* New York: Ballantine Books, 1998.

Hall, David and Roger Ames. *Democracy of the Dead: Dewey, Confucius, and the Hope for Democracy in China.* Chicago: Open Court, 2000.

James, William. *Pragmatism.* Ed. Bruce Kuklick. Indianapolis: Hackett, 1981.

WHOSE DEMOCRACY? WHICH RIGHTS? A CONFUCIAN CRITIQUE OF MODERN WESTERN LIBERALISM

Henry Rosemont, Jr.
St. Mary's College of Maryland

In the spirit of inter-cultural dialogue, this essay examines concepts of democracy and human rights through a series of lenses, including those of Classical Confucianism as well as ones more commonly associated with the Western intellectual tradition. Despite its apparent success and economic dominance, it is argued that the Western tradition is fundamentally flawed. The concept of human rights, even when buttressed with ideas like liberty, autonomy, and individualism, does not capture what it is to be a human being. At best, the Western approach vouchsafes first generation rights but falters in its attempt to take the next step, to second generation rights. If we are serious about moving beyond the limitations of Modern Western Liberalism we will do well to listen carefully to Classical Confucianism, which does not regard our most basic rights as civil or political, grounded in the view that we are autonomous individuals, but rather as natural consequences of our membership in a community, with each member assuming a measure of responsibility for the welfare of all other members.

Introduction

One of the major reasons for engaging in comparative philosophical research is to make a small contribution to the inter-cultural dialogues that are becoming a more prominent part of international affairs, especially those dialogues which take up basic human issues such as democracy, human rights and global justice; with the ultimate goal of these dialogues being to increase the probability that the 6+ billion human citizens of the global community will live more peaceably with one another in the twenty-first century than they did in the twentieth.

If this ultimate goal is to be realized it is essential that the dialogues be genuine dialogues, with give and take, and with all sides being willing to entertain seriously the possibility that their own moral and political theories might not capture the essence of what it is to be a human being.[1] The necessity of the dialogues being genuine is of especial importance to citizens of the United States, for it is clearly the most powerful voice in virtually every international gathering; the World Court would be a far more effective institution if the U.S. would agree to abide by its decisions, our oceans much more ecologically sound if it would sign the Law of the Sea, and the world safer if it would agree to the Comprehensive Test Ban Treaty it urges other nations to ratify. But if the U.S. is to become more internationally responsible, its regnant ideology must be challenged. We certainly have a monopoly on power, but once the political rhetoric is seen for what it is, it is by no means clear that we occupy a similar position with respect to concepts of truth, beauty, justice or the good.

The regnant ideology I wish to challenge may be loosely but usefully referred to as "modern Western liberalism," meaning by the expression support for a partial welfare state so long as it does not conflict with the basic concern of classical liberalism, namely, to protect individual freedom against the power of the state.[2] But challenges will come to naught if they are based on premises or presuppositions that are either factually mistaken, or embody basic values that modern liberalism finds abhorrent. Thus it will do no good to defend, for example, female genital circumcision solely on the grounds that it is embedded in a culture different from the West's but with its own integrity, and hence should be left alone to evolve in accordance with its own dynamics. Similarly, Western liberals—and many others—are rightfully sceptical of arguments that a particular people aren't ready for democracy yet, or that rights are a luxury the peoples of poor nations cannot afford. I wish, in other words, to question the conceptual framework of liberalism, but at the same time believe that those who accept the framework nevertheless have moral instincts that closely approximate my own.

To be at all useful then, a challenge to modern Western liberalism will have to show that certain values central to the Western intellectual tradition cannot be realized so long as other values championed by modern liberalism dominate our moral and political discourse, and that a rival tradition—in the present case, classical Confucianism—is superior to liberalism in this regard.

It is for this reason that I have entitled my paper to signal an indebtedness to the writings of Alasdair MacIntyre.[3] MacIntyre is, of course, as deeply suspicious of modern Western liberalism as I am. He is usually portrayed as an arch-conservative, fully committed to a modern version of Aristotelian Thomism. But he is not a relativist—pragmatic or otherwise—and unlike the great majority of "liberal" philosophers and political theorists, he takes Confucianism seriously as a genuine rival moral tradition.[4] Perhaps most important, he has argued well that incommensurable discourses between rival traditions can be made commensurable if certain conditions are met, and thus genuine dialogue can indeed take place. In his own words:[5]

> ... [T]he only way to approach a point at which our own [moral] standpoint could be vindicated against

some rival is to understand our own standpoint in a way that renders it from our own point of view as problematic as possible and therefore as maximally vulnerable as possible to defeat by that rival. We can only learn what intellectual and moral resources our own standpoint, our own tradition of theoretical and practical inquiry possesses, as well as what intellectual and moral resources its rivals may possess, when we have understood our own point of view in a way that takes with full seriousness the possibility that we may in the end, as rational beings, have to abandon that point of view. This admission of fallibilism need not entail any present lack of certitude, but it is a condition of worthwhile conversation with equally certain antagonists.

Most philosophical conversations of this kind, because of historical determinants, are being conducted in English, as are the great majority of the intercultural dialogues on human rights, democracy, and justice. This linguistic hegemony, if such it is, is not merely owing to the economic and military superiority of the West, for which English is now the *lingua franca*. It is deeply embedded in, and has established the agenda for the intercultural dialogues themselves. There are no traditional close semantic equivalents for "democracy," "justice," or "rights" in most of the world's languages; these are Western. The former two have their origins in Greek *demos* and *dike*, and "rights" we owe largely to the writings of John Locke, with conceptual roots that may go back to the *sokes* and *sakes* of late medieval England, and perhaps earlier.[6]

Thus, if we are to follow MacIntyre methodologically, we must allow the other their otherness, and, without in any way surrendering rationality, nevertheless allow for the possibility that not only don't we have all the answers, we may not have been asking all the questions in as universal a vocabulary as has hitherto been presupposed. Specifically for the early Confucians, there are, in addition to "rights," "democracy," and "justice," no analogous lexical items for most of the modern Western basic vocabulary for developing moral and political theories: "autonomy," "freedom," "liberty," "subjective," "objective," "individual," "rational," "choice," "private," "public," "dilemma," and—perhaps most eerie of all for a modern Western moral theorist—no term corresponding to English "ought," prudential or obligatory.[7] Thus the comparativist must be especially sensitive to the choice of terms employed in dialogue, so as not to beg the questions, for or against, the views under analysis and evaluation.

Another narrative difficulty facing the comparative philosopher is that the hypothetico-deductive, adversarial style of discourse common in Western analytic philosophical work is not found in most non-Western philosophical writings (which is why a great many analytically-trained Western philosophers do not take the non-Western writings seriously).

Still another narrative difficulty facing comparativists is that the texts they study do not as tidily separate metaphysical, moral, religious, political and aesthetic human concerns as do their Western counterparts. This problem is painfully acute for a student of classical Confucianism for, as I shall be suggesting in some of the pages to follow, much of the persuasiveness of the Confucian vision lies in its *integration* of these basic human concerns, rather than seeing them as disparate spheres of human life. But in order to make such a case, I cannot take up each of these areas in the depth they deserve, and as they are treated in specialized journals, without this essay becoming much longer than the entire anthology of which it is supposed to be only a small part.

Whose Democracy? Which Rights?

A final narrative difficulty facing (at least) the classical Chinese comparativist is that in the texts more purely philosophical statements are closely interwoven with judgements about current events in the lives of the writers, a style I shall follow, even though it is altogether alien to the modern Western philosophical tradition of discourse. (How much of the horror of the Thirty Years' War is discernible in Descartes' *Meditations*?)[8]

As a consequence of all of these methodological difficulties attendant on engaging in comparative philosophical dialogue, comparativists must steer between the Scylla of distorting the views, and the manner in which those views are presented, in the non-Western texts they study and the Charybdis of making those views, and the manner in which they are presented, appear to be no more than a socio-political screed, and/or philosophically naive to the analytically trained Western philosopher. All of the above is perhaps no more than to say that what follows is Confucian in narrative flavor (I think), but for all that, rational (I hope). My focus will be on the concept of what it is to be a human being, with special reference to human rights, and, to a lesser extent, to democracy. Current events loom large in my narration. I will employ the technical philosophical vocabulary of contemporary English as little as possible, and will run together the aesthetic, the political, the moral, and the spiritual in using a hurried sketch of the early Confucian vision to challenge modern Western liberalism in its variant philosophical guises, the challenge itself occupying center stage throughout.

Conceptual Background

Although the scholarly study of Confucianism in the West looks very different today than when it began with the first

Jesuit mission to China, at least one feature of those studies has remained constant: Western investigators have sought similarities and differences between Confucian principles and those principles embedded in their own Western conceptual framework.

Originally that framework was Christianity, and beginning with Father Ricci, running through Leibniz, and even extending in some circles to the present, many scholars have declared Confucianism—in either its classical or Song formulations, or both—to be compatible with basic Christian principles and beliefs.[9] Other scholars, beginning with Ricci's successor Nicolo Longobardi, running through Malebranche, and again, even extending to the present, found Confucian principles and beliefs sufficiently un-Christian to necessitate their rejection as a precondition for conversion.[10] But however much these two groups differed in their analyses and evaluations, they shared the same presupposition, namely, that the fundamental principles and beliefs of Christianity were universal, and, therefore, binding on all peoples.

To be sure, not all Christians agreed on what the fundamental principles and beliefs of their faith were, or ought to be; there was much room for theological and metaphysical debate. But at least a few beliefs were indeed fundamental, paramount among them being the Passion of Christ—from which much else of Christianity follows.

A somewhat different conceptual framework is employed by contemporary students of Confucianism. Most western scholars—and not a few Chinese—now seek similarities and differences between Confucian moral and political principles and beliefs and those embedded in a conceptual framework that clusters around the concepts of democracy and human rights. While Christian concerns may still underlie some research, they no longer have pride of place in the great bulk of comparative studies.[11]

This change has been significant, and it is equally significant, I believe, that many scholars have argued cogently that much of Confucianism is compatible with the modern Western moral and political principles and beliefs centered in the concept of human rights, and democracy.[12]

What has not changed, however (or so it seems to me), is that almost all contemporary scholars share a common presupposition, in this case the presupposition that the rights-based Western conceptual framework is universal, and therefore binding on all peoples.

To be sure, within this conceptual framework of rights, there is room for legitimate disagreement (just as in the framework of Christianity). For those who embrace deontological moral and political theories, especially of a Kantian sort, rights are absolutely central; whereas for most consequentialists, they are more adjunctive. But again, some things are fundamental, paramount among them being that human beings are, or ought to be, seen as free, autonomous individuals. If, for Matteo Ricci and his colleagues, the rejection of the Passion of Christ was tantamount to turning the world over to the Devil, so today the rejection of the free, autonomous individual seems tantamount to turning the world over to repressive governments and other terrorist organizations. But just as one can be skeptical of Christian theology without endorsing Old Scratch, so too, I believe, one can be skeptical of a rights-based conceptual framework, and a uniquely American notion of democracy, without giving any aid or comfort to the Husseins, Milosevics, or Li Pengs of this world.

In other writings, I have taken into account differences between rights theorists on such issues as natural rights, absolute rights, rights as "trumps," defeasible rights, and so forth, but herein want to concentrate on what binds them together (and binds them as well to most social scientists, especially economists): the vision of human beings as free, autonomous individuals, rational and self-interested.[13]

For myself, the study of classical Confucianism has suggested that rights-oriented moral and political theories based on this vision are flawed, and that a different vocabulary for moral and political discourse is needed. The concept of human rights, and related concepts clustered around it like liberty, the individual, property, autonomy, freedom, reason, choice, and so on, do not capture what it is we believe to be a human being; they have served to obscure the wrongness of the radical maldistribution of the world's wealth—both intra- and internationally—and even more fundamentally, they cannot, I believe, be employed to produce a coherent and consistent theory, much less a theory that is in accord with our basic moral intuitions, intuitions that have been obscured by concepts such as "human rights" and "democracy" as these have been defined for us in the contemporary capitalist West. Other definitions are possible.

Whose Democracy?

The basic moral ideal that underlies our espousal of democracy is, I suggest, that all rational human beings should have a significant and equal voice in arriving at decisions that directly affect their own lives.[14] This is indeed an ideal, for it does not seem to ever have been realized even approximately in any nation-state, with the possible exception of Catalonia for a few months in early 1937 before the

Whose Democracy? Which Rights?

Communists and the Falange combined to crush the anarchist cooperatives established there.[15]

If this be granted, it follows that all ostensible democracies are flawed, and consequently must be evaluated along a continuum of more or less. A basic criterion used in the evaluation will of course be how much freedom any government grants its citizens. By this criterion the so-called "democratic republics" of Vietnam, North Korea, and the Congo fare very poorly, and the United States ranks high.

But while a healthy measure of freedom is necessary for considering a state democratic, it cannot be sufficient. By many standards, the citizens of the U.S. enjoy a very large amount of freedom. But an increasing majority of those citizens have virtually no control over the impersonal forces—economic and otherwise—that directly affect their lives, and they are becoming increasingly apolitical. They have a sense of powerlessness, with good reason: democracy has been pretty much reduced to the ritual of going to the democracy temples once every four years to pull a lever for Tweedledee or Tweedledum, cynically expressed in the saying, "If voting could really change things, the government would make it illegal."[16]

My point here, however, is not simply to criticize the U.S. for the present sorry state of democracy within its borders. Rather is the criticism based on the slow evolution of the democratic ideal since 1789. The United States has always been a flawed democracy—slavery, institutionalized racism, lack of women's suffrage, etc.—but it was a fledgling democracy at least; most white males had some voice in political decisions that directly affected their lives. And of course democracy developed: slavery was abolished, women got the vote, and institutional racism was dismantled. Most of these evolutionary changes did not, however, come about by voting; slavery was effectively abolished on the battlefields of Shiloh, Antietam, and Gettysburg, not at the ballot box, and it was the courts that initiated the breakdown of the institutional racism it had earlier strengthened when Dred Scott and Plessy *vs.* Ferguson were replaced by Brown *vs.* Board of Education. And the rights of women, and all working people (now being lost), were obtained by their own militant organizing efforts.[17]

Given then that the U.S. form of democratic government has been in existence for over two hundred years, how much has been accomplished toward realizing the democratic ideal? That is to say, another criterion we must employ in evaluating nation-states with respect to democracy is the extent to which they nourish those qualities of character that enable their citizens to be self-governing, and sustain those institutions intermediate between the individual and the state—schools, local government, churches, unions, etc.—which are necessary for self-government to be effective, and hence for democracy to flourish.[18]

By these lights, the United States may well not be evaluated as at the higher end of the democratic scale, as the modern liberal tradition would have it. To see this point another way, let us contrast the U.S. with a very different contemporary state.

Malaysia's Prime Minister, Mahathir Mohamad, along with Singapore's Lee Kuan Yew, are usually portrayed in the West as advocating "Asian Authoritarianism"—more or less Confucian inspired—as against the liberal democratic tradition of the West. And Mahathir surely has been vocal in criticizing Western social, economic, and political institutions, as has Lee. But then what are we to make of Mahathir's "Asian Authoritarianism" when he says:[19]

Whose Democracy? Which Rights?

> When Malaya became independent in 1957, our per capita income was lower than that of Haiti. Haiti did not take the path of democracy. We did. Haiti today is the poorest country in all the Americas. We now have a standard of living higher than any major economy in the Americas, save only the United States and Canada.
>
> We could not have achieved what we have achieved without democracy.

Moreover, Mahathir has publicly criticized China for its policies on Tibet, the Indonesian government for its atrocities in East Timor, and the Burmese generals for their ill-treatment of Muslims; and of course there are contested elections in Malaysia: the opposition party Pas currently governs two provinces.[20] What, then, might "Asian Authoritarianism" mean, other than as a shibboleth?

If we assume that Mahathir was sincere in his statement, then we might see the policies of his "National Front" government as designed to foster self-government, and to foster many basic human rights as well. Malaysia—like Singapore and many other nation-states rich and poor—is multi-ethnic, and the avowed goal of the government was to achieve a strong measure of economic equity between the ethnic groupings so as to minimize communalist ethnic strife. Further, while Malaysia allows market forces to operate, the government requires major corporations to measure their success largely in terms of production and employment, rather than the way U.S. corporations measure their success in the market, i.e., by consumption and return on investment.

Malaysia remains a flawed democracy; its citizens are not as free as their U.S. counterparts: free speech has been restricted in the past on university campuses, and the government's prosecution of Anwar Ibrahim is surely deplorable. But it has given its citizens the franchise, and tolerated criticism, as has Singapore, despite its caning practices, and ban on gum-chewing; given how little a democratic base the Malaysian government had in 1957, (and Singapore in 1961), these countries have indeed come a long way socially, politically, and economically by their focus on equity across ethnic and religious boundaries, and have equally been encouraging of self-government within and between those communalist groupings. (In both countries today, and in Hong Kong, Taiwan, South Korea and Japan, there are strong and vocal opposition political parties, all of which criticize governmental policies).

If this be so, and when it is realized how many young nation-states are multi-ethnic today, then an argument can be made for Asian authoritarianism perhaps being not altogether authoritarian, but rather sensitive to cultural influences historically, yet supportive of a democratic ideal,[21] perhaps a better one than is insisted upon by the United States. And if this argument has merit, it will follow in turn that the fledgling democracies of East and Southeast Asia might provide a better model for the evolution of self-government than the U.S. model proffered by modern Western liberalism, and it may well fall to these Asian countries to be the true champions of democracy and human rights in the twenty-first century. This is precisely the claim—startling as it initially appears—made by political scientist Edward Friedman in an incisive recent article: [22]

> Since it is difficult to long maintain a fledgling democracy without economic growth ... dynamic Asian societies are seeking communalist equity ... [I]f the economic pie does not expand, then the only way the previously excluded can get their fair share of the pie is to take a big bite out of what established elites already have ... Lacking the benefits of East Asia's

> more dynamic, statist and equitable path to growth, a polarizing democracy elsewhere, in neo-liberalist guise, can quickly seem the enemy of most of the people. This has been the case with numerous new democracies in both Latin American and Eastern Europe.
>
> At the end of the twentieth century ... pure market economics further polarizes a society. What is emphasized in the post-Keynesian orthodoxy is containing inflation. What is rewarded is creating a climate welcomed by free-floating capital. The concerns of the marginalized, the poor, and the unemployed are not high on this agenda.... State intervention on behalf of equity—as with the way Singapore tries to make housing available to all, as with Malaysia's success with state aid to rural dwellers—is far more likely to sustain democratic institutionalization.

Without idealizing the governments of East and Southeast Asian fledgling democracies—some defenders of "Asian Authoritarianism" are indeed authoritarian and hostile to democracy—it remains that countries like Malaysia—and to a lesser extent, Singapore and the five "mini dragons"—have come a fair distance in nourishing self-government, and their record is especially impressive when compared to the U.S.: They began with much less, both economically and politically, and they have achieved much, both economically and politically, in only one-fifth of the time the U.S. has been at it.

To deepen our analysis of this state of affairs, and to bring the Confucian persuasion more directly to bear on the analysis, we turn now from this woefully brief consideration of democracy to the other issue central to inter-cultural dialogue today: human rights.

Henry Rosemont, Jr.

Which Rights?

A global concern for human rights has grown appreciably since the U.N. Declaration of 1948, with human rights activists found in every country, sufficient in quality and quantity as to render flatly wrong the view that human rights—and democracy—are simply Western conceits. There is increasing international insistence that human rights be respected, and democracy encouraged.[23]

In the course of these dialogues, and in recent political and moral theory, rights have been roughly placed in three categories: civil and political, social and economic, and solidarity rights. It is usually understood that each succeeding set of rights is a natural progression from the preceding set, evidenced in the terms by which we refer to them: first, second, and third generation rights.[24]

Unfortunately, upon closer examination it becomes less obvious that second generation rights are a natural conceptual progression from first generation rights. And if we are to understand the early Confucians, we must first come to appreciate the difference between the two.

For Locke, civil and political rights accrued to human beings as gifts from their Creator. But God is seldom invoked today to justify first generation rights. Instead, they are grounded in the view that human beings are basically autonomous individuals.[25] And if I am indeed essentially an autonomous individual, it is easy to understand and appreciate my demands that *ceteris paribus*, neither the state nor anyone else abridge my freedom to choose my own ends and means, so long as I similarly respect the civil and political rights of all others. But on what grounds can autonomous individuals demand a job, or health care, or an education—the second generation rights—from other autonomous individuals? There is a logical gap here, which no one has successfully bridged yet: From the mere premise of being an autonomous individual no conclusion can follow that I have a right to employment. Something more is needed, but it is by no means clear what that something might be, unless it conflicted with the view of human beings as basically autonomous individuals.

Put another way, jobs, adequate housing, schools, health care, and so on, do not fall from the sky. They are human creations, and no one has been able to show how I can demand that other human beings create these goods for me without them surrendering some significant portion of their first generation rights which accrue to them by virtue of their being autonomous individuals, free to pursue their own projects rather than being obliged to assist me with mine.

That I, too, can claim second generation rights to such goods is of no consequence if believe I can secure them on my own, or in free association with a few others, and thereby keep secure my civil and political rights. It is equally irrelevant that I can rationally and freely choose to assist you in securing those goods on my own initiative for this would be an act of charity, not an acknowledgement of your rights to those goods.

To see the logical gap between first and second generation rights in another way, consider this difference between them: 99% of the time I can fully respect your civil and political rights merely by ignoring you. (You certainly have the right to speak, but no right to make me listen.) If you have legitimate social and economic rights, on the other hand, then I have responsibilities to act on your behalf, and not ignore you. And what would it take for your social and economic rights claims to be legitimately binding on me?

Basically what is required is that I see neither you nor myself as an autonomous individual, but rather see both of us as more fundamentally co-members of a human community. No one would insist, of course, that we are either solely autonomous individuals or solely social beings. But if we believe we are fundamentally first and foremost autonomous individuals, then our basic moral obligation in the political realm will be to (passively) respect the first generation rights of all others. If we are first and foremost co-members of a community, on the other hand, our moral obligation to (actively) respect the second generation rights of all others will be binding—as it would be for Confucians.

A Confucian Response

Against this background let me quickly sketch my answer to the question of whether precursors of the concept of human rights—and derivatively, democracy—may be found in classical Confucianism. Unsurprisingly, my answer is "Yes and no." "No," if the most basic rights are seen as civil and political, grounded in the view that we are autonomous individuals; and "yes" if our most basic rights stem from membership in a community, with each member assuming a measure of responsibility for the welfare of all other members.

I do not believe much argumentation is necessary to establish that the classical Confucians did not focus on the individualism of human beings. *Ren*, the highest human excellence, must be given expression in interpersonal endeavors. Rituals (*li*), necessary for self-cultivation and the ordering of society, are communal activities. In order to exercise *xiao*, I must have parents, or at least their memory. This point is virtually a truism: in order to give human expression to the qualities inherent in being a friend, spouse, sibling, or neighbor, I must have a friend, spouse, sibling and neighbor, and these all-too-human interactions are not an accidental or incidental part of my life, for a Confucian; on the contrary, they are absolutely essential if I am to achieve any significant measure of self-realization.[26]

It is not merely that we are obliged, of necessity, to interact with others, we must care about them as well, and this caring, while it begins with the family, must nevertheless extend beyond it. The obligation to be attentive to the needs of all others in the community—large or small—can be traced as far back as the *Shu Jing*, in the well-known passage that "*Tian* hears and sees as our people hear and see …".[27]

This same theme permeates the *Lun Yu*, with Confucius insisting that even the humblest peasant was entitled to his opinions—which deserved attention—and insisting as well that the first responsibility of an official was to see that the people under his jurisdiction were well fed, with the attendant disgrace if he should be well fed when the people were not; and after they have been fed, they should be educated.[28] And that is exactly what is also required for generating those qualities of character that lead to public self-government—the democratic ideal. Moreover, think of how often the disciples ask socially-oriented questions: about government, about filial piety, about rituals, and so on. A very common question, of course, concerns the qualities of the *jun zi*, and in the overwhelming majority of cases, the Master places his response in a social setting: In the presence of superiors, the *jun zi* does X; in the presence of friends, Y and in the presence of *xiao ren* he does Z.[29]

Albeit in a semantically camouflaged way, Mencius justifies regicide when the ruler does not care for his people, and places him at the bottom of the moral hierarchy even when he does.[30] At a much more profound philosophical level, Mencius maintains that this caring for others is, to borrow Irene Bloom's felicitous term, a "foundational intuition"[31] in humans, as the child/well "gedanke experiment" is designed to establish.[32] And of course the "man in the street can become a Yao or a Shun."[33]

Moreover, this caring for all others was not to be only a personal excellence to be nurtured; it was to be institutionalized as well. Xun Zi's *Wang Zhi Pian* makes this point explicitly. To take only one example, after insisting that the ruler appoint ministers on the basis of their moral qualities rather than on the basis of lineage or wealth, he goes on to say:[34]

> When it comes to men of perverse words and theories, perverse undertakings and talents, or to people who are slippery and vagrant, they should be given tasks to do, taught what is right, and allowed a period of trial .... In the case of the Five incapacitated groups, the government should gather them together, look after them, and give them whatever work they are able to do. Employ them, provide them with food and clothing, and take care to see that none are left out.
>
> ... [L]ook after widows and orphans, and assist the poor...

This remarkable passage—and there are many others in a similar vein in the *Wang Zhi Pian*—requires comment. First, despite a number of semi-authoritarian pronouncements in this and other chapters, Xun Zi is clearly advocating the functional equivalent of job training programs, AFDC, welfare, and Medicare for the Chinese peoples; on this score he is far to the left of either Republicans or Democrats in the U.S. What makes this advocacy all the more impressive is that it requires the state to provide many goods and services to groups of people who cannot possibly pose a threat to that state's power; Machiavellian it is not.

Second, it is significant that Xun Zi's concern for the well-being of the sick, the poor, the marginalized and the unlettered is not mirrored in the political treatises composed by his near-contemporaries on the other side of the globe; we will read Plato's *Republic* and the *Laws*, and Aristotle's *Politics* in vain if what we wish to learn is the obligations of the state toward its neediest members.

Third, and perhaps most important in attending to this passage, and to the several others cited above, and to a great many others in the classical Confucian corpus, is it not possible to discern not only a sense of self-governance, but a sense of the importance of nurturing self-governance in others as well? Might we here be seeing a genesis for the development of social and economic rights, and for democracy? The answer, of course, is no, if our model of democracy is autonomous individuals freely exercising their franchise at the voting booth. Xun Zi's view of government is surely of the people and for the people, but not explicitly by the people. But bracket Lincoln and the U.S., and return for a moment to Mahathir Mohamad's Malaysia and Lee Kuan Yew's Singapore. If we agree that these countries, warts and all, are nevertheless fledgling democracies, whose theoretical perspective more significantly underlies the social, economic, and political progress that has been made, Xun Zi's or John Locke's?

As a final example of the Confucian claim that we cannot merely dwell among the birds and beasts—i.e., we are not autonomous individuals—and at the same time to meet the common objection that Confucian community norms are highly particularistic, let us examine a very familiar passage from the *Da Xue* for a moment. There is a strong spiritual dimension to this text, signaled by the large number of times words like "repose," "tranquility," "peace," and "the highest good"—*ding, jing, an,* and *zhi shan* respectively—appear in it.[35]

Its religious message is, however, singular; I know of no close parallel to it in other traditions. To find peace and to dwell in the highest good, as defined by the West, for example, we are uniformly instructed to look inward: to know our selves, as Socrates put it, or to know ourselves in relation to deity, as the texts of the three Abrahamic religions make clear. In the *Da Xue*, on the other hand, looking inward and coming to know our selves is more of a means than the ultimate end towards which we must strive. That goal is to augment *tian xia*, which may fairly be translated as "the world community," despite the monocultural orientation of the Han author(s) of the text. And we reach this goal by first shrinking our perspectives and activities from *tian xia* through the state, the clan, the family, and then to our own heart-mind. But once this task is accomplished, we must then begin to expand our perspectives and activities outward again, until they eventually encompass the world community.[36] Herein lies the highest good, to "serve the people" (*wei ren min*), Mao's abuse of the expression two millennia later notwithstanding.

There is a great deal more I could say to justify the claim that a sound conceptual basis for second generation rights, grounded in membership in a community, is contained in both the letter and the spirit of the classical Confucian writings. And I will go further, to also claim that if we can learn to read those writings against a global background that goes beyond modern Western liberalism, we may also see a basis for the development of democracies that is of direct relevance today. I am not suggesting that *"Alle Menschen werden Bruder"* is reflected in the classical corpus; to my knowledge, Zhang Cai's beautiful *Xi Ming* is the first text to do that. But "No man is an Island" thoroughly permeates classical Confucianism, and very probably we must fully appreciate Donne's vision before we can embrace Schiller's.

In sum, Confucian selves are much less autonomous individuals than they are relational persons, persons leading lives integrated morally, aesthetically, politically, and spiritually; they lead these lives in a human community. As Confucius said:[37]

> We cannot run with the birds and beasts
> Am I not one among the people of this world?
> If not them, with whom should I associate?

All of the specific human relations of which we are a part, interacting with the dead as well as the living, will be mediated by the courtesy, customs, rituals, and traditions we come to share as our inextricably linked histories unfold (the *li*), and by fulfilling the obligations defined by these relationships we are, for early Confucians, following the human way. It is a comprehensive way. By the manner in which we interact with others our lives will clearly have moral and political dimensions infusing *all*, not just some, of our conduct. By the ways in which this ethical interpersonal conduct is effected, with reciprocity, and governed by civility, respect, affection, custom, ritual, and tradition, our lives will also have an aesthetic dimension for ourselves and for others. And by specifically meeting our defining traditional obligations to our elders and ancestors on the one hand, and to our contemporaries and descendants on the other, the early Confucians offer an uncommon, but nevertheless spiritually authentic form of transcendence, a human capacity to go beyond the specific spatiotemporal circumstances in which we exist, giving our personhood the sense of humanity shared in common, and thereby a sense of strong continuity with what was gone before and what will come later, and a concomitant commitment to leave this earth in a better condition than we found it. There being no question for the early Confucians of the meaning *of* life, we may nevertheless see that their view of what it is to be a human being provided for every person to find meaning *in* life.[38]

This, then, is all-too-briefly a sketch of the conceptual framework of Confucianism, wherein rights-talk was not spoken, and within which I am not basically a free, autonomous individual. I am a son, husband, father, grandfather, neighbor, colleague, student, teacher, citizen, friend. I have a very large number of relational obligations and responsibilities, which severely constrain my choices of what to do. These responsibilities occasionally frustrate or annoy, they more often are satisfying, and they are always binding. If we are going to use words like "freedom" here, it must be seen as an achievement, not a stative term, as Confucius suggests in describing the milestones of his life. And my individuality, if anyone wishes to keep the concept, will come from the specific actions I take in meeting my relational responsibilities: there are many ways to be a good teacher, spouse, sibling, friend, and so forth; if Confucian persons aren't free, autonomous individuals, they aren't dull, faceless automatons either. As Herbert Fingarette has noted well, for the Confucians there must be at least two human beings before there can be any human beings.[39]

Furthermore, the language of Confucian discourse is rich and varied, permitting me to eulogize a Martin Luther King; it allows me a full lexicon to inveigh against the Chinese government for its treatment of Han Dongfang, Falun Gong members, and others; and against the Indonesian government for the horrors visited on the East Timorese people; I can express outrage at the rape of Bosnian women, and the NATO/US bombing of Kosovo and Serbia, and petition the Governor of Pennsylvania to grant a new trial to Mumia Abu Jamal; I can, in sum, fully express my moral sentiments in any democracy without ever invoking the language of first generation human rights.

Perhaps then, we should study Confucianism as a genuine alternative to modern Western theories of rights (and democracy), rather than merely as an implicit early version of them. When it is remembered that three-quarters of the world's peoples have, and continue to define themselves in terms of kinship and community rather than as rights-bearers, we may come to entertain seriously the possibility that if the search for universal moral and political principles—and a universally acceptable language for expressing these principles—are worthwhile endeavors, we might find more of a philosophical grounding for those principles, beliefs, and language in the writings of Confucius, Mengzi, and Xunzi, than those of John Locke, Adam Smith, and their successors. To emphasize this argument, let us return to the contemporary world.

Beyond the Liberal Tradition

The best way to go beyond modern Western liberalism in a global context is, I believe, to focus on economics. Large corporations are increasingly unrestrained in their behaviors both intra- and internationally, in an increasingly relentless drive for greater profits. The adverse social effects of this drive are obvious, yet we seem incapable of changing things; why?

One major reason, I submit, is that the Western—now international—legal system that is designed to protect the first generation civil and political rights of autonomous individuals equally protects the rights of autonomous individual corporations to do pretty much as they please, and the so-called democratic process, especially in the U.S., is so money-driven that those corporations can pretty much choose the candidates who will please them.

Consider a statement from Robert Reich, the former Secretary of Labor. Upon being challenged for expressing a measure of unhappiness at AT&T's decision to lay off 40,000 workers after declaring near-record dividends, he responded:[40]

> I don't question the morality of AT&T. In fact, I am very much against villainizing any of these people. And with regard to whether they did it wisely—the share price went up. By some measures, AT&T did precisely what it ought to have done. But the fundamental question is whether society is better off.

This is an astonishing statement. If society is better off for AT&T's action, then it would *prima facie* suggest the action was moral; and if society is worse off, then immoral. How, then, could Reich not wish to question the morality of AT&T's action? Worse, the answer to the "fundamental question" he asks surely appears to be that U.S. society is worse off for the job losses, even when we take shareholder gains into account: A great many AT&T shares are owned by a very few people.

In this light, we may better appreciate why the governments of the fledgling democracies in East Asia are so often called "authoritarian:" they enact laws prohibiting major corporations from laying off large numbers of workers in order to secure greater profits, and in this way, those governments restrict "free trade."

Japan, too, restricts free trade, which is at least partially responsible for the "Asian Authoritarian" label continuing to be affixed to the way the country is run. The curmudgeonly economist and political analyst Edward Luttwak has brought home succinctly the difference between a restrictive Japan and a free U.S.[41]

> When I go to my gas station in Japan, five young men wearing uniforms jump on my car. They not only check the oil but also wash the tires and wash the lights. Why is that? Because government doesn't allow oil companies to compete by price, and therefore they have to compete by service. They're still trying to maximize shareholder value, but they hire the young men. I pay a lot of money for the gas.
>
> Then I come to Washington, and in Washington gas is much cheaper. Nobody washes the tires, nobody does anything for me, but here, too, there are five young men. The five young men who in Japan are employed to wash my car are, here, standing around, unemployed, waiting to rob my car. I still have to pay for them, through my taxes, through imprisonment, through a failed welfare system. I still have to pay for them. But in Japan at least they clean my car.

Similarly, Clinton defended NAFTA by claiming that it would raise GNP and create more hi-tech jobs. But as Luttwak also noted, the U.S. already has the highest GNP in the world, and it is not important, for the vast majority of U.S. citizens, to give great weight to increasing it further. And to ascertain just how badly we need a lot more hi-tech jobs, just ask virtually any recent college graduate. What we do need is more decent-paying semi-skilled jobs for those five young men waiting to steal Luttwak's car, and for millions more young men and women just like them.

Perhaps I am mistaken here, we might indeed need to increase GNP and secure more hi-tech jobs. That is not my point. Rather do I wish to suggest a question: Why is it in this most free of all nations, we freely-choosing autonomous individuals have no democratic choice about whether we want to spend our money having our windshields washed, or building more prisons?

More directly: the anti-WTO demonstrations in Seattle made clear that many U.S. citizens would like to abolish the organization. Yet the four major candidates for the presidency in the year 2000—Gore, Bradley, Bush, and McCain—all support the WTO, as do the corporations which finance their campaigns; for whom can the Seattle demonstrators and other like-minded citizens vote to represent them in this "democracy?"

Consider the results of a poll conducted by the Preamble Center for Public Policy (completed shortly before President Clinton signed the end-of-Welfare bill): 70% of 800 registered voters believed corporate greed, not the global economy, was responsible for downsizing; and an equal number supported increased governmental action to curb that greed, and promote socially responsible conduct. Almost 80% favored obliging large employers to provide health benefits and pension plans, and equally favored "living wage" laws.[42]

As indicated earlier, one reason we have little or no real choice in such matters is that our legal system, significantly designed to protect and enhance the first generation rights of autonomous individuals, equally protects and enhances those rights for large corporations.[43]

Whose Democracy? Which Rights?

A related reason is a cardinal tenet of modern Western liberalism: the government, being public, must say nothing of the highest good; that is a private matter, for each autonomous individual to freely choose for him/herself. The state cannot legislate morality (which is why Secretary Reich did not wish to question AT&T's actions).

This is a powerful point, which contributes greatly to the support we are inclined to give to modern Western liberalism: we—especially we intellectuals—do want to be free to choose our own ends; we each have our individual hopes and dreams, and do not want our manner of expressing them dictated or altered by others. Herein lies, I believe, the basic appeal of the concept of civil and political rights for autonomous individuals.

But as Michael Sandel has argued in a recent work:[44]

> By insisting that we are bound only by ends and roles we choose for ourselves, [modern Western liberalism] denies that we can ever be claimed by ends we have not chosen—ends given by nature or God, for example, or by our identities as members of families, peoples, cultures, or traditions.

For the Confucians, this liberal denial is flatly mistaken at best, self-serving at worst, for human beings do indeed, they insist, have ends they have not chosen, ends given by nature, and by their roles in families, as members of communities, and as inheritors of tradition. The highest good is not many; it is one, no matter how difficult to ascertain, and it is communally realized in an intergenerational context. Confucius himself was absolutely clear on this point, for when a disciple asked him what he would most enjoy doing, he said:[45]

> I would like to bring peace and contentment to the
> aged, share relationships of trust and confidence with
> friends, and love and protect the young.

This, then, in far too brief a compass, is a sketch of a challenge to modern Western liberalism from a Confucian perspective. I believe I have met MacIntyre's criteria for intercultural discourse, for I have attempted to challenge contemporary Western liberalism largely on its own grounds, without recourse to any views liberals would claim to be patently false, and by appeal to a number of basic values the majority of liberals would endorse. And I have also attempted to show how those basic values cannot be realized in the modern liberal tradition owing to endorsing other values, namely, those that attach directly to autonomous individuals—and trans-national corporations.

If my challenge is at all sustainable, it suggests that either 1) the liberal or some other tradition must conceptually reconcile first and second generation rights claims much more clearly in the future than has been done in the past; or 2) that we must give pride of place to second and third generation rights in future intercultural dialogues on the subject, and future dialogues on democracy and justice as well; or 3) we might abandon the language of rights altogether, and seek a more appropriate language for expressing our moral and political concerns cross-culturally. But if either of the latter, it must follow that these dialogues can no more be value-neutral than can the governments of fledgling democracies in East and Southeast Asia, or in not-so-fledgling democracies like the United States.

The spell of the concept of autonomous individuals—once a needed bulwark perhaps against totalitarian regimes—is not confined to the economic and political dimensions of our (increasingly disjointed) lives; it affects us metaphysically and spiritually as well, which Aldous Huxley has well captured succinctly:[46]

> We live together, we act on, and react to, one another; but always and in all circumstance we are by ourselves. The martyrs go hand in hand into the arena; they are crucified alone.

Or as A.E. Housman put it:

> And here I am, alone and afraid
> In a world I never made

Much as I admire Huxley and Housman, this is a frightening universalist view to foist on the global community, and as most U.S. citizens and third-world peoples are beginning to understand, has the quality of being a self-fulfilling prophecy. Thus it seems imperative to challenge U.S. ideology at its moral, political and metaphysical roots, both for the sake of its citizens, and for the sake of the rest of the world, whose peoples share the burden of having to live with the untoward consequences of U.S. foreign policies defended by reference to that ideology.

There are alternatives to the Western liberal tradition, alternative visions which just might be endorsed by all people of good will, no matter what their cultural background.

There is nothing wrong with seeking universalist values; indeed, that search must go forward if we are ever to see an end to the ethnic, racial, religious, and sexual violence that have so thoroughly splattered the pages of human history with blood and gore since the Enlightenment. Rather does the wrongness lie in the belief that we—or any single culture—are already fully in possession of those values, and therefore feel justified, backed by superior economic and military threats, in foisting those values on everyone else.

Classical Confucianism proffers an alternative.[47]

NOTES

1. I appreciate that "essence" is a buzzword in most post-modern discourse today. For details, see my "Against Relativism" in *Interpreting Across Boundaries*, ed. G. Larwon and E. Deutsch. Princeton University Press, 1987.

2. The basic concern of John Rawls in his *A Theory of Justice* (Harvard University Press, 1970), most of the writings of Richard Rorty since 1980, Ronald Dworkin's *Taking Rights Seriously* (Harvard University Press, 1977), plus all the commentaries on these and related works over the years. My loose definition also parallels Michael Sandel's in "America's Search for a New Public Philosophy" in *The Atlantic Monthly*, March 1996, which is a lengthy excerpt from his book *Democracy's Discontent* (Harvard University Press, 1996).

3. See especially his *After Virtue, Whose Justice? Which Rationality?* and *Three Rival Versions of Moral Enquiry*, all University of Notre Dame Press, 1981, 1988, and 1990 respectively.

4. "Incommensurability, Truth, and the Conversation Between Confucians and Aristotelians about the Virtues" in *Culture and Modernity*, edited by Eliot Deutsch, University of Hawaii Press, 1991.

5. *Ibid.*, p. 21.

6. Others would trace the concept of rights to even earlier periods. See, for example, Brian Tierney, "Origins of Natural Rights Language: Texts and Contexts, 1150-1250," in *History of Political Thought*, vol. X, no. 4, Winter 1989; or *Nature, Justice, and Rights in Aristotle's Politics* by Fred D. Miller, Jr. (Clarendon Press, 1995).

7. I have argued this point in "Is There a Primordial Tradition in Ethics?" in *Fragments of Infinity*, edited by Arvind Sharma, Prism Press, 1991.

8. For properly contextualizing the cultural and historical milieu in which Descartes philosophized—or, more accurately, conducted his scientific work—I am indebted to Stephen Toulmin's *Cosmopolis*, Free Press, 1990. And the importance of current moral issues occupying an intellectual is not confined to the Confucians. Perhaps the greatest intellectual the U.S. has contributed to the world in the second half of this closing century of the millennium has said:

> The responsibility of the writer as a *moral agent* is to try
> to bring the truth about *matters of human significance to
> an audience that can do something about them.*

(Noam Chomsky, *Powers and Prospects*. South End Press, 1996, p. 59–italics in the original).

9 See the "Introduction" *to Leibniz: Writings on China*, translated by Daniel J. Cook and Henry Rosemont, Jr., Open Court Publishing Company, 1994.

10 *Ibid.*

11 An exception is Julia Ching's *Chinese Religions*, Orbis Books, 1993.

12 William T. deBary and Tu Weiming. eds., *Confucianism & Human Rights*, Columbia University Press, 1998.

13 "Rights-Bearing Individuals and Role-Bearing Persons" in *Rules, Rituals, and Responsibility*, edited by Mary I. Bockover, Open Court Publishing Company, 1991; "Why Take Rights Seriously? A Confucian Critique," in *Human Rights and the World's Religions*, edited by Leroy Rouner, University of Notre Dame Press, 1988. For an analysis of the role of individualism in modern Western philosophy, see C.B. McPherson, *The Political Theory of Possessive Individualism*, Oxford U. Press, 1962.

14 Following Sandel, "America's Search for a New Public Philosophy," *op. cit.*

15 See Noam Chomsky, "The Responsibility of Intellectuals" in his *American Power and the New Mandarins*, Vintage Press, 1969.

16 A bumper sticker put out by the Charles F. Kerr Publishing Company.

17 Some sources for these claims: P. Buhle and A. Dawley, editors, *Working for Democracy*, University of Illinois Press, 1985; Mari J. Buhle *et al*, editors, *Encyclopaedia of the American Left*, University of Illinois Press, 1992; Howard Zinn, *A People's History of the United States, 1492-1992*. Harper Collins, revised edition, 1995.

18 See n. 14.

19 Quoted in Edward Friedman, "What Asia Will or Won't Stand For: Globalizing Human Rights and Democracy," in the 1996 volume of the *Osaka Journal of Foreign Studies*.

[20] Kelantan has been in opposition hands for some time now, and in the recent (November 1999) elections, its eastern neighbor Teregganu also voted the Pas into power. It is equally important to note that despite his treatment of Anwar, Mahathir's National Front government won 56% of the popular vote. See the *Far Eastern Economic Review*, 12/9/99 for details.

[21] Although the ideal may have originally had economic more than moral and political roots. See my "Why the Chinese Economic Miracle Isn't One" in *Z Magazine*, October, 1995.

[22] See n. 19.

[23] For an excellent survey, see Sumner B. Twiss, "Comparative Ethics and Intercultural Human Rights Dialogue: A Programmatic Inquiry," in the volume edited by deBary cited in n. 12.

[24] *Ibid.*, especially pp. 17-19 for discussion and additional citations.

[25] For discussion, see my "Who Chooses?" in *Chinese Texts and Philosophical Contexts*, edited by Henry Rosemont, Jr., Open Court Publishing Company, 1991.

[26] A point now fairly well agreed upon in Confucian scholarship. See, for example, Tu Weiming's *Humanity and Self-Cultivation: Essays in Confucian Thought*, Asian Humanities Press, 1979; or *Thinking Through Confucius* by David L. Hall and Roger Ames, SUNY Press, 1987 (especially Chapters IV and V).

[27] James Legge, translator, *The Chinese Classics*, University of Hong Kong reprinting of the 1894 edition; volume III, *The Shoo King*, p. 74 and p. 292

[28] Some examples from the Lun Yu on these themes: 1:14, 1:15, 12:5, 12:7, 13:9. All citations are taken from *The Analects of Confucius*, trans. by Roger T. Ames and Henry Rosemont, Jr., Ballantine Books, 1998.

[29] See *ibid.*, pp. 48-65 for discussion.

[30] D.C. Lau, translator, *Mencius*, Penguin Books, 1970. On regicide, 1B8; on the moral hierarchy, 7A14.

[31] As employed in her contribution to the deBary volume cited in n. 12.

[32] *Mencius, op. cit.*, 2A6

[33] *Ibid.*, 6B2.

34 Translated by Burton Watson, *Hsün Tzu: Basic Writings*, Columbia University Press. 1963; pp. 34, 37.

35 Legge, *The Chinese Classics, op. cit.*, volume 1, pp. 357 ff

36 *Ibid.*

37 Lun Yu, 18:6.

38 This paragraph is taken from my contribution to the deBary volume cited in n. 12. The distinction between the meaning of life and meaning in life was first drawn by Kurt Baier in "The Meaning of Life" in *20th Century Philosophy: The Analytic Tradition*, edited by Morris Weitz, Prentice-Hall, 1966.

39 "The Music of Humanity in the Conversations of Confucius," in the *Journal of Chinese Philosophy* 10 (1983).

40 *Harper's Magazine*, May 1996, p. 38.

41 *Ibid.*, p. 47

42 Cited in the *Nation*, Aug. 26/Sept. 2, 1996, p. 5.

43 Mancur Olson makes clear the relation between the political and the economic with respect to first generation rights:

> A thriving market economy requires, among other things, institutions that provide secure individual rights. The incentives to save, to invest, to produce, and to engage in mutually advantageous trade depend particularly upon individual rights to marketable assets—on property rights. Similarly,...If there is no right to create legally secure corporations, the private economy cannot properly exploit ... productive opportunities ...

"Development Depends on Institutions," in *College Park International*, April, 1996, p. 2.

44 "America's Search for a New Public Philosophy," *op. cit.*, p. 70.

45 Lun Yu 5:26.

46 *The Doors of Perception*, Penguin, 1963, p. 12.

47 This paper will also appear in *Confucian Ethics: A Comparative Study of Self, Autonomy, and Community*, edited by Kwong-loi Shun and David Wong, Cambridge University Press, 2001. Some of the arguments advanced here were first presented at the Second Conference on Confucian and Human Rights at the East-West Center, May 22-24, 1996. I am grateful to Professor Barney Twiss for

comments and criticisms (and for many enjoyable conversations on these and related topics over the years). A fuller version was the text of my inaugural address upon being appointed the first George B. and Willma Reeves Distinguished Professor of the Liberal Arts at St. Mary's College of Maryland in 1997. The text was published in the College's *Mulberry Tree Papers* (Fall 1997), and reprinted in the *Raven* #39, Summer 1999. The present version was improved by comments from two anonymous referees for the Cambridge volume, and from editor David Wong. Again, I am deeply grateful to Ms. Mary Bloomer of St. Mary's College for preparing this manuscript for publication.

State University of New York
at Oneonta

Fifth Annual Undergraduate Philosophy Conference

March 31 – April 1, 2000

*Sponsored by the Philosophy Club,
the Student Association, Oneonta Philosophy Studies
the Ninash Foundation, the Philosophy Department
the Organization of Ancillary Services,
the Provost and Vice-President for Academic Affairs,
and the President of SUNY Oneonta.*

Oneonta Philosophy Club

The SUNY Oneonta Philosophy Club is pleased to sponsor our fifth annual Undergraduate Philosophy Conference. If there is anything we can do to make your time with us more enjoyable or intellectually satisfying, just let us know!

The Philosophy Club allows students, as well as faculty, to engage one another in academically and socially challenging discussion. Meetings, which are open to all members of the college community, are held Wednesday evenings at 8:00 p.m in the Hunt Student Union. We encourage you to come share your thoughts, interests, perspectives, and concerns in a comfortable environment of close student/faculty relationships. For more information: visit our web page, stop by the department office, or contact us at the email address provided below.

Sample activities include:
1) viewing and discussing films (*The Matrix, Woman in the Dunes, Heaven and Earth,* etc.),
2) guest presentations ("Our Environmental Destiny," Science and Spirituality," "Challenges in Contemporary China," etc.),
3) open discussions (ethics, life on other planets, the future of computers, etc.), and
4) field trips and excursions. For example, we are currently planning a visit to the Karma Triyana Dharmachakra Buddhist Monastery in Woodstock.

-- Don't Hesitate --
Join the Philosophy Club
"We're Waiting for You!"

Officers:	President	– Taylor Petekiewicz
	Treasurer	– Gotti Jicha
	Web Coordinator	– Kevin McGarry
	Faculty Advisors	– Achim Koeddermann
		– Douglas Shrader

Email: *philosc@oneonta.edu*
http://www.oneonta.edu/~philosc/philclub.html

SUNY Oneonta
Undergraduate Philosophy Conference
March 31-April 1, 2000

Friday

Registration and Opening Reception
(11:00 a.m. - 1:00 p.m.)
(Morris Conference Center Lobby)

**Yoga: A Philosophical Demonstration
and Guided Meditation**
Ashok Malhotra (SUNY Oneonta)
(1:00 - 2:00 p.m. Craven Lounge)

Session I (2:15 - 4:15 p.m.)
Philosophy and the Public Realm (Craven Lounge)

Session II (4:30 - 6:30 p.m.)
Language Games (Craven Lounge)

Dinner (6:30 - 7:30 p.m. Otsego Grille)

Words of Welcome (7:30 p.m. Craven Lounge)
President Alan B. Donovan

Keynote Address (7:30 - 9:00 p.m. Craven Lounge)
Pragmatism and the Future of Confucianism in China
Joanna Crosby (Morgan State University)

Reception (9:00 - 11:00 p.m. Lé Café)

Conference Program

SUNY Oneonta
Undergraduate Philosophy Conference
March 31-April 1, 2000

Saturday

Breakfast (9:00 - 10:00 a.m.)
   (Bacon Activity Center)

Session III (10:00 - Noon)
   Ethics: Theory and Practice (Craven Lounge)

Lunch (12:00 - 1:30 p.m.)
   (Bacon Activity Center)

Sessions IV & V (1:30 - 3:30 p.m.)
   Freedom, Happiness, and the Human Condition
      (Craven Lounge)
   Truth and Beauty (Room 103)

Sessions VI & VII (3:45 - 5:15 p.m.)
   Multiple Perspectives: The Search for
      Common Ground (Craven Lounge)
   Knowing Whereof We Speak:
      Language, Experience, and Truth (Room 103)

Keynote Address: (5:30 - 7:00 p.m. Craven Lounge)
   Whose Democracy? Which Rights?
   A Confucian Critique of Modern Western Liberalism
   Henry Rosemont Jr. (Saint Mary's College)

Awards Dinner (7:00 - 8:30 p.m. Lé Café)

Friday Afternoon

Inaugural Presentation
(1:00 - 2:00 p.m. Craven Lounge)
*Yoga: A Philosophical Demonstration
and Guided Meditation*
Ashok Malhotra
(SUNY Oneonta)

Dr. Ashok Malhotra is Professor of Philosophy at SUNY Oneonta. A recipient of the State University of New York Chancellor's Award for Excellence in Teaching, he has taught Philosophy and Yoga for over thirty years. Professor Malhotra is the director of Oneonta's Learn and Serve in India program, having conducted more than a dozen trips to India. His recent publications include *Transcreation of the Bhagavad Gita* (Prentice Hall, 1999) and *Instant Nirvana: Americanization of Mysticism and Meditation* (Oneonta Philosophy Studies, 1999). A new translation of the *Yogasutras* of Patanjali is forthcoming.

For the opening session of the conference, Professor Malhotra will:
1) provide an overview of the multidimensional nature of Yoga, including its popular versions in the west,
2) give demonstrations of some of the physical and meditative exercises associated with Yoga, and
3) invite the audience to participate.

Note: *For maximum benefit, wear loose clothing.*

Coffee, Exhibit, and Book Sale
(ongoing throughout the conference)
Morris 104

Take a coffee break, browse the book exhibit, and learn more about an exciting international program sponsored by SUNY Oneonta and the Ninash Foundation. Pick up some good books at great prices! All proceeds will be donated to the Indo-International School.

Learn and Serve in India

Students who want to encounter the real India in an intensive study abroad experience, while at the same time contributing their time and talents to help provide educational opportunities for impoverished and underprivileged children, are strongly encouraged to consider SUNY Oneonta's Learn and Serve Program in India. Program details and application forms are available from Professor Ashok Malhotra:

Department of Philosophy   malhotak@oneonta.edu
SUNY Oneonta   607 436-3220
Oneonta, NY 13820-4015

In January 2000, twelve students and six members of the local community helped finish construction of the Indo-International School in the village of Dundlod (Rajasthan, India.) After celebrating New Year's Eve and the arrival of "the New Millennium" in Agra (home of the Taj Mahal), they painted the new building, created a mural for an outside wall, cleared land for the playground, and helped purchase a year's worth of supplies for the 160 children served by the school. Their three-week trip also included a visit to Old and New Delhi as well as Jaipur (the "pink city" of India). Future plans include building a library for the children as well as three more classrooms. Additionally, the school will serve as a model for replication throughout India.

Friday Afternoon

2:15 - 4:15 p.m.   Session I

Philosophy and the Public Realm (Craven Lounge)

Chair: Gottlieb Jicha III

The Silence of Philosophy in Crito's Exhortation
   (Plato's Crito)
      Malinda Foster – University of Michigan, Dearborn
      Discussant: Mark Ayotte

Arendt, Heidegger, and the Decline of the Public Realm
      Katherine Collins – University of Massachusetts, Lowell
      Discussant: Amanda Rasnick

Political Noise and Vociferous Silence: Heidegger and Nazism
      Tamara Johnson – Binghamton University
      Discussant: Scott Fickboth

4:30 - 6: 30 p.m.   Session II

Language Games (Craven Lounge)

Chair: Cynthia Budka

The Mask Unmasked: The Role of Hypocrisy
   in the Dialectic of Thus Spoke Zarathustra
      John Kaag – Penn State University
      Discussant: Daniel Bristol

The Nature of Language: Public and Private
      Andrew Wilson – Macalester College
      Discussant: Yiannis Philippacopoulos

Wittgenstein and Naturalism
      Zachary Haines – Macalester College
      Discussant: Debbie Nickerson

Conference Program

Friday Evening

Conference Dinner
(6:30 - 7:30 p.m. Otsego Grille, Morris Hall)
Reservations Required

Words of Welcome
(7:30 p.m. Craven Lounge)
Alan B. Donovan
President of SUNY Oneonta

Keynote Address
(7:30 - 9:00 p.m. Craven Lounge)
Pragmatism and the Future of Confucianism in China
Joanna Crosby
(Morgan State University)

Dr. Joanna Crosby did undergraduate work in Philosophy and graduate work in American Studies at California State University at Fullerton. She graduated from Vanderbilt University with a Ph.D. in Philosophy in 1995 and has taught at Morgan State University, a historically black institution in Baltimore, MD ever since. Professor Crosby's work concerns critical social thought in the US, Europe, and Asia, including issues of class, race, and gender. Teaching, writing, and presenting papers on Confucianism for the last few years, her focus has centered on China. She spent the Fall 1999 semester teaching at Hubei University in Wuhan, China. She now resides in Baltimore with her husband and three feline companions.

For her Keynote Presentation, Professor Crosby will examine whether Pragmatism or Confucianism, both philosophies that emphasize practice over theory and actuality over metaphysics, can help heal the damage done to Chinese culture by the Cultural Revolution.

Friday Evening Social
(9:00 - 11:00 p.m. Lé Café)

Philosophy and the Public Realm

Saturday Morning

9:00 - 10:00 a.m.   Continental Breakfast
(Bacon Activity Center)

10:00 a.m. - Noon   Session III

Ethics: Theory and Practice (Craven Lounge)

Chair: Amanda Rasnick

Feminine Ethical Theories: Their Validity Tested
        Rachel Houchins – East Tennessee State University
        Discussant: Molly Maroldo

The Practice of Physician Assisted Suicide
  Supported by Kantian Ethics
        Seyra Ahmed – Virginia Commonwealth University
        Discussant: Ian Sherman

A Father's Rights in Abortion: Proof That He Has A Say
        Michael A. Payne – Virginia Commonwealth University
        Discussant: Cynthia Budka

12:00-1:30 p.m. Buffet Luncheon
(Bacon Activity Center)

Conference Program

Saturday Afternoon

1:30 - 3:30 p.m.   Sessions IV & V

Freedom, Happiness, and the Human Condition
(Craven Lounge)

Chair: Kevin McGarry

The Exhilarating Freedom! Hope in Existentialism
        Christine M. Cinquino – Saint Vincent's College
        Discussant: Rick Claypool/Stan Stepanic

The Problem of Happiness in Nietzsche's
    "Use and Abuse of History"
        Malinda Foster – University of Michigan, Dearborn
        Discussant: Gottlieb Jicha III

The Extraordinary: Movements in Dostoevsky and Nietzsche
        Eric Bergmann – Binghamton University
        Discussant: Katie Hapeman

Truth and Beauty (Room103)

Chair: Mark Ayotte

Towards a Processean Aesthetics
    Within a Whiteheadean Metaphysics
        Scott M. Gleason – SUNY Potsdam
        Discussant: Kevin Curran

On the Event of Truth: A Discussion of Art, Truth and the
    *Primal Conflict in Heidegger's **The Origin of the Work of Art***
        Iain Tucker Brown – St. Mary's College of Maryland
        Discussant: Eric Vanderbles

Tradition and Modern Meaning: Society and Relative Truth
        Jason Baumgarth – University of Minnesota, Duluth
        Discussant: Morgan Brenner

Late Saturday Afternoon

3:45 - 5:15 p.m.   Sessions VI & VII

Multiple Perspectives:
The Search for Common Ground
(Craven Lounge)

Chair: Daniel Bristol

Incommensurability, Normative Vices, and the
Comparative Language Game: A Wittgensteinian
Model for Comparative Philosophy
Erin Cline – Belmont University
Discussant: Kevin McGarry

The Environmental Crisis Through a Buddhist Perspective
Katherine Collins – University of Massachusetts, Lowell
Discussant: Tim Jones

Knowing Whereof We Speak:
Language, Experience, and Truth (Room 103)

Chair: Molly Maroldo

Religious and Non-Religious Language,
and Propositions About Human Rights
Jayson A. White – Iowa State University
Discussant: Justin Barrera

The Experience and Expression of Truth
Justin C. Maaia – Suffolk University
Discussant: Kari Smith

Conference Program

Saturday Evening

Keynote Address:
(5:30 - 7:00 p.m. Craven Lounge)
Whose Democracy? Which Rights?
A Confucian Critique of Modern Western Liberalism
Henry Rosemont, Jr.
(St. Mary's College of Maryland)

Dr. Henry Rosemont, Jr. received his Ph.D. from the University of Washington. He currently holds the positions at both Saint Mary's College of Maryland (George B. and Willma Reeves Distinguished Professor of the Liberal Arts) and Fudan University in China (Senior Consulting Professor). Professor Rosemont's interests include Chinese thought, logic and linguistics, and global justice. He is the author of more than fifty articles in scholarly journals and anthologies and editor of the Society for Asian and Comparative Philosophy's Monograph Series. His books include *A Chinese Mirror* (Open Court, 1991), *Leibniz: Writings on China* (Open Court, 1994) and *The Analects of Confucius: A Philosophical Translation* (Classics of Ancient China).

For his Keynote Presentation, Professor Rosemont will explore issues of human rights, freedom, and responsibility from a global, cross-cultural perspective.

Awards Dinner
(7:00 - 8:30 p.m. Lé Café)
Reservations Required

Abstracts

Seyra Ahmed
The Practice of Physician Assisted Suicide
Supported by Kantian Ethics
Virginia Commonwealth University

This paper attempts to establish the ethics of physician assisted suicide using Immanuel Kant's philosophical theories. Several arguments in support of and against this practice are evaluated using philosophical methods. Kant's theories help us realize the role of autonomy in defining us as human beings. By prohibiting physician assisted suicide, the ability of many individuals to exercise their autonomy is being lost. Furthermore, there is a contradiction in the action of physicians when they issue "do not resuscitate" orders while refusing to assist a patient in his or her request to die while they are still coherent. The possibility of coercion by the family or physician is also considered as a reason to continue the ban on physician assisted suicide. A case study and review of the physician assisted suicide system in place in Oregon is also included to help ground the debate in actual practice. After a philosophical consideration of these matters, the debate is resolved in favor of physician assisted suicide.

Jason Baumgarth
Tradition and Modern Meaning: Society and Relative Truth
University of Minnesota, Duluth

Kobo Abe and Walker Percy develop the ideas found in traditional Continental Existentialism in *The Woman in the Dunes* and *The Moviegoer*. Though not traditional philosophers, Abe and Percy provide Japanese and American perspectives on the problems which threaten the individual in modern society. Abe's *The Woman in the Dunes* addresses the confines of a society bound by tradition and the risks such a society poses to the individual. Percy's *The Moviegoer* examines the effects of American society on individual freewill and authenticity. Both Abe and Percy provide permutations to Continental Existentialism which reflect their respective cultures and further the ideas of writers such as Sartre and Camus. In helping to identify the downfalls of the society we have created, Abe and Percy add to the groundwork of Existential literature and begin the search for solutions to the problem of finding authenticity in a systematized world.

Eric Bergmann
The Extraordinary: Movements in Dostoevsky and Nietzsche
Binghamton University (NY)

Fyodor Dostoevsky and Friedrich Nietzsche—two great thinkers, two prolific writers of the 19th century. Nietzsche would discover the writings of Dostoevsky and speak favorably of them. Any critical reading of works by the two men will uncover parallels between thought; however, as much similar thought as one may notice, the differences should not be ignored.

This paper is an in-depth exploration of Dostoevsky's protagonist Raskolnikov, of *Crime and Punishment*, read against the thought of Nietzsche. Addressed are Raskolnikov's conception of the extraordinary man and his attempt at becoming this man, religion and the difference in Dostoevskian and Nietzschean portrayals of, and Nietzsche's thought pertaining to: herd mentality, the *Übermensch*, becoming, social values, and Will to Power. Although much of the paper is an attempt at consideration for what would in all probability be the thinkers' reactions to each other's thoughts, such considerations are defended and multiple possibilities are often left on the table. As well, the original thoughts remain untampered and untainted; these thoughts can speak for themselves, all extrapolation aside.

Iain Tucker Brown
*On the Event of Truth: A Discussion of Art, Truth,
and The Primal Conflict in Heidegger's*
The Origin of the Work of Art
St. Mary's College of Maryland

I attempt to bring to light three prominent questions from roughly two, highly significant yet extraordinarily difficult, sections of Heidegger's work *The Origin of the Work of Art*. My exploration into the text focuses on the following inquiries: 1) What is concealedness? 2) What is truth as unconcealedness? 3) How do we attain toward truth in the work of art? Without revealing too much, my intention is to illustrate, with the philosophical genius of Heidegger's aesthetic reflections, the function of art, not as a mere mechanism for the causal interpretation of thoughts and feelings that stand in relation to the aesthetic response or the artwork at hand, but rather as the impetus for a meaningful reconciliation between two dialectically opposed states of existence in the form of the event of truth. Art will be explored as a sort of story in which we, as characters, interact with ourselves and the world in order to resolve what Heidegger terms "The Primal Conflict."

Christine M. Cinquino
The Exhilarating Freedom! Hope in Existentialism
St. Vincent's College (PA)

In our age, following what Nietzsche metaphorically referred to as the "death" of God, it is common for individuals to feel lost in a philosophical environment where all values are considered relative and where absurdity and anxiety seem to be the most powerful feelings life has to offer. In this moral climate, a temptation exists for some introspective young persons, who may be experiencing a phase of mental and emotional anguish from recent life experiences, to give in to a form of pessimistic nihilism. However, accepting an existentialist perspective does not necessitate the surrender of humanistic faith in the value of persons or of a meaningful life. The existentialist claim that "existence precedes essence" challenges each individual to create personal meaning and to reveal the value of all human beings.

Erin Cline
*Incommensurability, Normative Vices,
and the Comparative Language Game:
A Wittgensteinian Model for Comparative Philosophy*
Belmont University (TN)

The examination of what might cause one to be "torn away" from a particular world view is essential to the construction of a Wittgensteinian model for comparative philosophy. In this paper, I discuss the obstacles which plague comparative studies and place Wittgenstein in conversation with other key thinkers on the subject of different world views. I give attention to Alasdair MacIntyre's discussion of inter-translatability, Donald Davidson's discussion of incommensurability, and to the normative vices proposed by Martha Nussbaum. I conclude my paper with an examination of a comparative language game, and the manner in which it is a process of refinement with many levels and characteristics.

Katherine Collins
Arendt, Heidegger, and the Decline of the Public Realm
University of Massachusetts, Lowell

Hannah Arendt's political philosophy can be described as an attempt to recover genuine political life from the isolating and alienating circumstances of modern capitalist society. However, even though Arendt's celebration of genuine political life can be traced back to Greek philosophy, an examination of her conclusions in *The Human Condition* makes it clear that, however much she drew from Plato and Aristotle, her political vision owes a great deal to the original thoughts expressed in Heidegger's *Being and Time*. In this paper I illustrate that Arendt's political theory rests fundamentally on her understanding, appropriation, and transformation of key Heideggerian concepts. Issues from Heidegger that Arendt appropriates are: Dasein, modernity and the public and private spheres. Finally I will demonstrate that both rejected the Marxist notion that we can achieve freedom by erasing bourgeoisie distinctions between the public and the private.

Katherine Collins
The Environmental Crisis Through a Buddhist Perspective
University of Massachusetts, Lowell

Although environmental degradation may not have been forefront in the mind of Buddha or his disciples, his teachings nonetheless provide lessons for contemporary society. Buddhism offers intriguing insights for a model of living that is compatible with the protection and preservation of the natural environment. There are also a number of apparent inconsistencies within a Buddhist environmental perspective. Whatever the limitations, by facilitating development of an ethic founded upon principles of sustainability, Buddhism can assist in the emergence of a clearer understanding of the environmental crisis.

Malinda Foster
*The Problem of Happiness in Nietzsche's
"Use and Abuse of History"*
University of Michigan, Dearborn

In my essay I aim to describe accurately the core issue in Nietzsche's "Use and Abuse of History" as seemingly indicated by Nietzsche himself: the problem of happiness. According to Nietzsche, in order for us to be happy in life we need history. Without history we will be unhappy. With too much history we will be unhappy. With just the right amount of history we may or may not be happy, but at least we will be tempted to think that happiness in life is possible–and the thought of that, Nietzsche says, will tend to make us rather happy.

I suggest further that Nietzsche's essay and its hortatory content are directed at young students. (Today, that would seem to translate into undergraduate students in particular.) These issues seem timely and appropriate because modern education, according to Nietzsche, leaves its pupils ignorant of the most important thing: the possibility of happiness in life.

Malinda Foster
*The Silence of Philosophy in Crito's Exhortation (Plato's **Crito**)*
University of Michigan, Dearborn

In my essay I argue that the *Crito* is an overtly political dialogue. Thematically central is the problem of obligation. The word "philosophy" is never spoken once. Philosophy unspoken, however, is in no way the same thing as philosophy absent. Considering, for example, the significant silence of philosophy in Crito's exhortation, I further suggest that when most people read *Crito* they tend to find two things most memorable: One is the speech on behalf of the laws. The other is Socrates' heroic resolve and determination. They tend to interpret these as examples of public and private excellence or political and philosophic virtue. What they forget, however, is that Socrates says what he says in response to Crito. But it seems appropriate to wonder if Socrates' response can only or best be understood in light of Crito and his own particular demands.

Additionally, it is a concern that after examining Crito's exhortation, we might be compelled to reinterpret those (once seemingly clear) examples of civic and philosophic virtue. For as we begin to look closely at what Socrates says, our understanding of civic virtue proves increasingly problematic. Furthermore, it seems to call into question and create a certain conflict with the idea that Socrates' willingness to stay in jail and face his immanent death is itself an example of philosophic virtue. The silent suggestion in Crito's exhortation is something very different; it seems to point away from politics proper and toward philosophy–but not just philosophy–Socratic philosophy. These issues seem relevant because they might teach us something about our own situation, living in a country at a time when the questions of virtue and civic-mindedness seem to be most pressing.

Scott M. Gleason
Towards a Processean Aesthetics
Within A Whiteheadean Metaphysics
SUNY Potsdam/Crane School of Music

Many philosophers engage in discussions of art and such considerations are, obviously, founded upon their metaphysical principles. Consequently, a vast and rich body of aesthetic investigation has risen, however, mostly within the static, dualistic ontologies characteristic of these philosophers. The work of Alfred North Whitehead (1861-1947) offers a decisive and rewarding framework with which to conceive of the nature of art and music, accepting many of the former principles of aesthetics, while at the same time challenging and revising them. Whitehead's metaphysical notions, so unique and compelling in their own right, abound with aesthetic implications and significance. However, Whitehead's discussions of art are fairly limited and beg for further investigation. To this end, this paper explores some notions regarding aesthetic experience that are latent in Whitehead's process metaphysics, and some of his more salient notions of art and its function. It is the central aim of this paper, then, to show that Alfred North

Philosophy and the Public Realm

Whitehead's metaphysics can be adventurously conceived of as a Processean Aesthetics.

Zachary Haines
Wittgenstein and Naturalism
Macalester College (MN)

Recently, philosophical texts have been based more and more on a naturalistic approach to philosophy. This interested me and I thought that it was the correct direction in which to move. One of the authors I read who instilled the belief that philosophy should be concerned with the way things are done, not with how they ought to ideally be done, was Ludwig Wittgenstein. I think that his *Philosophical Investigations* was not only a shift in philosophy of language methodology, but symbolic of the change occurring across the field of all philosophy. Philosophical inquiry is receiving more credibility with the layman because exploring the nature of things through empirical observation is done in place of normative, theoretical ideologies that would otherwise be produced. This is not to say that there is no place for theorizing about what should or could be done, but this is to come after what actually is done is examined.

Rachel Houchins
Feminine Ethical Theories: Their Validity Tested
East Tennessee State University

Numerous commentators agree that historically many ethical theories have not only excluded women, but also degraded them, portraying women as morally deficient. This theoretical tendency prompted Carol Gilligan, Nel Noddings, and many other women to attempt to remedy this deficiency by answering the question "How do women fit into ethical [or moral development] theory?" Although I applaud these efforts, I fear they perpetuate many detrimental assumptions about women, and thus indirectly support the subordination of women. Additionally, the ethic of care is not useful in many fields of applied ethics. This can be vividly demonstrated by studying the ramifications of the ethic of care on the field of bioethics. In a society where people are attempting to make medicine a more "caring" science, it is easy for many practitioners to find the ethic of care appealing, but it is, in fact, detrimental to both the patients and the health-care providers.

Tamara Johnson
Political Noise and Vociferous Silence: Heidegger and Nazism
Binghamton University (NY)

This paper addresses the main controversies surrounding the career of Martin Heidegger: his involvement with the Nazi party and the silence he maintained regarding said involvement. One may, with some justification, expect of a philosopher a higher standard of ethics and therefore feel especially appalled by Heidegger's relation to one of history's most nefarious evils. How could a philosopher, of all people, subscribe to such a heinous ideology? This is a exigent question to be asked as post modernism, which movement can be found to have roots in a great deal of Heidegger's writing, becomes one of the most dominant philosophies of our culture. If the relativism in Heidegger's existentialism allowed for genocide, what about the relativism that so permeates contemporary thought? I attempt to explain how it came about that Heidegger made such despicable choices by relating his philosophy of anxious authenticity and historicity to the philosophy of Hitler, hoping to thereby point out some of the strengths and weaknesses of Heidegger's thought.

John Kaag
*The Mask Unmasked: The Role of Hypocrisy in the Dialectic of **Thus Spoke Zarathustra***
Penn State University

The movement of Zarathustra is reminiscent of this classical content of the stage. The true essence of Nietzsche's ideal man is shrouded in the doctrine espoused by the acting vehicle of this ideal, the teachings of the acting "sage" (Nietzsche 227). Nietzsche assumes the position of the skilled choreographer. His "dance," the action and dialogue of Zarathustra, heralds its own destruction; the curtain must close on this act as well. The juxtaposition of atheistic sentiment and theistic method, draws Zarathustra to an explicit dénouement grounded in hypocrisy. The "playwright's" hypocritical blunder draws this curtain closed and strips the primary actor of his costume. The blunder, however, lies not in the process of the author, but rather in the eyes of an impatient audience. The life of the actor, the vitality of Zarathustra's teachings, fades, yet the overman is not destroyed by this unmasking. Man, once an actor, is "naked" (93), without costume or pretense. Nietzsche's reader is also robbed of his role as the passive student. The novel lends little to rely upon; it is an empty vessel which this active pupil must fill. It is, in fact, the essence of the Overman himself, in the reader himself, which is revealed.

Justin C. Maaia
The Experience and Expression of Truth
Suffolk University (MA)

Words are inadequate for expressing the Truth. This is characteristic of all forms of expression. While a word, a picture, or a song may act as a catalyst for another person to seek out the Truth, the medium itself cannot imbue someone with the understanding that the Truth itself can instill. This is why the only way to understand the Truth, or any other concept, is through direct experience. Any means of expressing it should be tailored to the purpose of inspiration. In this way can another person be convinced to seek out the truth. Attempting to capture its essence through some medium other than itself is futile. The truth cannot be communicated. It can only be experienced.

Michael Alan Payne
A Father's Rights in Abortion: Proof That He Has A Say
Virginia Commonwealth University

This paper will focus on case study 2:1 on page 75 of *Well and Good*, a book of medical case studies that takes an in-depth philosophical viewpoint. The paper will begin by giving an overview of the case study in question and will describe the family situation that we are dealing with. This situation, in which the father wishes to continue the pregnancy and the wife wishes to abort, casts a particularly intriguing view on current themes of abortion and has inspired the writer to question the rights of a father in the abortion decision making process. The paper ultimately takes a stance in support of paternal rights and cites several common place social acceptances and attitudes that reinforce these rights. The right to have a say is carefully looked at and is expressed, attacked, and rebutted by using popular arguments and proofs of philosophy common in Kantian, consequentialist, and teleological thoughts. The paper also expresses the main themes of autonomy, "safe sex," women vs. men in autonomy, and society vs. men in views towards abortion. The paper ends with a universalizable rule as well as a tangent that may be safely drawn from it.

Jayson A. White
*Religious and Non-Religious Language,
and Propositions About Human Rights*
Iowa State University

The distinction between religious and non-religious language is important, if not essential, to most Modern social and political dialogue. For any philosophical view attempting to exclude the use of any particular kind of thought or language ought to be able to give an account of what it is purporting to exclude. It seems clear that there is some significant difference between obviously religious and non-religious propositions. Identifying the nature of this difference or differences, however, proves to be a very difficult task. Moreover, many propositions (for example, references to human rights) which are not usually considered religious in any way seem to be subject to the same criticisms as analogous religious propositions. If one is to maintain the belief that propositions about human rights are meaningful in the sense that they are used in everyday language and are not subject to the same criticisms as propositions about karmic rights, then certain accounts of the difference between religious and non-religious propositions and certain theories of meaning and reference must be avoided.

Andrew Wilson
The Nature of Language: Public and Private
Macalester College (MN)

The confusion over the question of the privacy of language is to be attributed to the failure to recognize the fact that language can have both a public and a private aspect simultaneously, and, in fact, must have both if it is to function, and if its very existence is to be accounted for. A materialist account of mind, idealist skepticism, and empiricist epistemology, when joined with evolutionary logic, show clearly that each individual's meanings are necessarily private, but close similarities are necessary for practical communication to occur. This ambiguity has caused the confusion that has become the private vs. public controversy, while it is clear that close but nevertheless slightly different meanings must be present in order for meaningful communication to coexist with linguistic evolution.

✪ ✪ ✪

Four of the happy children who are receiving an education through the Indo-International School in Dundlod.

How You Can Help

The Ninash Foundation, a 501 (C)(3) charitable organization, hopes to raise $1 million dollars for new schools and facilities to educate the underprivileged children of India. Even small donations help purchase supplies and bring smiles to the faces of children like these. Contributions can be given to Professors Malhotra or Shrader, or mailed to:

Indo-International Schools Project
Ninash Foundation
17 Center Street
Oneonta, NY 13820

(Checks should be made payable to *The Ninash Foundation*.)

Participants

Seyra Ahmed (III)
Mark Ayotte (I, V)
Justin Barrera (VII)

Jason Baumgarth (V)
Eric Bergmann (IV)
Morgan Brenner (V)

Daniel Bristol (II, VI)
Ian Tucker Brown (V)
Cynthia Budka (II, III)

Christine M. Cinquino (IV)
Rick Claypool (IV)
Erin Cline (VI)

Katherine Collins (I, VI)
Joanna Crosby (Friday)
Kevin Curran (V)

Alan B. Donovan (Friday)
Scott Fickboth (I)
Malinda Foster (I, IV)

Scott M. Gleason (V)
Zachary Haines (II)
Katie Hapeman (IV)

Rachel Houchins (III)
Gottlieb Jicha III (I, IV)
Tamara Johnson (I)

Tim Jones (VI)
John Kaag (II)
Justin C. Maaia (VII)

Ashok Malhotra (Friday)
Molly Maroldo (III, VII)
Kevin McGarry (IV, VI)

Debbie Nickerson (II)
Michael A. Payne (III)
Yiannis Philippacopoulos (II)

Amanda Rasnick (I, III)
Henry Rosemont, Jr. (Saturday)
Ian Sherman (III)

Douglas Shrader (Saturday)
Kari Smith (VII)
Stan Stepanic (IV)

Eric Vanderbles (V)
Jayson A. White (VII)
Andrew Wilson (II)

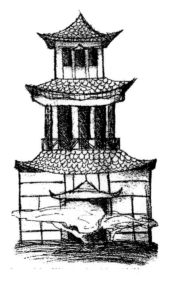

Acknowledgments

We are grateful to the following organizations
and local merchants for their generous support:

The Student Association
The Ninash Foundation
The Philosophy Club
The Philosophy Department
Organization for Ancillary Services
OAS Bookstore
Morris Conference Center
Oneonta Philosophy Studies
The Marketing Club
The Video Production Club
Hummel's Office Supply

Elena's Sweet Indulgence
Oneonta Bagel Company
Stewart's
Woody's Market
Hannaford Foods
P & C
Price Chopper
Subway
Wal-Mart
Gary's Flowers and Gifts
Stoeger's Florist
Wyckoff's Florist

We would also like to recognize the following individuals:

Joanna Crosby, Ph.D.
Alan B. Donovan, Ph.D.
Marjorie Holling
F. Daniel Larkin, Ph.D.
Ashok Malhotra, Ph.D.
Henry Rosemont, Jr., Ph.D.

Finally, a heartfelt **Thank You** to all the Presenters, Chairs, and Discussants — for without them there would be no Conference.

The Philosophy Conference Planning Committee:

Mark Ayotte
Morgan Brenner

Meghan Callahan
Gottlieb Jicha III
Molly Maroldo

Kevin McGarry
Amanda Rasnick

Cynthia Budka
student committee chair

Douglas W. Shrader
faculty advisor

ONEONTA PHILOSOPHY STUDIES
HISTORICAL AND CULTURAL PERSPECTIVES

Oneonta Philosophy Studies is a scholarly series that promotes exchange concerning traditional and contemporary issues in philosophy. Because comparative study often fosters appreciation and tolerance as well as understanding, special consideration is given to manuscripts that illuminate relationships between diverse or seemingly discrete views. Historical and cultural studies are especially welcome.

Submission is open to all —without regard to institutional affiliation, political preference, religious belief, gender, or national origin. Manuscripts are subject to external review. Published material does not necessarily reflect the views of the Editorial Board, the Philosophy Department, or the State University of New York.

A series such as this depends on the vision, good will, and labor of many. Special appreciation is extended to the *Asian Studies Development Program* (ASDP), *Institute of Global Cultural Studies* (IGCS), *Society for Ancient Greek Philosophy* (SAGP), *Society for the Study of Islamic Philosophy and Science* (SSIPS), and the State University of New York at Oneonta—especially Michael Merilan (Dean of Science and Social Science), F. Daniel Larkin (Provost and Vice President for Academic Affairs) and Alan B. Donovan (President).

DOUGLAS W. SHRADER
EDITOR IN CHIEF

Books

✤ **Virtue, Order, Mind:**
Ancient, Modern, and Post-Modern Perspectives
Peter Vincent Amato, editor

On Choosing a Teacher: Plato's *Protagoras* (MARIE I. GEORGE); Words of Love: Rhetoric and Eros in Plato's *Phaedrus* (DOUGLAS W. SHRADER); Tragic *Katharsis* (MARTHA HUSAIN); *Metaphysics* Z and H: Spurious V. Genuine Genera (WALTER E. WEHRLE); Aquinas, Aristotle, and the Convertibility of Being and Truth (JAMES T. H. MARTIN); Toxic Shame and the Lonerganian Concept of Conversion (DENNIS D. KLEIN); Jonas on the Crisis for Modern Man (OSCAR MOHL AND ANGELO JUFFRAS); A Roadmap for Ethics in the Twenty-First Century (EDDY SOUFFRANT); Communicative Rationality, Communicative Ethics and the Political Space of the Public Sphere (EVANGELOS KOBOLAKIS); A Pragmatic Reading of Gadamer's Philosophical Hermeneutics (VINCENT MARK VACCARO); Reconceiving Power and the Social Through Baudrillard (MARC HANES); A Feminist Analysis of Value-Neutral Observation (MAUREEN LINKER); Modernity, Kolakowski and Myth (PETER VINCENT AMATO).
1994 – 203 pages – ISBN 1-883058-16-3

✤ **Essays in Islamic Philosophy, Theology, and Mysticism**
Parviz Morewedge

Basic Dimensions of Islamic Theology; Basic Concepts of Neoplatonism; Greek Sources of Some Islamic Philosophies of Being and Existence; Substance and Process Theories of the Self in Islamic Mysticism; Mystical Icons in Rumi's Metaphysical Poetry: Light, the Mediator and the Way; Sufism, Neoplatonism and Zaehner's Theistic Theory of Mysticism.
1995 – 265 + xxviii pages – ISBN 0-9633277-7-1

The Fractal Self

✤ **Jean Paul Sartre's Existentialism
in Literature and Philosophy**
Ashok Kumar Malhotra

This book offers innovative approaches to the reading of the novel *Nausea*, considering it as a philosophical and a psychological novel, and as a work of art. After depicting the existential themes in *Nausea*, the author compares the existential philosophy of *Nausea* to that of *Being and Nothingness*, and then deals with the ethical and social dimensions of Sartre's philosophy before exploring the interconnection between philosophy, art, and literature.
1995 – 154 + x pages – ISBN 1-883058-14-7

✤ **Seeds of Wisdom**
Douglas W. Shrader, editor

Biological Research and Feminist Obligation (JENNIFER BURKE); Subjective versus Objective Reality: An Examination Through Physics and Philosophy (MICHAEL JOSEPH); Exploring the Universe: From Plato to Einstein and Beyond (ALEX SLATER); Observing, Observability, and the Importance of a Smiler: A Partial Defense of Strawsonian Events (DAVID MIGUEL GRAY); Follow Your Bliss: The Philosophy of Joseph Campbell (ANGELA CASE); Concepts of Self: East and West (GABRIELLE LEVIN); Quality, Love, and Madness: Pirsig versus Plato (KERRI NICHOLAS); Nietzsche's Appropriative Representation *or* Is the Overman a Hermaphrodite? (JOHN DEVINE); The Impossibilities, Irrationality, and Contradictions of Immanuel Kant's Ethical Theories (DAVID SCHAAF); Descartes and Nietzsche (TATIANA ZELIKINA)
1997 – 167 + xii pages – ISBN 1-883058-08-2

Oneonta Philosophy Studies

✤ Language, Ethics, and Ontology
Douglas W. Shrader, editor

Between Eastern and Western Thought: Individuation in a Western Setting (JOHN R. HARTMANN); The Paradigm of Emptiness: A Commentary on the *Diamond Sutra* (DANIEL J. BRISTOL); Rational Systematic Thought: Aristotle and Ancient Cultures (JOHN F. VELONA); Evolution of the One During the Early Medieval Period: Plotinus to Proclus (DAVID SCHAAF); Inversion of Fate: Boethius' Philosophy From Within (DAVID JUSTIN HODGE); The Nature of Rhetoric in Plato's *Gorgias* (ANNA CHRISTINA S. RIBEIRO); Discussing an Education, as Found in the *Phaedrus* (KEVIN GOETZ); Existence Communication and the Arbitrary Nature of Language (JEFFREY F. DUECK); On the Priority of Epistemic Issues to the Metaphysical Issues of Realism (DARIN SOMMA); Surface Spectral Reflectance and Color Objectivism (CHRISTOPHER O'CALLAGHAN); Events, Objects, Tropes, and Explanation (DAVID MIGUEL GRAY); Nietzsche and the Eternal Recurrence (DAVID MORGAN SVOLBA); The Possibility of Permissible Suicide Within Kant's Ethical Theory (PAUL NGUYEN); Emotions, Gender, and Kantian Morality (EMILY D. PORTER); Woman Philosopher: An Oxymoron? (HAZEL E. BARNES)
1998 – 352 + xvi pages – ISBN 1-883058-74-0

✤ **Children of Athena**
Douglas W. Shrader, editor

Temporal Incongruity in Zeno of Elea and its Philosophical Consequences (JEFFERY M.J. MURPHY); Does the Ontological Argument Need Salvaging? (ERIN KATHLEEN CARTER); Putnam, Realism and PERCEPTION (CLINTON TOLLEY); Great Perfection: The Practical Phenomenology of Tibetan Buddhism (DANIEL J. BRISTOL); Counter-Intuitive Ethics (MEGHAN TADEL); The Thinker as Poet (ROBB E. EASON); Nietzsche's Use of Metaphor (JOHN HARTMANN); Wittgensteinian Hermeneutics? (KEVIN GOETZ); "Hear Say Yes in Joyce": Otherness, Gender, and Derridian Repetition (LITIA PERTA); A Critical Re-Evaluation of the Esoteric Character of Maimonides' Guide of the Perplexed (MICHAEL FRAZER); Apollonian, Dionysian and Socratic Views: A Nietzschian Exegesis (G. J. SCHWENK); Anti-Essentialism and Re-Identification (MICHAEL D. DAY); Contemporary Analytic Philosophy as Reflected in the Work of Monty Python (GARY HARDCASTLE); When Artists Read Philosophers: From Modernism to Postmodernism (JERE PAUL SURBER)
1999 – 334 + xxii pages – ISBN 1-883058-67-8

✤ **Instant Nirvana:**
Americanization of Mysticism and Meditation
Ashok Kumar Malhotra

Mysticism in the Hindu Tradition; Instant Nirvana: Hindu Mysticism in the West; Meditation: Yoga, Zen, and T.M.; Encounters and Experiences with the Gurus.
1999 – 128 + xvi pages – ISBN 1-883058-01-5

✤ **The Fractal Self**
Douglas W. Shrader, editor

Hegel And Shankaracharya: On the Non-Dualistic 'I' (PRIYADARSHI SHUKLA); The Nature of Mind in Tibetan Buddhist Ethical Theory (DANIEL J. BRISTOL); Buddha, Kant, and the Ethical Consequences of Suicide (KATHERINE COLLINS); Justice Outside the Polis in Aristotle's *Politics* and *Nicomachean Ethics* (TARA K. HOGAN); The Freedom That Fear Has Wrought (BRETT BISGROVE); An Analysis of Deontic Logic and Chisholm's Paradox (MATTHEW A. FERKANY); Contextual Influences on Wittgenstein's Philosophy (JONATHAN C. MESSINGER); Intuitions in Conceptual Shape? Misconceptions and Motivations (NATHAN C. DOTY); An Attack On Tradition (ROBERT ERLEWINE); Nietzschean Christology (CHRISTOPHER RODKEY); Heidegger, Lao Tzu and Dasein (CHRISTOPHER MARTIN); The Fractal Self and the Organization of Nature: The Daoist Sage and Chaos Theory (DAVID JONES AND JOHN CULLINEY); Reading Socially Engaged Buddhism in Modern America: A Case Study of Tibet/Tibetan Buddhism (JENNIFER MANLOWE).
2000 – 286 + xxii pages – ISBN 1-586840-42-8

✤ **Strange Birds from Zoroaster's Nest:**
An Overview of Revealed Religions
Laina Farhat-Holzman

The Mystery of Human Religion; The Common Stream of Human Religion; Beyond Priests and Human Sacrifice: Human Responsibility; Good and Evil: No Shades of Gray; Unforeseen Consequences: The Transformed Message; State Religion: The Kiss of Death; The Role of Zoroastrian Heresies in Shaping Later Monotheistic Religions; Zoroastrian Concepts in World Religions; Zoroaster's Mark on the Secular World; The Modern Dilemma: A World Religion?; Epilogue: The Future of Religion; Appendix: Zoroastrian Texts and Scholarly Disagreements.
2000 – 236 + xiv pages – ISBN 1-586840-31-2

The Fractal Self

✤ Philosophy and the Public Realm
Douglas W. Shrader, editor

The Exhilarating Freedom! Hope in Existentialism (CHRISTINE M. CINQUINO); The Problem of Happiness in Nietzsche's "Use and Abuse of History" (MALINDA FOSTER); Tradition and Modern Meaning: Society and Relative Truth (JASON BAUMGARTH); Ethical Theory Reconsidered: An Evaluation of the Ethics of Health Care (RACHEL HOUCHINS); Proof of Paternal Rights in Abortion (MICHAEL ALAN PAYNE); Political Noise and Vociferous Silence: Heidegger and Nazism (TAMARA JOHNSON); Incommensurability, Normative Vices, and the Comparative Language Game: A Wittgensteinian Model for Comparative Philosophy (ERIN CLINE); Wittgenstein and Naturalism (ZACHARY HAINES); The Mask Unmasked: The Role of Hypocrisy in the Dialectic of *Thus Spoke Zarathustra* (JOHN KAAG); The Experience and Expression of Truth (JUSTIN C. MAAIA); On the Event of Truth: A Discussion of Art, Truth and the Primal Conflict in Heidegger's "The Origin of the Work of Art" (IAIN TUCKER BROWN); Towards a Processean Aesthetics Within a Whiteheadian Metaphysics (SCOTT M. GLEASON); Pragmatism and the Future of Confucianism in China (JOANNA CROSBY); Whose Democracy? Which Rights? A Confucian Critique of Modern Western Liberalism (HENRY ROSEMONT, JR.).
2001 – 302 + xxvi pages – ISBN 1-586841-16-5

Oneonta Philosophy Studies

Journal

✤ **East-West Connections: Review of Asian Studies**
David Jones, editor
Volume 1, Number 1: 2001 – ISSN Pending

Research Papers

✤ **The Logic Beneath the Caution: An Analysis of
the Buddha's Responses to Questions About the Self**
Douglas W. Shrader
1992 – 22 pages – ISBN 0-9633277-3-9

✤ **On Hindu Philosophies of Experience:
Cults, Mysticism, and Meditations**
Ashok K. Malhotra
1993 – 75 pages – ISBN 1-883058-03-1

✤ **Near-Death Experiences:
Scientific, Philosophical, and Religious Perspectives**
Douglas W. Shrader
1995 – 56 pages – ISBN 0-9633277-9-8

Department of Philosophy
SUNY-ONEONTA
Oneonta, NY 13820-4015

http://www.oneonta.edu/~shradedw/ops.html